Chicken Soup for the Soul®

READER'S CHOICE

Chicken Soup for the Soul: Reader's Choice 20th Anniversary Edition
The Chicken Soup for the Soul Stories that Changed Your Lives
Jack Canfield, Mark Victor Hansen, and Amy Newmark

Published by Chicken Soup for the Soul Publishing, LLC www.chickensoup.com
Copyright © 2013 by Chicken Soup for the Soul Publishing, LLC. All Rights Reserved.

The publisher gratefully acknowledges the many publishers and individuals who granted Chicken Soup for the Soul permission to reprint the cited material.

Front cover photo courtesy of GettyImages.com/nicolas hansen, E+.

Book covers on interior pages 5, 14, 19, 31, 37, 80, 85, 102, 126, 146, 168, 174, 224, 231, and 286 designed and produced by Brian Taylor.

Cover and Interior Design & Layout by Brian Taylor, Pneuma Books, LLC.

Distributed to the booktrade by Simon & Schuster. SAN: 200-2442

Publisher's Cataloging-in-Publication Data
(Prepared by The Donohue Group)

Chicken soup for the soul : reader's choice 20th anniversary edition :
  the Chicken Soup for the Soul stories that changed your lives /
  [compiled by] Jack Canfield, Mark Victor Hansen, [and] Amy Newmark. --
  20th anniversary ed.

     p. ; cm.

  ISBN: 978-1-61159-912-1

  1. Spiritual life--Literary collections. 2. Spiritual life--Anecdotes. 3. Anecdotes. I. Canfield, Jack, 1944- II. Hansen, Mark Victor. III. Newmark, Amy. IV. Title: Reader's choice 20th anniversary edition

BL624 .A122 2013
158/.12   2013937400

PRINTED IN THE UNITED STATES OF AMERICA
on acid ∞ free paper
22 21 20 19 18 17 16 15 14 13   01 02 03 04 05 06 07 08 09 10

Chicken Soup for the Soul®

20th Anniversary Edition

READER'S CHOICE

The Chicken Soup for the Soul Stories
that Changed Your Lives

Jack Canfield
Mark Victor Hansen
Amy Newmark

Chicken Soup for the Soul Publishing, LLC
Cos Cob, CT

Contents

❶

~Epiphanies~

❷
~Attitude Adjustments~

3
~Great Advice~

❹

~Motivation~

❺

~Doing Good~

❻

~Amazing Connections~

Introduction

S torytelling has been mankind's most effective way of passing on wisdom, advice, and culture throughout history. It is the best way for us to learn things. Most successful self-help authors or motivational speakers use storytelling to illustrate their points and deliver their messages in a way that resonates with people.

Our books are primarily composed of stories written by ordinary people who have had extraordinary experiences. These people unselfishly share their stories with our readers. Sometimes they even reveal deeply personal moments in their lives that they have never shared with anyone before, not even their families or friends. Our contributors write the stories for two reasons: 1) to share their stories with strangers who may benefit from hearing of someone else's experience, and 2) because writing the stories helps them—it is therapeutic to get stories onto paper. Writers tell us that even though their story wasn't chosen for one of our books, it was still a great experience putting it on paper.

I love our approach because we give our readers 101 personal, revealing stories from different people in every book—and that way everyone is likely to find an approach that works for them, or a story that causes a shift in their attitude, or a story that provides them the support they need during a challenging time. Our books are like portable support groups, with your peers eagerly sharing their stories and offering to help you.

Picking stories that will influence people's lives is a big responsibility. We get e-mails and letters all the time from people telling us that we have stopped them from committing suicide, reassured them that they are doing the right thing in their personal lives, given them a friend when they thought they were all alone, caused them to pick up the phone and call an estranged relative or friend. They tell us that our stories have inspired them to change their jobs, embrace a volunteer activity, try again to reach a long-ago abandoned goal, or have reinvigorated their lives.

We've been publishing our books and changing lives one story at a time since 1993. As part of our twentieth-anniversary celebration, we asked our readers to write about how their favorite Chicken Soup for the Soul stories affected them. You'll find the stories in pairs in this volume — a new story written just for this book, followed by the story or poem that the reader found so inspiring in one of our past 250+ titles.

The stories that you'll read cover the whole gamut of Chicken Soup for the Soul's history, from the very first *Chicken Soup for the Soul*, which has sold more than eight million copies in the U.S. and Canada, to books you may have never seen that are focused on specific topics. It's interesting that my own favorite comes from a book called *Chicken Soup for the Soul: Hope & Healing for Your Breast Cancer Journey* that we created with Dr. Julie Silver of Harvard Medical School. No one in my family has ever had breast cancer, but this story is a standout for me because I feel that it applies to all of us.

In "Eliminate the Negative, Accentuate the Positive," Georgia Shaffer writes about what happened when she had a recurrence of her breast cancer. A friend drove her to chemo one day but spent the entire time talking about people who had died of cancer. As Georgia says:

"I learned the hard way that I needed to protect myself as much as possible from contact with that kind of negative or thoughtless person... I had never realized that just like the weeds in a garden rob the flowers of vital moisture, nutrients and sunlight, so too the 'weeds' in my life were robbing me of the vital energy I needed to fight cancer and heal. I could not afford to allow interactions with negative people to steal the few resources I had left... I needed to eliminate the negative as much as possible and then accentuate the positive. Like the flowers in my garden turn toward the sun, I decided to focus on the loving, beautiful connections in my life."

I am so busy in my job as publisher, author, and editor-in-chief of Chicken Soup for the Soul that I too have found that I need to focus on the people who can cast sunshine into my own life. I don't have as much time as I would like for interaction with family and friends, so I want to make the most of the time that I have outside the office.

And when I am at the office, one of my jobs is to introduce you to the positive people who write for us. They give us stories that are empowering and uplifting, encouraging our readers to look within themselves for the keys to being happy, productive, and purposeful. I love stories from people who have been through enormous challenges and yet have maintained a positive attitude, filled with gratitude for the good things they still have.

In this book, you'll meet one of our favorite contributors of all time, twenty-year-old Angie Sayers, who bravely wrote about her terminal cancer and changed many lives, including that of Susan Smith, who used Angie's example to overcome her panic disorder. You'll meet Sophfronia Scott, who learned from a story in the original Chicken Soup for the Soul about the power of smiling to change her life, even in impersonal New York City. It changed her life, and I happen to see Sophfronia now and again and can report that she is always smiling.

You'll also read one of the classic self-esteem boosters that we published, by Virginia Satir, and discover how it helped Annabel Sheila turn her life around after a divorce. And you'll read about Tracy Fitzgerald, whose story gives me chills. One night, Tracy read a story in Chicken Soup for the Military Wife's Soul and mentally prepared herself in case she ever got "the phone call" and learned her husband had lost a limb in Afghanistan. She got the phone call the very next morning.

You'll read about a woman who was reunited with the daughter she gave up for adoption twenty-three years earlier, all because of a connection made in one of our stories. You'll read about the medevac crewmember who read a story in *Chicken Soup for the Veteran's Soul* and realized that he was reading about one of the soldiers he saved in Vietnam, who went on to win four Super Bowls.

The list goes on. We have enjoyed a wonderful trip down Memory Lane putting this volume together for you, and we are gratified to see the effect that our stories have had on so many lives.

As Jack Canfield says, "There are essentially two things that will make you wise — the books you read and the people you meet." We hope to make you doubly wise — by reading our books and by meeting hundreds of new people through them, so that their life experiences become part of your life experience and wisdom.

Mark Victor Hansen says, "Get started now. With each step you take, you will grow stronger and stronger, more and more skilled, more and more self-confident and more and more successful." We wish you happy reading and an enjoyable journey through these powerful stories, and we hope that we contribute to your strength, self-confidence and success, whatever your endeavors.

~Amy Newmark

Eliminate the Negative, Accentuate the Positive

I always plucked a thistle and planted a flower
where I thought a flower would grow.
~Abraham Lincoln

O ne chilly January day twenty-two years ago, I sat in an examining room, waiting for the results of yet another biopsy. Six months earlier, at the age of thirty-eight, I had been diagnosed with breast cancer, and had a mastectomy and reconstruction. But a suspicious rash had appeared on my reconstructed breast and I was waiting to hear the results of the lab report.

My doctor entered the room with a look of concern. "Georgia," he said, "I'm sorry but it's a recurrence of breast cancer."

My head started to spin and I felt that familiar awful ache in the pit of my stomach.

But my feelings were not exactly like the first time I was told I had cancer. There was no shock. There was no numbness. There was no denying what was happening. It was serious and I knew it.

Although I can't recall everything the surgeon said that day, I do remember what happened when he left the room. His nurse, Vickie, who was only a few years younger than I was, looked over at me with deep concern.

My eyes met hers and I burst into tears. "I don't want to die. My son is only nine years old," I sobbed. "I want to live to see him graduate from high school." I started rocking back and forth and kept repeating, "I just want to see my son graduate from high school."

Vickie didn't tell me I would see my son Kyle graduate. She didn't tell me I wouldn't. She listened, held me tightly and handed me one tissue after another.

I don't know how long I stayed in that examining room, but I do know that she stayed with me and she ached with me.

During the days that followed, I discovered I had a slim chance of being alive in ten years. My only hope for long-term survival was chemotherapy, radiation and a bone marrow transplant.

I had all those treatments. When they were complete, my cancer was in remission, but I was a mere shell of a person. As Kyle said years later, "Mom, you were a ghost in a shell."

Through my experience with cancer, I learned the powerful impact of one caring person. Whether that person is a doctor's assistant like Vickie, a counselor, a friend or a relative — it's one person who can make a positive difference.

The harsh reality is that I also became painfully aware that some people are not positive and life giving. Rather, their negative or thoughtless interactions are draining and, in some cases, toxic.

For example, one day a "friend" took me to a chemotherapy treatment. For the 50-minute drive, she told me one painful story after another about people who had faced cancer. At one point I asked, "Can we talk about something besides cancer?"

She did. For five minutes. And then the litany began again.

After previous treatments, I had never gotten sick. After that treatment, I was sick for two days.

I learned the hard way that I needed to protect myself as much as possible from contact with that kind of negative or thoughtless person. At the very least I had to distance myself from certain people and acquire the ability to say no. This was especially difficult because I had been taught to be kind to everyone. I had never recognized the importance of setting clear boundaries with some people. I had never realized that just like the weeds in a garden rob the flowers of vital moisture, nutrients and sunlight, so too the "weeds" in my life were robbing me of the vital energy I needed to fight cancer and heal. I could not afford to allow interactions with negative people to steal the few resources I had left.

In a perfect world, everyone gathers around cancer survivors and supports them in the way they need to be supported. Since this isn't a perfect world, I needed to make two changes. I needed to eliminate the negative as much as possible and then accentuate the positive. Like the flowers in my garden turn toward the sun, I decided to focus on the loving, beautiful connections in my life. I chose to truly appreciate and treasure the people who cared for me and doted on me. I know I would not be here today without all the support I received.

Seventeen years later, I called Vickie the nurse and asked to meet with her.

"Vickie," I said when we met, "I want to thank you again. You have no idea of the impact that your warmth and compassion made in my life." Tears of gratitude streamed down my cheeks.

She looked at me and shook her head in amazement. "You just never know, do you? I had no idea what that meant to you that day."

Like Vickie, many people give us a hug, make an affirming comment or lend a helping hand and never think about it again. They don't realize that it makes all the difference to us as cancer survivors when we sometimes wonder how we'll make it through another day. It's that positive nurturing connection, that heart-to-heart connection, that not only will counteract all those sterile needles or machines we have to face, but will continue to warm our hearts years later even on the chilliest of winter days.

~Georgia Shaffer

Chapter
1

READER'S CHOICE

Epiphanies

Gratitude bestows reverence, allowing us to encounter everyday epiphanies, those transcendent moments of awe that change forever how we experience life and the world.

~John Milton

Living by the Light
of a Smile

Sometimes your joy is the source of your smile,
but sometimes your smile can be the source of your joy.
~Thich Nhất Hạnh

I moved to New York City after college. I quickly learned that smiling, for the most part, was not a good thing. A smile attracted unwanted attention, especially from men who equated it with an invitation and who would send catcalls my way as I walked down the street. Being an inexperienced young woman, I didn't know how to deal with such behavior. I felt annoyed, harassed, and powerless. Eventually I cultivated a kind of neutral expression that I wore every time I went outside. If I smiled at a stranger it was forced, a polite return of a smile. My true smile came out only with my loved ones.

In 2002 I began training to become a life coach. Many of my teachers and fellow classmates recommended the original *Chicken Soup for the Soul* book. I had heard of The New York Times bestseller, but I'd never read it. I figured I should read it if only to have the text "under my belt" as part of my personal-development knowledge base. I had read only thirty-seven pages when I came across the story that changed my outlook about the way I looked as I walked through the world: "The Smile."

Contributor Hanoch McCarty told the story of Antoine de Saint-

Exupéry, who wrote *The Little Prince* as well as a lesser-known piece, "The Smile," that was possibly based on Saint-Exupéry's own experience as a captured fighter pilot in the Spanish Civil War. The pilot, nervous and frightened because he's certain he will be executed the next day, finds a cigarette in his pockets and asks his jailer for a light. The jailer agrees and comes forward with a match. As he gets closer, he looks at his prisoner and their eyes lock unexpectedly. The pilot smiles at him. In that moment it's as though the prisoner, not the jailer, has ignited a light. The jailer warms to him. The two men begin to discuss their families and even share pictures. Later the jailer decides to release the pilot and lead him to safety. I remember being absolutely stunned by the words: "My life was saved by a smile."

McCarty goes on to say that when the pilot smiled it was a "magic moment when two souls recognize each other." I recognized that moment too and to me it felt so full of hope and possibility. The next morning on my way to work I stopped in a deli and bought a cup of tea. When the server handed me the cup I smiled and said thank you. He stepped back and for a moment looked confused. Then he smiled and said, "I've been doing this all morning, but you're the first person to smile at me." I just nodded, smiled again and left.

I couldn't believe how good I felt — I actually felt more like myself! As I continued to smile throughout the days, weeks and months I noticed an amazing cycle: The more I smiled, the friendlier everything seemed; and the friendlier everything seemed, the more I smiled. It also seemed to me that the smiles I received in return were not just polite smiles. I felt a momentary connection with the person, as though we had come to an agreement that all was right with the world.

Before reading McCarty's story I had thought that a smile made me passive and powerless, and invited unwanted attention. Afterwards my view was just the opposite. Smiling gave me strength. I could change myself, and the people I encountered, by simply smiling. In fact over the years I've come to observe how, as Andy Andrews say in his book, *The Traveler's Gift*, "My smile has become my calling card. It is, after all, the most potent weapon I possess." Boxers lead with their left or right jabs. I lead with my smile.

Here's an example. Recently I became a substitute bus driver in my son's school district. The more I drove the more I heard the other drivers complain about a new crossing guard, the person who controls the flow of traffic so the huge fleet of buses can get in and out of the school's driveways quickly and safely. The guard, an older man, seemed unsure in his decision making, which often resulted in long lines of backed up traffic. Most days he looked harried and worried. He knew he wasn't doing a good job. I would see buses pass by him with the drivers looking impatient, annoyed or downright angry. I wanted things to be different for the guard. I felt bad that all these people were sending such negativity in his direction.

Then I realized I did have the power to change at least one interaction in his day. One morning when the crossing guard signaled me to pull into the school, I inched the bus forward. Then, just before I began my turn, I made eye contact, gave him a tiny wave and a big smile. He saw me. His face softened and something like relief washed over his features. He waved back with his own smile as I continued my turn.

That's it. That's all it took. I knew I had made a difference in his day just by that one "magic moment" of connection. And even though I have yet to speak a word to this man, I know he recognizes me because we repeat this little ritual each time he sees me behind the wheel.

Now, take that one moment and multiply it by the millions of times I've smiled since reading the Saint-Exupéry/McCarty story. That's a lot of magic conjured by the spontaneous flashing of teeth. I can't speak for the people who have been on the receiving end of these smiles, but I can say this for myself: my life is so much brighter, so much more joyous, that I can't imagine how I lived without such light. I hope I can inspire others to share their happiness just as freely. I smile just thinking about it.

~Sophfronia Scott

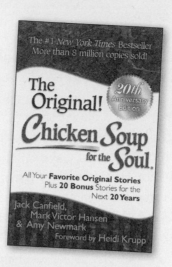

The Smile

Smile at each other, smile at your wife, smile at your husband, smile at your
children, smile at each other—it doesn't matter who it is—and that will
help you to grow up in greater love for each other.
~Mother Teresa

Many Americans are familiar with *The Little Prince*, a wonderful book by Antoine de Saint-Exupéry. This is a whimsical and fabulous book and works as a children's story as well as a thought-provoking adult fable. Far fewer are aware of Saint-Exupéry's other writings, novels and short stories.

Saint-Exupéry was a fighter pilot who fought against the Nazis and was killed in action. Before World War II, he fought in the Spanish Civil War against the fascists. He wrote a fascinating story based on that experience entitled *The Smile (Le Sourire)*. It isn't clear whether or not he meant this to be autobiographical or fiction. I choose to believe it is the former.

He said that he was captured by the enemy and thrown into a jail cell. He was sure from the contemptuous looks and rough treatment he received from his jailers that he would be executed the next day. From here, I'll tell the story as I remember it in my own words.

"I was sure that I was to be killed. I became terribly nervous and distraught. I fumbled in my pockets to see if there were any cigarettes that had escaped their search. I found one and because of my shaking hands, I could barely get it to my lips. But I had no matches; they had taken those.

"I looked through the bars at my jailer. He did not make eye contact with me. After all, one does not make eye contact with a thing, a corpse. I called out to him 'Have you got a light, *por favor?*' He looked at me, shrugged and came over to light my cigarette.

"As he came close and lit the match, his eyes inadvertently locked with mine. At that moment, I smiled. I don't know why I did that. Perhaps it was nervousness, perhaps it was because, when you get very close, one to another, it is very hard not to smile. In any case, I smiled. In that instant, it was as though a spark jumped across the gap between our two hearts, our two human souls. I know he didn't want to, but my smile leaped through the bars and generated a smile on his lips, too. He lit my cigarette but stayed near, looking at me directly in the eyes and continuing to smile.

"I kept smiling at him, now aware of him as a person and not just a jailer. And his looking at me seemed to have a new dimension, too. 'Do you have kids?' he asked.

"'Yes, here, here.' I took out my wallet and nervously fumbled for the pictures of my family. He, too, took out the pictures of his *niños* and began to talk about his plans and hopes for them. My eyes filled with tears. I said that I feared that I'd never see my family again, never have the chance to see them grow up. Tears came to his eyes, too.

"Suddenly, without another word, he unlocked my cell and silently led me out. Out of the jail, quietly and by back routes, out of the town. There, at the edge of town, he released me. And without another word, he turned back toward the town.

"My life was saved by a smile."

Yes, the smile — the unaffected, unplanned, natural connection between people. I tell this story in my work because I'd like people to consider that underneath all the layers we construct to protect ourselves, our dignity, our titles, our degrees, our status and our need to be seen in certain ways—underneath all that, remains the authentic, essential self. I'm not afraid to call it the soul. I really believe that if that part of you and that part of me could recognize each other, we wouldn't be enemies. We couldn't have hate or envy or fear. I sadly conclude that all those other layers, which we so carefully construct through our lives, distance and insulate us from truly contacting others. Saint-Exupéry's story speaks of that magic moment when two souls recognize each other.

I've had just a few moments like that. Falling in love is one example. And looking at a baby. Why do we smile when we see a baby? Perhaps it's because we see someone without all the defensive layers, someone whose smile for us we know to be fully genuine and without guile. And that baby-soul inside us smiles wistfully in recognition.

~Hanoch McCarty

My Wakeup Call

The struggle ends when the gratitude begins.
~Neale Donald Walsch

The spring and summer of 2008 was a time that changed my life. I was sick during this time and no matter what I did I just wasn't getting any better. I was scared to leave the house, I didn't want to drive, I didn't eat, my mind was spinning out of control and before I knew it I sank into a depression. I needed help and fast, as my life was in a downward spiral. I went to the doctor and was diagnosed with panic disorder. The doctor prescribed antidepressants and counseling. The first set of antidepressants did not work, so he gave me another prescription and between that prescription and counseling my condition dramatically improved. I was doing so well that my counselor successfully completed my program and my doctor weaned me off the medication.

Let me now take you to the spring and summer of 2012. I relapsed, and although I wasn't as sick as the first time, I felt like my world was coming to an end. All I kept thinking was "Why me?" and "What did I do to deserve this?" My attitude was so negative that it drove everyone around me crazy. I went back to the doctor and he put me back on the medication, but that is not what helped me get my act together. My help came from my friend and from a young woman I never met. I asked my friend to pick out my next book to read and she picked out *Chicken Soup for the Soul: Find Your Happiness*.

I am really glad she picked that book because the first story, titled "My Epiphany," by Angela Sayers gave me the attitude adjustment I needed.

Angela was a remarkable young woman with an amazing attitude. She was terminally ill and the doctor didn't give her a lot of time, but she did not let that stop her from living. She lived each day to the fullest and like it was her last. Although I never met her, she taught me a very valuable lesson. As I read her story, I reflected on my life. My illness was so minor, and yet I was acting like it was the end of the world. I realized that there were so many people out there that were sicker than me, but had a better attitude. I should have been happy that there was nothing seriously wrong with me and that I had all my body parts and that my organs functioned normally.

I learned to accept that even though I have panic disorder, it does not have me. I have days when I feel down and depressed and there are even times when I feel my mind spinning out of control, but when I begin to feel like that I do two things: I talk to my friend because she is amazing and supportive, and I think about Angela and everything she went through and how courageous and positive she was. That is enough to bring a smile to my face and turn my attitude around real fast.

~Susan Elizabeth Smith

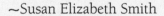

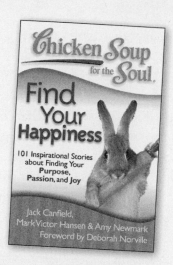

My Epiphany

With the past, I have nothing to do; nor with the future. I live now.
~Ralph Waldo Emerson

It seems that when something awful happens to me, my mind just shuts down. These things change the way I think for a period of time after they happen. Somehow, I find a way to keep it all together by reverting to my "one day at a time" motto, but really, inside, I'm freaking out. Sometimes I'm freaking out and I don't even realize it yet. I've discovered lately that moving on from those difficult times really is a process.

These days, I am in the final stages of my long battle with osteosarcoma, a bone cancer, which made its appearance when I was fourteen years old, claimed one of my lower legs and a lung along the way, and recently spread to my brain. The doctors found three or four new tumors in my brain. This news was a terrible blow since it meant two huge things. It meant that one, along with the nodules that I already had in my single lung, the Thalidomide I have been trying isn't doing a single thing for me. And secondly it officially marked me as terminal. The doctors told us that they thought I probably had less than a month to live.

It has now been longer than a month, and I am still here and still feeling well. Nothing has truly changed about my situation. I am still taking medication for the headaches, and sometimes my breathing is a lot more strained than it used to be. Although I do have a cold, which could be part of it, it's most likely that the cancer is progressing. There is nothing in my situation that has changed. I know that I probably won't make it, still. But there is something different now about the way I look at things. I *feel* different. I feel inspired! I feel invigorated! I don't feel like I'm just sitting around waiting to die anymore. I feel infused with life. There's a reason I have already beaten the odds. There's a reason it's not time yet.

I don't know what came first—the changes to my daily routine, or the changes to my perspective. But somehow they're working together to be just what I needed. During the past week or so we've been making small changes to my medications since I've been doing so well. The first thing we did was drop the nausea medicine I'd been taking on a schedule with the pain medication. It turns out that I don't really need it at all, since I haven't had any nausea since. We also started weaning me off the steroid I'd been taking to control swelling, which makes me eat everything in sight and makes me swell up like a balloon. Somehow, and the only thing I can think to attribute it to, is that by getting rid of those two medications, I am feeling a little more like myself. I haven't had to take a nap in ages! My eyes, which had been blurry and unfocused, are doing so well that I finished a book that I was reading... on my Kindle! My computer screen no longer tries to flip letters around. But that's not all—a few days ago Mom convinced me to put my prosthetic leg on for a while. It didn't take too much cajoling, since it was something I'd been meaning to try since I have been feeling better. It doesn't quite fit right because I haven't worn it in a month. Right now because I haven't been wearing it, I have no leg muscle to even hardly hold it up. But I can kind of walk on it, with my crutches, and I have hope and faith that before long I'll be able to use it again for a short time.

I'm not sure where it came from, this sudden epiphany I've had. But something inside me has clicked. It reminds me of a story my pastor told me when he came by for a visit, about a man who was pronounced terminal. Another person asked him, "What are you doing right now?" And the man who was dying answered, "Well I'm terminal, I'm dying." The first man either asked him again what he was doing right now or informed him somehow that he was wrong. The man who was terminal wasn't dying just then, just at that moment he was living. And as long as he was breathing he would be living. That's the epiphany I've had. Right now, regardless of the things to come, I'm living! I'm not sitting around waiting to die. My entire perspective has changed. I'm alive right now. I'm living.

So, today I leave you with this message, one that I can hardly believe that I went this far without. Cherish every single day. It is one of those things that is easier said than done. The way that something feels is all about perspective. Sometimes our hearts don't need a miracle. Sometimes there just aren't any miracles and the world around us feels like there can never be any happiness in it again. I know how that feels. I have had some dark days these last few months. I won't lie. It's difficult to know that eventually I won't feel good. It's hard to know that essentially I'm just sitting around waiting for the cancer to progress.

I can't think like that anymore. I have to think about the things that I can do. The life that I can live. I may not be able to go on the ski trip this month, but I'm still doing better than expected. I'm still here. I'm still living. Life is precious, whether you have a straight road stretched before you as far as the eye can see, or whether, like most people, your road turns and bends into the undergrowth and you have no idea where it leads. Follow that bend, and your heart, no matter where it goes. Mine may go on, to places unmentionable, but everyone's does, eventually. All roads lead to the same bend, and although we can't see around the corner, I know there are people who have gone before me that will help me when I get there. But for now, I'm not there yet. Today I'm living, and my heart sings with joy for the days that follow.

For anyone going through a difficult time, I want to pass on the list of ten steps that I composed. These steps have helped me move forward in the past. I'm not a professional and I have no claim to fame, but these steps have helped me and I want to share them with other people. Here are my Ten Steps to Moving Forward:

1. Cry, Yell, and Grieve: The first step can make you feel like you are taking a few steps back, but it is necessary. I think when something happens that reroutes your entire life and the direction you were going previously, it is normal to grieve and be sad. Because I believe that whenever you go through a difficult time, it changes you. It changes the way you think and perceive things, and the first step to acceptance of the new reality, whatever it is, is to mourn the past and the person you used to be. So, let yourself grieve for as long as you need to, and when you're able, you'll find the next step.

2. Talk When You're Ready: Sometimes you feel like talking things through and sometimes you don't. When you're ready to talk, find someone who you can talk to as an equal and whose opinion you value, and pour your heart out. Sometimes, just having someone who cares and who is there for you, no matter what, gives you the boost you need, to move on from the first step (even though you may feel still the need to grieve from time to time).

3. Escape When You Need To: but not too often. Sometimes life just takes a dump on you, and your heart and mind are too full to process things in a healthy way. In these moments, escape is essential; watch a TV show or movie, read a book, or veg out on the Internet. Take a break from the things that are weighing you down, and come back to them later with a fresh outlook. But I caution you on escaping too often, because escaping never makes your problems go away, and you always have to deal with them eventually.

4. Start Small: If the big things are too overwhelming at any given moment, start small. Instead of worrying about a huge appointment next week that you're afraid might hold bad news (perhaps similar to where you just were) try to focus on smaller more attainable goals.

Rather than brooding about the appointment, focus on your exercises, your chores, or even your homework assignments. You'll get there in the same amount of time, whether or not you worry about it.

5. Find Your Muse: Your muse is the source of your inspiration. Find the thing, or things, that inspire you the most, and absorb them into your world. These could be anything. For some, it could be their children, others music or nature, and for people like me, poetry or literature.

6. Reach Out: Interaction is an important thing in any person's life. Reaching out doesn't necessarily mean telling everyone about your struggles, rather it means finding people you enjoy, and spending time with them. It can mean laughing and teasing each other, but it also means support. Maybe not support like that of step two, but support that lets you know that they care and that they're thinking of you. This kind of support is a bulwark that can bolster you through any storm. These are the people who know how to cheer you on, when you're going through a hard time.

7. Channel Your Nervous Energy: Often you may find yourself stressing out and worrying. The best way to prevent this is to throw yourself headlong into another project, albeit a more relaxing one. For me, this usually means writing, scrapbooking, or artwork of some kind. I actually find that some of my best poetry is written when I'm trying not to freak out.

8. Help Someone Else: Helping someone else is actually a great way to help you deal with tough things that are going on your own life. It may sound selfish, in an ironic way. But not only does helping someone through their problems distract you, it also fills you with a pleasant satisfaction. Plain and simple; it feels good to help someone else out.

9. Focus on the Good Things: If you go through life with a "woe is me" attitude, things can seem harder than they really are. Granted, I'm finding that optimism comes more easily to me than most, but I cannot help but feel that some optimism is imperative to dealing with any situation. By focusing on the good things in your life, you can muster up enough strength to hope. And I believe that hope is ultimately what allows you to move on.

10. Take One Day At a Time: We spend so much time worrying about things that are far in the future, that we miss the things that are happening in the moment. Even if the moment you are in seems difficult, and there are things on the horizon that seem even more difficult, it is important to focus on the moment you are in. We can't worry about things that haven't happened yet, or that may or may not happen. If you must worry, worry about the day you are in, and worry about tomorrow, well, tomorrow. But remember also, no matter what you're going through, that you will get through. No matter how hard it seems in that moment, or how bleak the future looks, time will move you forward against your will. Eventually you'll find that things don't seem as hard, or hurt as bad, and life will take on a new routine. And you'll be okay. Or... at least that's the way it's been for me.

~Angela Sayers

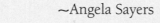

Ask for Help

A friend is the one who comes in when the whole world has gone out.
~Grace Pulpit

The curse of the over compulsive and the addict is the belief that we can rein our behaviors in—all on our own—especially if the behaviors, such as mine, are done in secret. In the beginning my maneuverings afforded me some measure of comfort, helping to ease my mental pain. But in the end, choosing addictive compulsions instead of doing the real work of facing my fears and inadequacies pulled me into the dark underworld of self-loathing.

What had formerly eased my pain was now actually making it worse! Oh what a hellish concoction I had mixed for myself. How I loathed the way my behaviors commanded my will, the way they mocked me. I felt like they were talking to me and saying: "Loser."

I began plotting and planning ways to break free. I battled my secrets by buying books and CDs, consuming reams of information, believing that if I could just find that one bit of information—that one key that fit my lock—then I would be free. I truly believed that I could tame these compulsive addictions all by myself.

Of course, I was wrong. Instead, for many years, the torture of my secret battle raged on.

Then I came across a copy of *Chicken Soup for the Recovering Soul* and realized I had never acknowledged the most liberating bit of information. I could ask for help!

In "Friends of Bill W., Please Come to the Gate..." a flight attendant who is a recovering alcoholic is having a hard time passing the bar in an airport, so in a moment of inspiration, she pages "friends of Bill W." throughout the airport. More than a dozen people come to her aid, even at the risk of missing their own flights, to talk her through her craving for alcohol.

The most important sentence in the story for me was: "Grace had a moment of sanity, realized she could not do it on her own, took the action of asking for help and received it immediately."

I began to weep. I finally understood that I could not rein in my destructive behaviors on my own. Alone was my mortal flaw!

I would not be here today if it were not for eye to eye, soul to soul contact with people who were familiar with my condition and helped me.

The road to self-respecting freedom begins by telling someone, "I am powerless. Help!"

~J. Fullerton

Friends of Bill W., Please Come to the Gate...

Once you learn to walk, crawling is out of the question.
~James D. Davis

Sometime in the early 1990s I was treating a woman in an intensive outpatient chemical dependency group. Let's call her "Grace." Grace was a flight attendant and had been suspended from her job with a major airline due to her untreated alcoholism. She had been stealing the miniature liquor bottles, drinking in airport bars in uniform, and so on. Her employer, realizing she needed treatment, sent her to us.

After the eight-week program, I suggested to her it might be a good idea to solidify her foundation in recovery before returning to work, as she would be working in a high-risk environment (serving alcohol, being out of town alone, etc.). Grace did, however, return to work shortly after completing outpatient treatment. One day while she was departing from a plane at the end of a long day, a major craving for alcohol overpowered her. There she was, in the Los Angeles International Airport, pulling her roller-bag behind her when this massive craving to drink came over her. She tried to just "think through it, " or "just forget about it, " but it was way too powerful. It was so powerful, in fact, that she was resigned to the fact that she would just go drink.

Grace thought, *Oh, the heck with it, I'll get another job… or maybe no one will find out anyway.* But deep down inside, Grace did not want to drink. She truly had wanted to stay sober, but she was in trouble.

On her way to the bar in the airport, Grace had a moment of sanity. She stopped, picked up the airport paging phone and said, "Will you please page friends of Bill W., " she paused, quickly looking around for an empty gate, "to come to Gate 12?"

Within minutes, over the paging system in the L.A. International Airport came, "Will friends of Bill W. please come to Gate 12? Will friends of Bill W. please come to Gate 12?" Most people in recovery know that saying you are a friend of Bill W. is an anonymous way to identify yourself as a member of AA.

In less than five minutes there were about fifteen people at that gate from all over the world. That brought tears of amazement, relief and joy to Grace. They had a little meeting there in that empty gate, total strangers prior to that moment. Grace discovered that two of those people had gotten out of their boarding lines and missed their flights to answer that call for help. They had remembered what they had seen on many walls of meeting rooms: "When anyone, anywhere reaches out their hand for help, I want the hand of AA to be there and for that I am responsible."

Grace did not drink that day. I would venture to guess that none of the people who came to Gate 12 drank that day either. Instead Grace had a moment of sanity, realized she could not do it on her own, took the action of asking for help and received it immediately. This help is available to all of us if we want it and sincerely ask for it. It never fails.

~Jim C., Jr.

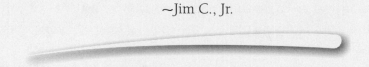

Sticks and Stones

*Let's not forget that the little emotions are the great captains of our lives
and we obey them without realizing it.*
~Vincent van Gogh

"Sticks and stones may break my bones, but words will never harm me," is an old adage my fourth-grade teacher once told me. This saying has been etched in my memory, and I have reflected on this saying many times since I read the story "Two Little Words with a Big Impact" by Linda O'Connell in *Chicken Soup for the Soul: My Resolution.*

I grew up thinking that as long as people didn't physically hurt each other, hurtful words were to be tolerated, but I changed my mind after reading Linda's story. She discusses two words: "and" and "but" and she explained how "but" can be one of the most destructive words in the English language.

I realized that I had felt the sting of the word "but" many times, and that I had wounded others, too, by using the word thoughtlessly. For example, when I was a teacher and edited my students' stories, I would always tell them their content was good, but then I would add comments such as "but you need to proofread your paper more than once" or "but you need to make your characters more realistic." I could have said, "Your content is good, and proofreading will make it even better," or "Your content is good and making your characters even more believable will increase your chances of publication."

In setting up guidelines for critiquing writers, I now realize that we need to praise each other, make helpful comments, and then praise each other again, without using the word "but." I remember a college professor who said, "There is no such thing as constructive criticism. Criticism is criticism." She has now passed on, but her words will remain with me always.

While listening to the service taken from the Book of Common Prayer in church, I listened for the word "and" and "but." For the first time, I noticed that the word "and" was used countless times; but the word "but" was never mentioned. "How positive," I thought.

When a friend once cooked a scrumptious meal and baked a cake for my husband and me, I told her the meal looked delicious, but she was two hours late. As she lifted a perfectly cooked roast from the oven, I saw the look on her face turn from joy to disappointment. I thought I was just being truthful and meant no harm.

I could have said, "The table is beautiful all decked out in fancy linens and your best china. The food smells and looks delectable. You must have spent hours preparing for us, and it's been worth waiting for." Proverbs 12:18 says, "Some people make cutting remarks, but the words of the wise bring healing."

I have watched a smile come to the faces of my own children and grandchildren when I praised them and put their art projects on the refrigerator. I have seen that a loving and nurturing word like "and" will lift their spirits and build their self-esteem as they proudly present me a paper they have improved on.

My fourth-grade teacher's quote was aimed at what she thought was harmless playground teasing, but she was wrong. Even teasing hurts. And today, the news relates many stories where young people have committed suicide because they were the victims of ugly words.

Now I realize the importance of thinking before speaking, even to avoid seemingly inconsequential words like "but." Sticks and stones break our bones, but thoughtless words also do harm. They can leave scars for a lifetime.

~Janet N. Miracle

Two Little Words with a Big Impact

Too many people miss the silver lining because they're expecting gold.
~Maurice Setter

I have always considered myself a positive thinker, an upbeat person and an optimist. I try to find the best in every situation. I've recently become aware of how two little words in my vocabulary have had a tremendous impact on people. I didn't even realize it.

I've been listening to myself lately, and I don't like the way I sound. As a veteran teacher, I know that praise can be a huge motivational tool. I realize the importance of developing a child's self-esteem. I generously sprinkle uplifting comments around my classroom like I am fertilizing flowers. Each new school year brings a garden variety of students, and they all blossom with praise and encouragement. I know how to thank my grown kids, my grandkids and my husband for a job well done. I toss compliments to the unsuspecting if it appears someone needs a lift. I also yo-yo my positive comments right back when I use the word that makes my preschoolers giggle—BUT.

When one of my students attempted to print her name, I oohed and ahhed. "Wow! That is a great A, and your letter D is nice and tall, but your letter E should be short; can you erase it and try to make it shorter?" I asked. She wasn't crushed by my comment. She tried to live up to my expectation. I thought I was helping, preparing her for kindergarten, showing her the difference in size between upper case and lower case letters. I don't believe that my comment would have any long term affect on her self-worth. I imagine though, if I'd substituted the word BUT with the word AND, she'd have been proud of her accomplishment instead of questioning the "right way" to print her name. I wish I had said, "I like your nice tall letters, AND I like how hard you are trying to make your letter E."

My recently divorced daughter called to tell me about a house she was interested in. I listened to her. I applauded her for moving forward with her life, and I said, "Honey, I am glad that you've found something you like, but...." There, I did it again! "Don't you think, with the gas prices, you might want to buy closer to your work?" As she told me all about the prospective house, I could hear the excitement and joy in her voice. The moment I spoke the word, BUT, it was as if I pricked a balloon with a needle. I could hear her slowly deflate. I sure wish I'd used the word AND. "Honey, I'm glad you found a house in your price range, AND I'm happy for you." She knows I freely express my opinions, and I know she's used to my mouth. I suspect that if I had leashed my tongue, her emotions wouldn't have flip-flopped, and we'd have both hung up feeling better.

Recently I visited my son and his six-year-old little boy and six-month-old daughter. I scooped up my grandchildren and bragged. He babysits while my daughter-in-law works weekends. I told him he was a great father; I praised him for his devotion to his family. He beamed as though he was a little boy, and then I flubbed. "You should be commended for spending your whole day taking your little boy to his sports events, but don't you think he might be worn out and ready for a bath?" There I was with my bad word again! My son's smile slid away, and he said, "He'll be fine. I'll get him to bed soon." I planted an ounce of doubt, when I should have been planting the seeds of confidence. I wish I'd said, "You're a good father,

AND I admire your ability to recognize the children's individual needs."

My granddaughter showed up at my door dressed like a princess on her way to the prom. I told her how beautiful she looked. I told her I was proud of the young lady she has become, and I said, "Sweetheart, I want you to have a great time, but please don't drink tonight." I know she doesn't engage in risky behavior; she's responsible and sensible and trustworthy. She looked as though I'd snatched her crown. "Nana!" The tone of her voice indicated how I'd made her feel. How I wish I'd said, "I want you to have a great time, AND I trust you."

My dear husband helps around the house; he did the dishes, emptied the dishwasher, and folded the laundry. I was thrilled he had lightened my workload. I thanked him. I told him how wonderful he is, and I used that naughty word again. "BUT, why did you leave crumbs all over the counter?" Why? Why? Why didn't I say, "Thank you, AND I appreciate all you do around the house."

I've been doing some self-reflecting. I've given up on losing those twenty pounds. I've decided a walk around the neighborhood is a good substitute for vigorous exercise. I've watched dust bunnies cuddle under the sofa. I've prayed in the dark instead of at church more often than not. In other words, all those New Year's resolutions are now null and void. I lose a pound; I eat a chocolate; I gain a pound. The bar on my treadmill makes a nice rack for hanging laundry. I've attended church for grandchildren's christenings, and I pass the sanctuary on my way to the church office. I vacuum on weekends. I figure if the dust bunnies don't mind snuggling for another day, I don't care either.

My house isn't spotless, my thighs are heavy, my soul, like my face could use some uplifting, but I have decided that I simply cannot keep all those resolutions I made on January 1st. I'm ready for some spring cleaning. I'm tossing those old resolutions out and I am making one, just one, which I intend to keep. I am going to refrain from using the B word. I think I can do it, and I am going to give it my best. I know it will have a positive effect on others. BUT if I mess up, I will try again, and again, and again to remove that naughty little word from my vocabulary. I resolve to replace it with the word AND. This is a resolution I intend to keep!

~Linda O'Connell

The Room Decorated with Love

In time of test, family is best.
~Burmese Proverb

Jeannie Lancaster's story called "Entering the Thankful Zone" in *Chicken Soup for the Soul: The Power of Positive* took me back nearly five years to when my eighty-nine-year-old father entered the hospital for the last time.

"Your father won't last another two weeks," the doctor said, the sympathy in his eyes at odds with the stark words.

My sister Carla and I clung to each other. "What can we do for him?" I asked.

"We can't do anything more for him here," the doctor said. "I suggest placing him in a care facility where he will be well looked after."

We reviewed the local care centers and chose one. Within a day, we knew we'd made a mistake. The staff, though professional, was overworked and didn't have the time to give our father the attention he needed.

"This isn't working," I whispered.

Carla nodded. "Let's take Dad home."

With the help of hospice, we brought Dad home the following day.

Several grandchildren and great-grandchildren lived close by and visited him when he felt up to it. The great-grandchildren drew pictures and made cards. What these crayon and watercolor drawings lacked in artistic talent, they made up for with enthusiastic color and unbridled imagination.

Just as Jeannie Lancaster decorated her husband's hospital room with index cards of gratitude, we tacked these cards and pictures to the walls, set them on tables, surrounding Dad with love.

I encouraged family members who lived in other states to send cards as well. More handmade cards and pictures went up until Dad's room resembled a Hallmark store.

Carla and I took turns staying with our father. I read the cards to him and we laughed over the exuberant and improbable drawings of two-headed horses and pink cows. "These are one-of-a-kind originals," I said to Dad, who rewarded me with a smile.

Dad didn't last the expected two weeks. Within five days of our bringing him home, he passed away, there in the room we had decorated with love.

Over the years, occasional doubts assailed me over our decision to bring Dad home, taking him away from the care of professional nurses and attendants. Had we done the right thing?

Jeannie Lancaster's story reassured me that we gave Dad what he needed most: family and love.

~Jane McBride Choate

Entering the Thankful Zone

If you want to turn your life around, try thankfulness.
It will change your life mightily.
~Gerald Good

One by one we wrote upon the 3x5 index cards and then taped them to the closet door across from my husband's hospital bed. On the card at the top was written "God's Love," on another "Each New Morning."

It was Thanksgiving Day 2011, and my husband and I were celebrating the holiday alone in his hospital room. He had been admitted a couple of weeks earlier, after his AML (acute myeloid leukemia) had roared out of remission. Our adult children, who lived with us, were spending the day with friends in our town an hour to the north.

Earlier that morning, as I prepared to leave home and head to the hospital, I found myself grumbling about the fact that we wouldn't be together as a family; this would not be the kind of Thanksgiving we had hoped for. A specter of worry about my husband's health hung over the day. But then, I had an idea!

I raced about our home gathering supplies and printing things out on the computer. As I did so, I found my attitude changing and a sense of anticipation and gratitude replacing my darker thoughts.

Later that morning, I walked into my husband's room and pulled out a sign I had printed. I announced, "We are declaring this room the 'Thankful Zone.'" I taped the sign to the outside of his door, where anyone coming into his room would see it. It read, "You are now entering the 'Thankful Zone.' Admittance is an Attitude of Gratitude."

I handed my husband a pen and some of the 3x5 cards I had brought with me, and we proceeded to reflect on the things that we were most grateful for. The list grew as the day passed.

"Hope," "Faith" and "Love" were placed at the top of our list. "Good friends" and "Dear family" also held places of honor.

My husband, who could not leave the medical unit he was on, wrote that he was grateful for "Sunshine," for "Moonless nights, when you can see the stars" and for "The smell in the air after rain."

He laughed, but wholeheartedly agreed when I added "anti-nausea drugs" and the name of the sedation drug that he was given before each of his many bone marrow biopsies.

Something happened as we added each new item. We were able to step back from the horror of cancer and see that even in the midst of great adversity there can also be great blessings. Among the many blessings were "Laughter," "Music" and through it all "Each other."

Our changed attitude affected everything around us. We even found ourselves thankful for the delicious hospital dinner of turkey and stuffing and the hands that had prepared it. We recognized the blessing of the amazing nurses and doctors who were caring for my husband.

At the day's end, the closet door was overflowing with written reminders of the many things we were thankful for. No, we had not been able to spend a traditional Thanksgiving with family and friends, but we had experienced a day overflowing with giving thanks. Simple things such as "Warm showers" and "Dancing with the one you love" can make life an unexpectedly sweet journey.

~Jeannie Lancaster

The Living Room

Kids spell love T-I-M-E.
~John Crudele

When I read the poem called "The Play's the Thing" in *Chicken Soup for the Mother's Soul*, I realized my life was very similar to that of the author, Jayne Jaudon Ferrer. Every day was a routine for me. I cleaned, cooked, and spent time on chores that didn't have to be done at that very moment.

I had always been so paranoid that someone would come over and see shoes on the floor, books off their shelves and toys everywhere that I was cleaning at the expense of my son. He would throw a ball at me while I was washing dishes and I wouldn't even react. While I was vacuuming, my son would hold up his bear and make those adorable baby talk noises. Did I put the vacuum down? No. I said, "Oh what a pretty bear," and continued disinfecting my home.

After I read the poem one night when William, my son, was asleep, I teared up and resolved to change. It wasn't that easy. The next day, I forced myself not to pick up the two toys he brought into the living room, not to hover over him with a mop smelling of floor cleaner in case of spills, and not to insist that he eat his snack in our designated eating spot. Instead, I played trucks, danced with him in a circle in the living room, and made a mess baking brownies for him. It was a great day.

So now, every day, we play bears or trucks, dance to Lady Gaga, and just have fun. At night, when he is asleep, I clean like nobody's business. I have also discovered that just because there are a couple of shoes in the wrong place, or some toys are scattered in my living room, it doesn't mean our house is dirty. It just means that we are actually living here.

~Brittany Perry

The Play's the Thing

It is a happy talent to know how to play.
~Ralph Waldo Emerson

Forgive me, Lord,
for all the tasks
that went undone today.
But this morning when my child
toddled in and said, "Mommy play?"
I simply had to say yes.
And between the puzzles and trucks
and blocks and dolls and old hats and
books and giggles,
we shared a thousand special thoughts,
a hundred hopes and dreams and hugs.
And tonight, when prayer time came
and he folded his hands and softly whispered,
"Thank you, God, for Mommy and Daddy and
toys and French fries, but 'specially
for Mommy playing,"

I knew it was a day well wasted.
And I knew You'd understand.

~Jayne Jaudon Ferrer

Joining the Family Business

You have to decide what your highest priorities are
and have the courage—pleasantly, smilingly, nonapologetically—
to say "no" to other things. And the way to do that is by having
a bigger "yes" burning inside.
~Stephen Covey

Fifteen years ago, the most important story of my life was being written... but I was oblivious. It was a story overflowing with love, bleeding with sacrifice, and brimming with hope. It was my mother's story – "Résumé of the Heart"—written for me, about me, and in spite of me. "Look!" said Mom one day with a hint of humble excitement as I returned home from school. I was a preoccupied preteen at the time, more concerned with boys and the color of my backpack. "One of my stories was just published in *Chicken Soup for the Mother & Daughter Soul!*"

I had to admit that I was pretty impressed. My mom was published in a real live book. I celebrated with her as any twelve-year-old with her head in the clouds would. I grinned at her name in print, showed off her copy of the book to friends, and quietly glowed with pride and excitement. But it has taken me fifteen years to understand the real moral of the story—that even as I read my dear mother's words and failed to grasp their true significance, she was writing my own story, too.

I'd read the words, but didn't realize how my mom's heart

continued to ache as she flashed her encouraging smiles that propelled me forward. She watched me grow through high school, giving me nudges now and then, and stayed strong as I spread my wings to soar toward every mother's worst nightmare—the military. And my mom kept sacrificing, standing steady as my rock, as I soared through four strenuous years at West Point, the successful start to my Army career, my wedding, and the birth of my first child.

Mom was always there for me, no matter what I needed. When driving around hopelessly lost, I knew my mom would drop what she was doing to answer my phone call and help navigate from a distance. My dad joked that I'd never need OnStar; I had MomStar. She became Dial-a-Recipe when I wanted to master her special dishes, my greatest prayer buddy when I sent out pleas for prayer, and she had burned a path to the post office sending morning sickness remedies when I was pregnant.

Yet it was only as I looked into my beautiful newborn daughter's eyes four years ago that my mother's story really hit home for the first time. I finally began to understand her words—or rather, live them. I was a woman in the workforce suddenly losing my heart to the most fragile miracle I had ever encountered.

I'd come face to face with the disconnect between the world's standard of a successful professional and my new role as a mother. My five-year military service contract guaranteed a comfortable salary and ample opportunity for advancement. I spent every day working among heroes. I answered to "Captain," and my soldiers recognized me as a leader.

My résumé was nothing short of impressive. But as I returned to work, I realized that more than anything I wanted to turn right back around and stay home with my daughter—witnessing her first words, watching her first steps, responding to her every need. I ached for those things that my mother had written about. Her words were becoming my own, and as our family grew, they burned their way into my heart. Despite my extensive education and diverse opportunities, I longed for the tiniest increments of time with my children, when I could lend a helping hand, open a storybook, or share in the discovery of a moment. I began counting the days until my service commitment would end so I could finally be a stay-at-home mom—it seemed the day couldn't come soon enough.

Thankfully, that day did come. I am blessed to spend each day with our three beautiful children. I answer to "Mommy" now. I am finally the one kissing boo-boos to make them better. I push aside my own dreams to encourage those of my children. But with my résumé buried at the bottom of the pile, my mother's words ring truer than ever. When my daughter's school registration form demands to know my profession, it's difficult to ignore the inner twinge as I write "Homemaker" instead of "U.S. Army Officer." I'm met with the humbling realization that the world doesn't always understand the merits of my new job—one of the most important in the world.

No, I'll never be featured as *Time* magazine's person of the year, nor will my résumé boast any great accomplishments beyond the career I so quickly left behind. But I do know that I have gained my own "Résumé of the Heart"—the one, I am learning, that will count most in the long run. As my mother so eloquently put it fifteen years ago as she wrote our story:

"Mine is the kiss that melts away the pain of a scraped knee. Mine is the heart that swells while witnessing each new triumph. Mine is the smile that bravely encourages independence, while silently wrestling with the ache of letting go. After all, there's nothing heroic about hugs—unless you're on the receiving end."

~Megan C. Hjelmstad

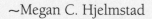

Résumé of the Heart

Being a full-time mother is one of the highest salaried jobs in my field,
since the payment is pure love.
~Mildred B. Vermont

My daughter waited while I stitched the final threads, anchoring a button to the shirt she was about to put on. As her nimble fingers tucked the last button through its hole, I reached up and untangled the golden strands of her ponytail. I wrapped my arms around her in a hug. Then she disappeared through the doorway and onto the waiting school bus.

I knew in that moment that my accomplishments of the past years would never be listed in the *Who's Who* of life. I loved being a mother. Still, I often witnessed the puzzled faces as unknowing souls asked, "What do you do all day?" Most people could not understand my choices; after all, there's nothing heroic about hugs—unless you're on the receiving end.

Despite an extensive education and diverse opportunities, my résumé couldn't tout prestigious positions or high salaries. Instead, it was marked by the tiniest increments of time when I'd lent a helping hand, opened a storybook or shared in the discovery of a moment.

I'd spent endless hours taxiing between practices, applauding little accomplishments and discerning temporary hurts from great big wounds of the heart.

Mine was the kiss that melted the pain of a scraped knee. Mine was the heart that swelled while witnessing each new triumph. Mine was the smile that bravely encouraged independence, while silently wrestling with the ache of letting go.

There is no place on a résumé for the wisdom of life experiences, compassion or nurturing relationships. The logic of my choices over the years would be appreciated by only a few, and never in the *Who's Who* of life.

But as my front door opened again later that afternoon and growing arms embraced me, I knew I had been blessed with a résumé of the heart. The real *Who* in life had already given me just enough prestige and salary to be the Who I was meant to be.

~Kathleen Swartz McQuaig

Chapter

2

READER'S CHOICE

Attitude Adjustments

If you don't like something change it;
if you can't change it, change the way you think about it.

~Mary Engelbreit

I Am Me and I Am Okay

Respect yourself and others will respect you.
~Confucius

In 1988, at the age of thirty-four, I divorced a man who had been lying and cheating on me for years. And as the old story goes, I was the last to know. I'll never forget his hurtful remark, as I threw his sorry butt out the door, "You are what I am." At the time I knew it wasn't true, but his words planted a seed of doubt in my very fragile self-esteem that festered and changed me into someone I didn't want to be.

Thank goodness two wonderful children had come out of my sixteen-year marriage, because for a very long time after the divorce they were the only light I could see from the dark emotional abyss I'd slipped into. My self-esteem had taken a nasty hit, and I encased myself in a bitter shell I vowed no man would ever break through again. My self-preservation instinct had kicked in big time.

It was a struggle raising children alone, and my ex-husband turned out to be a deadbeat father the children never saw again. During those first five years after the divorce I prayed more than ever before. I prayed for the courage to face my life and be a good mother to my children. Life was hard and there were times we didn't have much, but we had each other and our little family circle was secure. I also prayed for the wisdom to put the bitterness in the past and leave it there.

One day in 1993 I was in the local department store, waiting in line for the cashier, and there on the shelf beside the checkout was a book titled *Chicken Soup for the Soul*. I picked it up and randomly opened the pages to a story called "My Declaration of Self-Esteem." There were six or seven people ahead of me in the line and of course the one at the cashier needed a price check. So I figured I had time to read the short two-page story. And it changed my life!

The book was a luxury I really couldn't afford on my meager salary, but I knew I had to have it. That little story made me square my shoulders and look everyone in the eye on the way home.

That night, after the children were settled in their beds, I crawled into mine and picked up my new book. I must have read "My Declaration of Self-Esteem" a dozen times or more! I read each line carefully, absorbing the wisdom in every word, and understanding how unique I was and that I was the only one who could control my destiny. The last line — "I am me and I am okay" — was something that would reverberate in my head for years to come.

Before long, there were so many dog-eared pages in that book it ended up twice as thick as it was when I bought it. Simply oozing inspiration, the positive reinforcement on each and every page was indeed chicken soup for my soul, and I re-read the stories again and again whenever I was troubled or life just got too difficult.

My investment in that little book turned out to be one of the best I've ever made because the stories in it helped me learn to love myself, and once that happened my life began to change for the better. I finally realized I was a good person, worthy of the best, and the past was just history!

Today I am happily married to the love of my life, and he's a good man I trust with all my heart. He loves me unconditionally and that love is reciprocated without hesitation. I know I am where I was destined to be!

After a multitude of moves, nineteen years have come and gone since I read the original *Chicken Soup for the Soul* and I still have that book. From time to time I pick it up and re-read the stories; however I always come back to the one that helped me change my life and embrace a positive attitude. I would strongly recommend "My Declaration of Self-Esteem" to anyone that needs a nice warm cup of chicken soup for the soul.

~Annabel Sheila

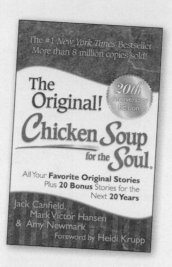

My Declaration of Self-Esteem

What I am is good enough if I would only be it openly.
~Carl Rogers

The following was written in answer to a 15-year-old girl's question, "How can I prepare myself for a fulfilling life?"

I am me.

In all the world, there is no one else exactly like me.

There are people who have some parts like me but no one adds up exactly like me. Therefore, everything that comes out of me is authentically mine because I alone choose it.

I own everything about me—my body, including everything it does; my mind, including all my thoughts and ideas; my eyes, including the images of all they behold; my feelings, whatever they might be—anger, joy, frustration, love, disappointment, excitement; my mouth and all the words that come out of it—polite, sweet and rough, correct or incorrect; my voice, loud and soft; all my actions, whether they be to others or myself.

I own my fantasies, my dreams, my hopes, my fears.

I own all my triumphs and successes, all my failures and mistakes.

Because I own all of me, I can become intimately acquainted with me. By so doing, I can love me and be friendly with me in all my parts. I can then make it possible for all of me to work in my best interests.

I know there are aspects about myself that puzzle me, and other aspects that I do not know. But as long as I am friendly and loving to myself, I can courageously and hopefully look for the solutions to the puzzles and for ways to find out more about me.

However I look and sound, whatever I say and do, and whatever I think and feel at a given moment in time is me. This is authentic and represents where I am at that moment in time.

When I review later how I looked and sounded, what I said and did, and how I thought and felt, some parts may turn out to be unfitting. I can discard that which is unfitting and keep that which proved fitting, and invent something new for that which I discarded.

I can see, hear, feel, think, say and do. I have the tools to survive, to be close to others, to be productive, to make sense and order out of the world of people and things outside of me.

I own me and therefore I can engineer me.

I am me and I am okay.

~Virginia Satir

Lunch with David

Reality is the leading cause of stress amongst those in touch with it.
~Jane Wagner

The very first story I wrote for the *Chicken Soup for the Soul* series appeared in *Chicken Soup for the Caregiver's Soul*. When my copy of the book arrived, I immediately sat down to read the entire volume. Early on, I came to Teri Batts' story called "Lunch with Grandma" and I began to laugh out loud. My chuckles turned to guffaws and the noise wafted through the house. Curious, my husband came upstairs to see what had amused me, but when I tried to read the story aloud to him, I couldn't control my own chortles. In truth, I could barely breathe as I laughed and shared this wild adventure of Teri taking her grandmother, afflicted with Alzheimer's disease, out to lunch.

Little did I guess that a few years down the road I would step into the role of caregiver again. This time it was my cousin who needed help. David was only fifty years old when doctors diagnosed him with Pick's disease. Similar to Alzheimer's, this form of dementia affects the frontal and temporal lobes of the brain. The lobes slowly shrink and steadily impair the ability to recognize faces and find the right word. In David's case, after a few years he could no longer distinguish the faces of people he loved. When I visited, he did not know if I was his cousin, his sister, his daughter or his wife. Simple words like "clock" and "glass" fled from his mind and left him groping for weak substitutes that could express his needs.

In his earlier years, my cousin had amazing gifts. For example, when he was an eighth-grade student, he took a woodshop class at school and, for his class project he decided to build a harpsichord. Not a walnut bookshelf, like his classmates made. Not a pair of oak candle sticks. A full-sized musical instrument. For years I listened to David play the keys of that instrument every time I visited his home. His fingers flitted across the keyboard and produced sounds that set my heart dancing.

Today, that harpsichord sits in the front hall of his home, a mute reminder of the woodworking talents my cousin once had.

When he grew up and graduated from college, David became a successful director of a well-known museum near my home. His knowledge of history and his passion for facts made him well respected in his field. He served as president of a national historical society. The onset of the Pick's disease forced him to leave these roles.

Today, when I visit him on the dementia ward, he can't remember what he had for breakfast.

At first I watched the slowdown of David's mind from a distance. His wife bore the brunt of caring for him during those early years. As the task of looking after David began to weigh heavier and heavier upon her, I gave her a copy of *Chicken Soup for Caregiver's Soul*, hoping the stories would encourage her.

But a time came when she was no longer able to care for her husband at home. She moved him to a care facility nearer my home. She visited several times each week. I promised to visit regularly too.

David's new home was lovely. The staff was friendly and unfailingly patient with the residents. I was amazed how each member of the staff knew the names of all the residents. As David and I walked the halls outside the dementia wing, even the people sweeping the floors and preparing meals waved and greeted David by name. The staff set aside a place for David to have his own woodshop where he could continue to work on simple projects with his hands. The meals were good and the rooms clean.

Still I found the environment depressing. I asked a friend who worked on a similar unit in another care facility how she coped with the melancholic atmosphere. She surprised me by saying how much she enjoyed the ward. "In the nursing wing, the people have active minds but their bodies are failing. Many of them truly are depressed and they often complain. But here on the dementia unit? The people don't realize that their minds have gone. They are grateful for each activity and take each day as it comes."

Could it be true? I was so focused on what David had lost. I thought back to Teri Batts' story of taking her grandmother to lunch. Instead of grieving over what no longer was, Teri entered into her grandmother's new world. She joined her grandmother as she crawled across the floor of the restaurant avoiding "danger." Instead of tears of grief, Teri produced tears of laughter.

These days I still visit David regularly. Occasionally he sits down at the piano in the group activity room. His nimble fingers pull harmonies from the old instrument. That portion of his brain remains intact. I rejoice in the pleasure he gives his listeners. A fellow resident begins singing a tune. David and I enjoy a meal together. A female resident walks off with his dessert. He responds with a gentle smile.

I remember better days, but I do not grieve. Thanks, Teri, for the reminder that laughter is still the best entree on the lunch menu.

~Emily Parke Chase

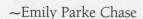

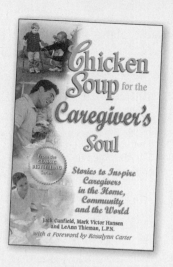

Lunch with Grandma

Laughter is the sun that drives winter from the human face.
~Victor Hugo

Although uncertain, unprepared and unaware of the challenges of Alzheimer's disease, I headed to Charlotte to help Mom care for Grandma. With my usual upbeat, positive attitude, I rose the first morning full of enthusiasm and knowing exactly what to do, or so I thought.

But before my first cup of coffee, I entered the bathroom to find Grandmother attempting to brush her teeth with a razor. Shocked and near hysterics, I yelled for my mother while trying to retrieve the razor without hurting Grandmother or myself. Mom quietly walked into the room, confiscated the razor and took control with a smile and what looked like an invisible tear. Tears were many as the day went on. The "tuff one," as I had been called, had met her match.

A few days passed and I became more confident as Mom and I realized that Grandma did things born of habit. So we began playing on her habits—messing up the living room so she could straighten up again and again, assigning her the chore of sweeping the porch, and washing unbreakable plates and cups as I dried them and put them away.

My confidence grew. I decided to take Grandma to lunch, just the two of us. Against mother's better judgment, I decided to take her to a steakhouse with a salad bar, so Grandma could pick out what SHE wanted to eat.

Riding to the restaurant was no problem; she just loved these new-fangled vehicles. Happily, we entered the steakhouse, got our plates, and ventured to the salad bar. But Grandmother didn't know what anything was, not even a roll. She refused to eat anything except the pretty "red stuff" that wiggled. Finally, with only gelatin on her plate, we sat down and had a wonderful lunch. She swirled the good "red stuff" around in her mouth, thoroughly enjoying herself.

All of a sudden, she grabbed my arm and yanked me to the floor, pulling me under the table. I was too shocked to scream. I took her arm and gently coaxed her to stand, but she clutched my arms with a surprising strength and jerked me back to the floor. "Indians!" she cried out. "We must escape!"

Trying desperately to understand, I said, "Where are the Indians?"

Frightened, she pointed to a group of people that had just entered the restaurant. Then she started crawling on the floor, dragging her purse behind and motioning me to follow her.

"Come on!" she commanded, her irritation and my embarrassment mounting.

What the heck, I thought, swallowing any pride I had left. I crept behind her between and under empty tables, making our way through the great Wild West toward the salad bar. Once we arrived safely, she pulled me toward her and said, "That way to the door! We can make it," she said. "Be brave!"

Off we went in a fast crawl, her in her dress, me in cut-off blue jeans, both of us dragging a purse and turning our heads from side to side as we went. She was looking for danger and I was looking to see who was staring. Just when we were getting close to the door, the manager came from behind the counter. Terrified, Grandma flung herself over my body to protect me.

The manager gazed down at the two of us piled in a heap on the floor and asked, "Can I help you ladies?"

I burst out laughing. Grandma pulled herself up and bent over to help me since I was laughing so hard I couldn't stand. She brushed me off and asked me, "Are you okay, honey?"

The confused manager asked the obvious question. "Is anything wrong?"

"Of course, everything is quite all right," Grandma said, "now that you are here, Marshall Dillon."

Grandma pulled me to the door as I laughed. Once she got there, she turned back to the manager and said, "I'm sorry, sir, we forgot to pay." She took a dime out of her purse and placed it on the counter.

"Thank you, ma'am," he said and gave her a big smile.

By now I was laughing so hard I could hardly breathe. My grandmother gripped my arm and jerked me toward the door. "We have to get out of here, Teri," she said. "You're embarrassing me."

~Teri Batts

The Tipping Point

If at first you don't succeed, do it like your mother told you.
~Author Unknown

Most of my adult life has been spent in and out of prison, and 2008 was no different. That was the year I began serving this seven-and-a-half-year sentence for charges stemming from problems I've had in my life with addiction. Only this incarceration would prove to be a major tipping point for my loved ones.

After endless disappointments, the last of my family and friends had finally had enough. They gave up hoping I'd realize the errors of my ways. I was entirely on my own—completely and absolutely alone.

Loneliness can do one of two things to a man. It can cause him to give up, abandoning all hope for his own self, or it can instill in him a drive to find something better, no matter how much negativity he must first overcome.

For the first year and a half I had succumbed to a very depressing, dark time. That was until I found a reason to demand better of myself thanks to the book *Chicken Soup for the Prisoner's Soul*.

I had heard of the series but never read a *Chicken Soup for the Soul* book and had no idea how much of an impact one would have on my life. The first time I read *Chicken Soup for the Prisoner's Soul*, I was in solitary confinement. If there was such a thing as rock bottom,

I was certainly there. In such a cold, bleak environment, the stories I read were like a campfire, warming me deep down to my core.

One story in particular—"Success—Who Can Judge?"—influenced me the most. It was written by Tom Lagana, who also was one of the coauthors of *Chicken Soup for the Prisoner's Soul*. The story was about a man named Rick who, much like myself, spent most of his life incarcerated. With so much time I still had to serve, this story helped me to see that there was real opportunity in front of me… an opportunity for major, positive changes. At my absolute lowest point, there I sat, greatly inspired by Rick and all he had overcome. His story was a mirror image of my own, and I began to think, "If this guy can make the changes needed in his life, why not me?" So I decided to focus on finding something I could feasibly accomplish while incarcerated.

While reading *Chicken Soup for the Prisoner's Soul*, I also noticed that the cartoons included were created mostly by people who were incarcerated. Matt Matteo's cartoons appeared frequently throughout the book. As an artist myself, I was amazed by his talent and reach. Here was a guy who was incarcerated making very valid strides toward more positive things. I realized then that I wanted to do the same thing. I wanted my life to have purpose and meaning, even while I was a prisoner. That passion became my focus.

Thanks to the contact information in the back of the book, I began corresponding with Tom Lagana and Matt Matteo. Both provided me with invaluable insight as to how to start creating my own cartoons, as well as uplifting words of encouragement and kindness. I created cartoons at a frantic pace and even began submitting my work to many different publications. It gave me a great sense of accomplishment.

Now I am more than four years into my incarceration journey, still creating cartoons, and have found direction in my life. I've set realistic goals I plan to achieve once released and work daily toward showing my loved ones I have the capability to be successful.

I realize now that there was another tipping point to this story… one I so desperately needed so that I could find reason to change my life for the better. That tipping point was *Chicken Soup for the Prisoner's Soul*. Thanks to Rick's story, cartoonist Matt Matteo, and coauthor Tom Lagana, I found hope in a seemingly hopeless situation.

~Joseph P. Guerrero

COULD YOU MENTION THAT I'VE BEEN
READING "CHICKEN SOUP FOR THE
PRISONER'S SOUL?"

Chicken Soup for the PRISONER'S Soul

101 Stories to
Open the Heart and
Rekindle the Spirit of
Hope, Healing and
Forgiveness

Jack Canfield, Mark Victor Hansen
and Tom Lagana

Success—
Who Can Judge?

While awaiting sentencing, I decided to give stand-up comedy a shot.
The judge had suggested I get my act together, and I took him seriously.
~Tim Allen

n September 1997, I coordinated a project to bring a group of motivational speakers into prison for Make-a-Difference Day. The warden had given me a list of specific criteria each speaker needed to meet in order to gain entrance to the prison for that program. The first item on that list was: "No criminal record."

I had volunteered in this prison for the past five years, and when I decided to coordinate this program, I had immediately thought of many potential speakers—including several former inmates. I had been especially excited about inviting one in particular to speak—Rick.

Rick had spent most of his adult life in prison. It appeared he was on the in-and-out plan. First he would be in, then he would be out—released just long enough to get himself sentenced to be in again. But two years earlier he had been released, and he had not returned. He had finally found a way to become successful in society. I was proud of him. I believed his story could help make a difference to the current inmate population in a way no other motivational speakers could. After all, Rick had been there, and now he was a success—on the outside.

So I asked the warden to make an exception. "Obviously, he has found a way to live successfully and responsibly," I pleaded. "I'm sure his message could move these inmates like no one else's."

"Tell me the name again," the warden requested.

"Rick," I said, and I gave his full name.

"But Rick is in Booking right now—he was brought back in last night."

I felt my heart drop. I must have been wrong. Rick wasn't a success after all. He had been out of jail for two years—but now he was back. And probably for life. Hadn't the judge warned him at his last sentencing? If he was arrested and convicted again, he would be sentenced to a life term as a habitual criminal.

I was beyond disappointment. Part of me felt like chucking it all. Make-a-Difference Day? Hummphh. Apparently, nothing made a difference. But I kept working at the arrangements anyway—halfheartedly.

A week later, I ran into Rick at the weekly meeting I sponsor in the prison. I was both happy and sad to see him. I greeted him with my standard big hug, and I told him how I felt.

"I was so sure you had made it! I was certain you were a success! What happened? I'm so disappointed."

Rick's answer surprised me: "But Tom, I am a success. In forty-four years, this is the longest time I have ever been out of jail. I was responsible! I paid my electric bills and phone bills—for two years! I have been clean, drug-free and sober for all this time. I did a stupid thing, yes. But that is nowhere near as stupid as the stuff I used to do. And I'm only sentenced to four months for a parole violation. Me? I can still walk with my head held high. I am a success."

I'm not ashamed to tell you that the next thing he said brought tears to my eyes. "Please don't be disappointed—so much of my success is because of you! The way you always showed up, week after week, and helped us put this program together. The way you always greeted me with a smile and genuine concern about how I was doing. The way you believed in me even when I couldn't believe in myself. Maybe those couple of hours every week weren't such a big deal to you, but to me, they were everything."

He was right. He was a success. He was a success because he saw himself as one. Rick had changed.

The funny thing was, now that Rick was back inside the walls, I didn't need any special permission to make him a speaker at the Make-a-Difference Day program. Maybe his parole violation actually served a greater purpose, after all. And as I listened to him, the truth dawned on me: Rick didn't need to wait the four months of his sentence to regain his freedom. His perception of himself had already set him free.

~Tom Lagana

Fearing the Scar

Now my belly is as noble as my heart.
~Gabriela Mistral

I was pregnant with twin girls. My first pregnancy had ended in a miscarriage, so I was very apprehensive.

As the pregnancy progressed, my doctor brought up the fact that the practice preferred to deliver twins by C-section due to the possible complications that could arise from giving birth twice in a row. Naturally, I would do what it took to give my daughters the best possible chance at a healthy birth. But I was very worried about the C-section, and especially about the scar.

I was blessed with a wonderful husband who had seen past my insecurities and self-esteem issues surrounding my weight for fourteen years. Michael had always loved me for who I was and thought I was beautiful. However, would he feel the same after I had a large scar?

Someone (unfortunately I don't remember who) gave me *Chicken Soup for the New Mom's Soul* and I devoured it! I loved reading all the stories of women who had faced hardships, uncertainties and even humor during their own crazy pregnancies.

Then I found the story "Because He Loved Me" by Ginger LeBlanc. It spoke to my exact fears and described my exact feelings. I was reading my own story! As she described how her husband reacted to her after a C-section, my body shook as I sobbed. Michael read it. I confessed my fears to him. While he tried to reassure me, I couldn't shake the fear.

Before dawn on the morning before Mother's Day, at thirty-six weeks pregnant, my water broke. We knew that one of the girls was sitting in the breach position, so there was no way to avoid a C-section. When the doctor at the hospital confirmed that was the only option, I hesitated and looked helplessly at Michael. The doctor followed my gaze and asked him, "Do you want to take none of your girls home… or all three?"

"All three, of course," he replied.

"Then we need to do a C-section. Now."

And off we went.

On Monday I was told I could finally shower. This was the moment I had been dreading—the moment of truth. I shuffled to the bathroom while he pulled the girls' cradles to the bathroom door so we could hear their tiny cries if they woke up. Slowly, Michael helped me bathe while telling me how beautiful I was and how much he loved me. He named specific things he loved about me, both in my physical appearance and in my personality, and thanked me for each little thing he could think of that I did to care for him and our adopted son. Finally, he addressed the real issue: "And your incision is beautiful because you worked so hard to care for our daughters."

I sobbed. But it gave me a new perspective on my incision and what it represented. It was not a grotesque disfiguration, but a sign of love and life. Ginger LeBlanc's story had given my husband guidance on how to encourage me in what he knew would be an unbelievably emotional time. She helped us prepare for something the mommy-to-be books don't address. I am everlastingly grateful.

~Aletheia D. Lee

Touching Stories About the Miracles of Motherhood

Jack Canfield, Mark Victor Hansen,
and Patty Aubery

Because He Loved Me

If I know what love is, it is because of you.
~Herman Hesse

Jude had been out of my body for two days. He lay in his little clear plastic "case" next to me, sleeping mostly. I'd often slip my finger into his soft, tiny hand and stare at him when I wasn't entertaining all the visitors we had.

And yet, the crushing bubble was already welling up inside me, the bubble that would burst soon after I came home. I could feel the pressure of emotions filling up my rib cage. It wasn't just that I felt so fat and so exposed; I felt incapable. I felt more overwhelmed than I'd ever felt about anything—even the cancer I'd dealt with. At least with cancer it was just the disease and me. This time another person was thrown into the mix. A person that I would be responsible for, whose character I would be largely accountable for molding and shaping, who might or might not give me heartfelt Mother's Day cards at some point in his life.

What if I messed it all up? A million and one scenarios raced through my mind, which was growing ever manic.

And, as if my mind weren't in enough pain, my body had

discovered a whole new level of anguish. I would complain. And then I would feel guilty, because, after all, I did get a baby out of the deal, and women didn't always have it so "easy." And then time would pass and I'd repeat that cycle of complaining and guilt.

So it was on day two, around 7:00 p.m., that one of the crabbier nurses on staff came in and announced very flatly that I had to take a shower. That night. I could sense a hint of disgust in her voice, and I, of course, took that very personally to mean that I especially had to hurry up and shower because of my size.

The bubble of panic inside me grew ever larger.

My stepmom, Sara, was staying with me that night so that Chad could go home and get some real rest. Before I could even think about crying, the tears were streaming down my face. I began to choke back sobs. The nurse looked at me, expressionless, and left the room.

I knew I couldn't shower by myself. I could barely walk. Someone would have to help me, and I didn't want anyone to see me looking this enormous, swollen, bruised, and disgusting, my lower abdomen stained dark orange from the Betadine covering my C-section incision. I only wanted the help of one person, and he'd just left.

My head was exploding with protests: *I'll just refuse! They can't make me! They can't! I can't let anyone see me like this. I'll die of shame. I'll never stop crying.* And then I remembered that the walk from my hospital room to the parking garage was quite a long one. Maybe Chad hadn't made it to the car yet. Maybe he'd come back and help me.

I frantically dialed his cell phone from my hospital line. I could hear the echo of the parking garage in his voice, and he could hear the panic and sorrow in mine. He hadn't left yet and he'd be right back. I was flooded with relief.

I started crying again the minute I saw his face.

Sara said she'd watch the baby while he helped me take my shower.

Chad helped me to the bathroom. I hobbled more with each step, my breath hissing out of me. He helped get my gown off. I grimaced and apologized, but he only shook his head and told me not to worry about anything.

I didn't really want him to have to see me like this, but I couldn't think of anyone else I needed more.

"It's going to be okay," he whispered. "I'm going to help you. Don't worry."

But I worried in spite of myself. I wondered if he'd ever be able to put the horrific picture of what I looked like at that moment out of his mind. I wondered if this moment would forever taint our love life.

He literally had to lift each of my legs into the shower, one at a time, because I was so weak. The warm water felt surprisingly good, but I was terrified of doing anything with my incision. The nurses had told me that I had to soap up the stapled gash and softly scrub it with a washcloth. I didn't even want to know how painful that was going to be. I was shaking from weakness and fear.

"Just tell me what to do," he said softly.

And so I guided him. He gently washed my hair first and for a moment, I felt like a little girl again. Then he slowly lathered the rest of my body, avoiding the incision until I was ready.

He was standing outside of the shower and his shirt was soaked.

"You're getting all wet," I said, my voice shaking.

"It's okay. Don't worry about me."

"I guess we need to wash my incision," I said weakly.

Our eyes locked and I began sobbing. I was so afraid and felt so wounded and exhausted. He put his arms around me as I sobbed on his soaking wet shoulder.

"I didn't want you to have to see me like this. I can't believe you have to help me like this. I didn't think that..."

"I love you," he said. "You're so beautiful to me. I'd do anything for you. No matter what."

I sobbed even harder. I'd never felt so loved in all my life.

Moments later, he very gently cleaned my incision and surprisingly, the pain was minimal. It was something I didn't think a husband should ever have to do, but he did it with such love and compassion. He uttered not one complaint.

He helped me ease out of the shower and wrapped me in a towel. We stood there just holding each other for what seemed like a million years.

I knew having the baby would change our lives forever, but this moment changed our love forever. In those moments, we developed a bond so deep it takes my breath away just thinking about it.

~Ginger LeBlanc

Good Morning, Grandma

Nobody grows old merely by living a number of years.
We grow old by deserting our ideals. Years may wrinkle the skin,
but to give up enthusiasm wrinkles the soul.
~Samuel Ullman

In 2011, Chicken Soup for the Soul published *Chicken Soup for the Soul: Inspiration for the Young at Heart*. I jumped at the chance to contribute a story. I so wanted to help get the word out that gray hair and wrinkles do not an old soul make. We're as young as we feel, and it's time the world knows it. No more birthday cards making fun of a person for getting a year older. No more of those condescending looks.

I wrote about doing my first marathon at sixty-five and was thrilled when my story was accepted. Little did I realize how much more thrilled I'd be when reading through my copy of the book and finding Robert Tell's poem, "Mushy Face Is No Disgrace." It changed my outlook forever.

I'm not sure when it started, but I do remember my shock one morning when I glanced in the bathroom mirror and saw my long-dead grandmother staring out at me. What was she doing in my mirror?

I didn't feel old. I was still physically active and had all my marbles. I traveled, volunteered, wrote and taught writing. My days were crammed with new and interesting things to do. I wasn't like my old stay-at-home Grandma, who in my childhood had seemed ancient to me. How could I look like her?

I washed up in a grumpy mood. I felt depressed, then angry. I railed against Mother Nature. Why should I look like my years instead of how I felt inside? I started to feel irritated when people offered me help with a heavy package or a hand to step up into their SUV. I'd tell myself, "They see my wrinkles so they think I'm old. They think I can't do it myself."

Looking back, I feel ashamed at how I allowed that angry, defensive mood to persist so long. I was slowing down, but I refused to see it. I gritted my teeth at the airport employee returning with an empty wheelchair who offered me a ride. "It's a long way to baggage from here and we're going the same way. Hop in," he said. I smiled lamely, shook my head and kept walking, dragging my heavy carry-on behind me. "You may have trouble with that suitcase on the escalator. I'm headed for the elevator. You'll find it easier."

He was right, but he couldn't convince me. I didn't want to act like the little old lady he thought I was. I'd show him he was wrong. "No, thanks. I always use the escalator. It's not a problem," I said and hurried on.

I was lying. The escalator was always a problem for me. With my vertigo, getting on without being able to immediately grab the rail was scary. I'd hesitate, while people behind me grew impatient. If someone said, "Let me help you with that bag," and pulled it on for me, I'd mumble a thank you but inwardly wince. I'd want to turn around and say, "Don't judge me by a few wrinkles. I'm as young as you are inside."

When I began reading Robert Tell's delightful poem, I found it comforting. I wasn't alone! This guy looked in his mirror and was just as shocked as I was. As I read on, I found affirmation in this verse:

> In the mirror is a face
> Of a man you can't replace;
> Though it sags from ear to ear,
> Not yet will it disappear.

At first, I nodded in agreement. He's right, I thought. I am in my eighties and wrinkled, but I'm still here. He too is here and shocked at what he sees in the mirror because he doesn't feel old and useless either. He still feels like himself. He's defiant about those wrinkles, just like me.

Then I realized: no, not like me. Not at all like me. I've been defiantly angry, but he's defiant in an affirmative way. He sees his aging face and graying hair and accepts them as a small price to pay for the blessing of still being able to wake each morning to life. Another day to enjoy friends, play with a grandchild, glory at the sunset, tell someone you love them. He is thankful where I have been vain. He's right. I'm wrong. It's not my appearance that needs a facelift. It's my attitude.

I continued reading and found myself laughing out loud by the end of the poem. Humor. How could I have forgotten its healing power? How could I have slipped into such a black mood over resembling my grandmother? How could I have not noticed the wonderful fact that I was alive to see myself turn into my grandmother?

I have a new morning ritual for washing up now. I start with a look in the mirror, a look long enough to begin my day with a cheerful, "Good morning, Grandma," as the faucet starts to run.

~Marcia Rudoff

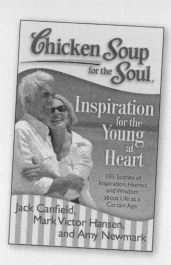

Mushy Face
Is No Disgrace

Inside every older person is a younger person wondering what happened.
~Jennifer Yane

In the mirror is a face,
Oh my goodness what a face!
Used to be so firm and full.
Hair as coarse as new clipped wool;
Now it's gone from black to gray,
Incremental, day by day.

Mushy face is no disgrace;
Loss of tone is commonplace.
Still, it's interesting to see
My youth vanish by degree.

In the mirror is a face
Of a man you can't replace;

Though it sags from ear to ear,
Not yet will it disappear.

Droopy cheeks and widow's peaks,
Older than valued antiques;
Strange that this image I see
Represents reality.
Really now, how can it be
That this old fossil face is me?

~Robert Tell

Detours

Happiness is a form of courage.
~Holbrook Jackson

t was hard not to notice her sitting at the table. Not only was she beautiful, but she had a sweet, gentle aura about her.

"I'm so sorry," she said, motioning towards the man seated next to her. "I didn't know the Chicken Soup for the Soul author lunch was for contributors only." I am not sure anyone would have thought twice about the handsome man, who looked to be in his late twenties, except that he was the only man at a table full of women. Like mother hens, the rest of us all reassured her that it was not a problem. We especially didn't want her to feel bad because it was obvious that her guest had some physical challenges, not unlike someone who might have suffered a stroke. She went on to introduce him as her husband.

I wondered what had happened. They both seemed so young—him, too young to be a stroke victim, and her, too young to be a caretaker. I watched as she lovingly prepared a plate of food for him, watched the way she included him in conversation, checking every so often to be sure all his needs were met. We learned her name was Penelope and that her husband didn't have a stroke, but suffered several aneurysms that left him physically impaired and with many needs.

"What book are you in?" I asked her.

"*Chicken Soup for the Soul: Family Caregivers*," she said.

"Me, too! What's your story title? I can't wait to read it." I was excited that I already had a copy of the book and vowed to read her story as soon as the luncheon was over. It was hard not to be impressed with Penelope, even without knowing her full story yet. She exuded an air of peace and joy, in spite of what must have been a serious trial in her life.

As the luncheon began to come to an end, Penelope graciously rose from her chair, helping her husband with his cane.

"We need to get home to our son," she said somewhat apologetically.

A son? All this and they had a son, too? Now I really needed to read her story!

Her story, "A Season to Be Strong," was in the chapter entitled "Perseverance." Seeing that she and her husband were still on the long journey of rehabilitation, the choice of perseverance seemed so appropriate. I read Penelope's story and learned that she and her husband were dancers who traveled the world until they met with a life-altering detour. With a young son at home, she and her husband found themselves on a road neither of them had anticipated—the road to recovery. She now found herself having to step up in ways she never anticipated. But what really made an impression on me was the grace and faith that Penelope exhibited as her life took this unexpected detour.

I have known people who have also faced unexpected life detours but were left feeling bitter and victimized. I, myself, have been forced onto unexpected paths. I wish that I could say I exuded grace, peace and faith during my journey—but often, that wasn't the case. Often, it was more like sniveling and whining.

I wish that everyone who reads Penelope's story could have had the opportunity to sit at her table at the Chicken Soup for the Soul contributors' luncheon. The words in her story are poignant and powerful, but her presence, so filled with peace, was a true testament to faith and unconditional love.

Now when I encounter a roadblock in life and find myself

tempted to sit on the side of the road and have a pity party, I think back to Penelope's story. I think about that graceful woman with a dancer's body and hope in her eyes. I think about the loving way she cared for her husband. I remember her perseverance and belief that one day her road will lead her to that beach where she will have that lazy day with her husband. I remember and I am inspired to embrace my detours with more peace and faith, knowing that there can be beauty in a change of scenery, if I look for it.

~Lynne Leite

A Season to Be Strong

Being deeply loved by someone gives you strength, while loving someone deeply gives you courage.

~Lao Tzu

'm twenty-eight years old and my husband and I have been married four years. We have traveled the world dancing professionally. We were performing off-Broadway together when we found out I was pregnant with our first child. We had made a point to really enjoy each other in the first years of marriage and we were ready to settle down and start a family. It was the beginning of a new season in our lives.

When my son was ten months old, we celebrated our first Father's Day together. My husband woke up to breakfast in bed and received a gift that my son and I made for him. It was a good start to the day. My husband hadn't been feeling well five days before. He came home from dance practice and was throwing up and having terrible headaches. We weren't sure what was going on but didn't pay too much mind to it considering injury is very common to dancers. We planned to take him to the doctor on Monday morning, but we weren't going to let it ruin our first Father's Day together.

On our way to church, shortly after breakfast, my husband start-ing acting a little weird. He didn't feel like driving and wanted me to hold our son. It was during the service that I was called from the nursery because my husband had passed out. I knew something was terribly wrong when I looked into his eyes as he was being helped onto a gurney. He was completely pale. I immediately felt a knot in my stomach and began to cry.

My first instinct was to start praying with whoever was around me. We were taken to UCLA where we learned that my husband had a ruptured aneurysm. He had suffered from two ruptures, the first being at dance practice five days before and the second at church when he passed out. He had been walking around with a bleed in his brain, not feeling well, but functioning.

I was in shock and couldn't believe this was happening to us. My husband is a good person. Patient, loving, generous, selfless, a leader, wise, humble, humorous and a very talented dancer and actor. He had never been sick in all the time that I had known him and now this horrible thing had happened.

My husband had a third rupture on the table during brain sur-gery and they were unable to operate. They had to go in with a dif-ferent plan and you can imagine my reaction when they called me for my consent. All I wanted to hear was that everything went well but that wasn't the case. And I'd like to say that it got better after that but it was only the beginning of a long summer of surgeries, setbacks and multiple complications.

I could see that this was going to be a long road and my husband would only want me to be strong and apply our faith. We are both believers and my husband has spent a lot of time sowing wisdom, patience and faith into me. He has prayed for me and has set the bar for what kind of wife he wants me to be by being an example as a good husband. Not having my husband to lead me through this because he isn't neurologically all there was tough. So I had to change my attitude and thought process. I had to step into a leadership posi-tion. It is difficult to see your better half in a vulnerable position. I had to make medical decisions to save his life and on top of it all take care of our baby, bills, home, work, etc. I could have easily had a mental breakdown but I wanted to handle this the way I know my husband would have if the roles were reversed.

My family, friends, and I stayed with my husband throughout his whole time in ICU. My husband wasn't alone for nine weeks. It was important to keep him surrounded by people who loved him and who would pray over him. I didn't want him to feel alone or fearful and wanted him to know what he was fighting for. My son's first birthday came and I organized the biggest first birthday that I had ever been to, but I wanted my husband to be a part of that too. Although he may not remember it, we opened presents and sang happy birthday to our son Elijah in the ICU. Even the doctors and nurses came in to join us.

My son took his first steps at the hospital. He was growing before my very eyes and it made me sad that my husband was missing that. I didn't want anything else in our life to have to suffer because of this circumstance. I had been breastfeeding at the time and I had no intention of stopping. It added a little more stress to worry about pumping and then eating right so my milk wouldn't dry up, but I was determined to keep some sort of normalcy for my son. One of the harder decisions I had to make was sending my son off with my mom for several weeks. Would that ruin our bond? Would I have to stop breastfeeding? Would that traumatize our son? These were the questions running through my mind, but I had to prioritize, and although my baby needed me, my husband needed me more.

Since my son was with my mom, I was able to be more present with my husband. Not just physically but mentally as well. I supported him as he was beginning his physical, occupational and speech therapy. He had to learn how to walk and talk again. His progress improved when I was there for his therapy, so I tried not to miss any sessions, but that became more challenging over time. I had to start working and that pulled me away from spending as much time with my husband.

Eventually my son came home and I had to balance learning how to be a single mom, take care of the house, work, and go back and forth to the hospital to support my husband through his rehabilitation. Sometimes I wish there were five of me, and one of me would be sleeping on a beach somewhere, but I know this is just a season in my life and I have to keep pushing through.

A lot of people tell me I'm strong and that they couldn't do it if they were me. The truth is that when you're put in this position, you just do it. You have no other choice but to step up. It's hard and ugly but it builds character. I know I can handle anything after going through this and I look forward to taking that nap on the beach with my husband by my side.

~Penelope Vazquez

An Honors Class
for Remedial Dieters

Shoot for the moon. Even if you miss, you'll land among the stars.
~Les Brown

I eyed the name of my next patient on the schedule and groaned. Maggie Nelson. Why did I even bother trying to help her? Talk about a waste of time. I had spent hours over the years counseling, encouraging, guilt tripping, and attempting to motivate the butterball to lose weight. Diabetes, high cholesterol, high blood pressure, worn-out knees—the woman needed to drop a good ninety pounds—but I might as well have instructed a Macy's mannequin for all the results I'd seen. She couldn't afford Weight Watchers, her insurance didn't cover gastric bypass, her knees ached so she couldn't exercise, broccoli made her bloat, and artificial sweeteners gave her a headache. When it came to excuses, Maggie could write a bestseller.

I inhaled a deep breath and forced myself to enter Maggie's exam room. I perused her chart and scowled. As expected, not only had she not lost a single ounce, she'd actually gained a whopping ten pounds. Next came her lame excuse: she'd had out-of-town company and how could I expect her to lose weight around her birthday and anniversary? Then she claimed she "ate like a bird." Right! An ostrich, maybe. My favorite excuse? She had to keep freshly baked chocolate chip cookies around the house in case the grandkids paid a visit. When I asked how often the grandkids came, she hemmed and hawed and finally admitted they lived out of state.

We danced the same worn-out waltz, Maggie and I. I'd counsel her to exercise more and cut down on her sweets and soda and she'd nod, promise to do better, and waddle out of my office, both of us knowing nothing would change.

Then I read Jennie Ivey's story, "The Honors Class," in *Chicken Soup for the Soul: The Power of Positive*, a story about a class of remedial history students whose teacher had been falsely informed the class was filled with academic superstars—the "Honors" students. Because of her high expectations and the extra effort she poured into these supposed "gifted" scholars, not only did all the students pass, but the majority earned A's and B's. Wow! Remedial students acing Honors History? Unheard of.

A twinge of guilt pricked my conscience. Had I prematurely given up hope for patients like Maggie? Did the quote about "the soft bigotry of low expectations" apply to me? Truthfully, I'd given up on Maggie years ago. But what if I treated my obese diabetics with the same high expectations and extra effort with which Jennie Ivey treated her remedial History students? What if I treated my failing dieters as though they were "Honors" patients?

You'll just be wasting your time, my inner cynic insisted. *No harm trying*, my conscience countered.

First, I researched everything I could find from reputable journals and books about people who had lost at least fifty pounds without surgery and maintained the loss for over a year. I discovered the National Weight Loss Registry, which researched and followed over three thousand people who met these criteria. Then I created a notebook of all the winning advice from these weight loss champions. Weekly group support proved helpful to many successful dieters so I'd start a weight loss support group where I'd teach the principles of the Weight Loss Registry.

At Maggie's next clinic visit, I told her about the group and encouraged her to join. I offered the class for free so money wouldn't be an excuse. She claimed she didn't want to face rush hour traffic every week. That's when I took her to task. "Maggie, you claim you desperately want to lose weight, but you aren't willing to make any sacrifices. If you seriously want to get off insulin and be healthy, you won't let rush hour traffic keep you from participating."

Arms crossed, Maggie glared at me. "I've lost forty pounds three times before. It never stays off."

I put a hand on her arm. "It came back because you returned to your old eating habits."

She moaned. "I've failed so many times before. I guess I don't believe I can do it." She glanced up at me, tears in her eyes. "You really think I can lose this weight and get off insulin?" Her eyes registered a glimmer of hope.

I squeezed her arm. "I know you can, Maggie. But it will take sacrifice, time, and hard work. Just think, you could be fifty pounds lighter by this time next year. Think how much less your knees would ache."

She hesitated, fear etched across her face.

"You can do this, Maggie. I'll help you."

She glanced up, grinning. "Alright, I'll do it."

Thus, every week we weighed ourselves, recorded our food intake, wore pedometers, ate high protein breakfasts, and explored the emotional triggers behind our overeating. We learned to distract ourselves when tempted to snack.

When Maggie lost three pounds the first week, you'd have thought she'd won an Olympic gold medal. Within a month, she'd lost ten pounds and proudly demonstrated to the group how the waistline of her pants was now loose.

I wanted to cartwheel across the room the week Maggie announced her husband had bought her an exercise bike for Christmas. She was cycling thirty minutes each morning while watching the *Today* show.

There were some setbacks along the way, however. Three months into the group, Maggie gained two pounds after a family reunion. She hung her head in shame and said nothing during the meeting. Her face, however, screamed, "I'm a failure."

After class, I took her aside. "Maggie, I'm so proud of you."

Her eyes widened. "Proud of me? Why? I ate like a pig and gained two pounds."

"But you showed up tonight, didn't you? That shows you're committed—even when you've messed up. Champions don't quit, they learn from their mistakes. They keep trying until they succeed."

She smirked. "I learned to stay away from the cobbler and ice cream."

I laughed. "You're my star pupil and you've proven it tonight—you didn't quit. You may have failed at dieting before, but you're an Honors student now."

In four months, Maggie lost thirty pounds and cut her insulin dose in half. Her knees no longer ached. When her grandchildren came to visit, she informed me, "I served them turkey slices and baby carrots for a snack and they liked them just as much as the cookies." She said she wanted to teach them healthy eating habits.

After she'd lost the thirty pounds with no signs of reverting to her old eating habits, Maggie announced she was starting a support group at her church. "I want to teach others everything you've taught me. They're all asking how I lost my weight."

Everyone applauded.

Her face beamed. "If I can do it, anybody can. People just need somebody to encourage them along the way."

Amen!

Jennie Ivey would probably be shocked to learn that fifteen "remedial" dieters lost over two hundred pounds of fat because of her story. Amazing what raising the bar on low expectations can do! Thanks, Jennie!

~Sally Willard Burbank, MD

The Honors Class

Don't live down to expectations. Go out there and do something remarkable.
~Wendy Wasserstein

The motley looking group of eleventh graders didn't look like any "honors" U.S. History class I'd ever imagined. They shuffled into my classroom, which I'd painstakingly decorated with Presidential portraits and colorful maps and framed copies of the Declaration of Independence and the Constitution, with an "attitude" that was apparent even to a rookie teacher.

Which is exactly what I was. Fresh out of college with a degree in history, a teaching certificate, and not a lick of experience. I was grateful to have a job, even if it was in one of the rougher high schools in the city where I lived.

"Good morning," I said brightly. I was greeted with vacant stares. "I'm so excited to have been selected to teach this honors class," I continued. "They usually don't let first-year teachers do that."

Several of the students sat up straighter and cut their eyes at each other. Too late, I wondered if I should have tried to hide the fact that I had zero teaching experience. Oh, well. "We're going to do things a little differently in this class because I know that all of you want a challenge."

By now, every student was staring at me with a puzzled expression.

"First off, let's rearrange these desks," I said. "I like lots of class discussion, so let's put them in a big circle so we can all see each other's faces." Several of the kids rolled their eyes, but they all got up and began scooting the desks out of the traditional straight rows. "Perfect! Thanks. Now, everybody choose a seat and let's play a game. When I point to you, tell me your name. Then tell me what you hate most about history."

Finally, some smiles. And lots more as our game progressed.

Amanda hated how history seemed to be all about war. Jose didn't like memorizing names and dates. Gerald was convinced that nothing that had happened in the past was relevant to his life. "Why should I care about a bunch of dead white guys?" was how he put it. Caitlyn hated tricky true-false questions. Miranda despised fill-in-the-blank tests.

We had just made our way around the circle when the bell rang. Who knew fifty minutes could pass so quickly?

Armed with the feedback my students had given me, I began formulating a plan. No teaching straight from the textbook for this group. No "read the chapter and answer the questions at the end" homework. These kids were bright. They were motivated. My honors class deserved to be taught in a way that would speak to them.

We'd study social and economic history, not just battles and generals. We'd tie current events into events from the past. We'd read novels to bring home the humanity of history. *Across Five Aprils* when studying the Civil War. *The Grapes of Wrath* to learn about the Great Depression. *The Things They Carried* when talking about Vietnam.

Tests would cover the facts, but also require higher level thinking skills. No tricky true-false questions. No fill-in-the-blank.

At first, I was surprised by how many of my students used poor grammar and lacked writing skills. And some seemed to falter when reading out loud. But we worked on those skills while we were learning history. I found that many of the kids were not only willing, but eager to attend the after-school study sessions I offered and to accept the help of peer tutors.

Four of my students came to love the subject matter so much that they formed their own "History Bowl" team and entered a countywide contest. Though they didn't take first place, they were ecstatic over the Honorable Mention trophy they brought home to our classroom.

The school year came to an end more quickly than I could have imagined. Though I had grown fond of many of my students, the ones in the honors class held a special place in my heart. Most had earned A's and B's. No one had averaged lower than a C.

During our final teacher workday before summer break, the principal called me into her office for my end-of-the-year evaluation.

"I want to congratulate you on a great rookie season," she said with a smile. "Especially on how well you did with your remedial kids."

"Remedial kids? I don't understand. I didn't have any remedial classes."

Mrs. Anderson looked at me in a strange way. "Your first period class was remedial. Surely you saw that indicated at the top of the roll." She pulled a file folder from a drawer and handed it to me. "And you must have suspected the students in that class were below average by the way they dressed and the way they carried themselves. Not to mention their terrible grammar and poor reading and writing skills."

I opened the file folder and removed a copy of the roll from my first period class. There at the top, plain as day, was the word HONORS. I showed it to Mrs. Anderson.

"Oh, dear," she said. "What a huge mistake! How did you ever manage, treating slow students as though they were…"

I couldn't help but finish the sentence for her. "As though they were bright?"

She nodded, looking more than a little sheepish.

"You know what, Mrs. Anderson? I think we've both learned

a lesson from this. One they didn't teach in any of the education courses I took. But one I'll never forget."

"Nor will I," she said, circling the word HONORS with a red marker before placing the paper back in the folder. "Next year, I may just have this printed at the top of all the class rolls."

~Jennie Ivey

The Rescue of a Worrywart

Do not anticipate trouble or worry about what may never happen.
Keep in the sunlight.
~Benjamin Franklin

was born a worrier. If my cries in the delivery room had been translated, I'm sure I was saying, "Careful, Doc. Don't drop me! Watch out for that table edge!"

I worried all through elementary school, especially when I had a substitute teacher. I panicked, my stomach churned, and I felt sick and ready to throw up. With each substitute, the school had to phone my mother to come and get me. Once I was safely home, I instantly recovered.

I worried when it stormed. (What if the water rose up and we drowned? Yes, even in our hilltop house!) I worried when I met new people. (Would anyone want to know me?) And later I worried when I went on a trip. (Had I left some electric appliance turned on that would burn down the house while I was gone?)

Then, one day, life smacked me in the head with a genuine problem.

The phone rang, and the doctor on the other end said, "You have invasive breast cancer."

My worrying went into overdrive, keeping me awake at night and following me during the day.

It was at that point I read *Chicken Soup for the Cancer Survivor's Soul*. One particular page contained advice that seemed as if it had been written just for me.

The short piece was called "Two Things Not to Worry About," and said, in effect, hey girl, don't worry about things you can't change, because what's the use? And don't worry about the things you can change; instead get busy and change them.

The words rang true, nestled in my brain, and calmed my anxious heart. They made me realize that I was accomplishing nothing with my worrying except upsetting myself. Worry wouldn't solve problems, heal my cancer, or change anything. It was a complete waste of energy.

In accepting the advice in the book, I felt a huge burden lift from my shoulders. I was freer than I had ever been.

During long days of chemotherapy and radiation, I carefully divided everything into two camps: the things I could do something about, and those I couldn't.

When I entered what I call the second phase of my life (life after cancer), I approached it with a new attitude and a lighter spirit. And to remind myself, in case I fell into my old ways, I printed out the advice from the book and added it to a poster board on which I had pasted pictures of things I wanted to accomplish—a kind of a pictorial "bucket list."

Now, fourteen years later, when I look at what I still want to do or places I want to go, I am reminded that in this life of mine, I can't control everything. Some things still simply are what they are, and worrying won't change them. The rest? The things I can control? I need to get off my butt and do something about them.

It's only a change in attitude, but the words I read that afternoon while in the middle of the worst crisis of my life have made all the difference in how I am living the rest of it.

~Michele Ivy Davis

Two Things
Not to Worry About

Worry is a misuse of imagination.
~Dan Zadra

In my life, I have found there are two things about which I should never worry.

First, I shouldn't worry about the things I can't change. If I can't change them, worry is certainly most foolish and useless.

Second, I shouldn't worry about the things I can change. If I can change them, then taking action will accomplish far more than wasting my energies in worry.

Besides, it is my belief that, nine times out of ten, worrying about something does more danger than the thing itself. Give worry its rightful place—out of your life.

~Source Unknown

Moving Forward

The foolish man seeks happiness in the distance;
the wise grows it under his feet.
~James Oppenheim

The story that changed my life is called "Dancing in the Rain" by Jeannie Lancaster and appeared in the book *Chicken Soup for the Soul: Think Positive*. I read the entire book cover to cover. There were many stories that resonated with me but that story in particular made me smile and I keep going back to it.

The key phrase that captured me was "Life isn't about waiting for the storm to pass. It's about learning to dance in the rain." The story talked about how the author discovered a plaque with those words and how she bought it to constantly remind herself to implement that attitude into her daily life. The story also mentions how too often people put conditions on their own happiness. That's my problem. I tend to be a "glass is half empty" kind of person. Too often when things aren't going the way I plan, I basically take a back seat in my life and wait for everything to magically start getting better and work itself out on its own. Of course I am always disappointed when nothing happens or more often than not, things get worse.

I read the story a couple of weeks ago. It has stuck with me and I say the quote to myself several times throughout the day: "Life isn't about waiting for the storm to pass. It's about learning to dance in the rain." Just repeating that sentence over and over again makes me feel more positive and changes how I feel and react to situations that I am not normally happy with.

A couple of years ago my cousin Jenny and I had some sort of falling out. I am not even sure what it was about at this point. All I know was that Jenny had been my best friend, my maid of honor at my wedding and the godmother of my first-born child. I had thought of her every now and then. After our spat, I had been invited to her wedding but didn't go out of spite. I kept waiting for her to apologize or something. After reading the story I felt like a spoiled brat. How much time do we really have to cultivate relationships and do all the things we want to do? The fact is we really don't know.

I realized that I missed her friendship; this whole situation was completely silly. I was ashamed of myself for not going to her wedding. "Enough," I told myself. "This foolishness has to stop here and now. I am tired of missing out on my own life."

I sat down and wrote a note to Jenny. I told her that I wanted to start over, call a truce and I apologized for not being at her wedding. I mailed the letter and I waited. Would she return the letter unopened? Would she contact me? What if she didn't contact me?

A week later the phone rang. I asked my daughter to answer it because I was dealing with a flood in the basement. A sock had gotten stuck in the washing drain and I was busy reminding myself to dance in the rain! Jenny was calling to thank me for my letter. She was happy to hear from me and we talked on the phone for over an hour, until the battery died in my phone. She is planning on visiting us in the next couple of weeks. I will finally get the pleasure of meeting her husband, son and daughter for the very first time. I have learned to move forward now and to actively pursue my happiness. After all, "life isn't about waiting for the storm to pass. It is about learning how to dance in the rain."

~Catina Noble

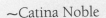

Dancing in the Rain

Anyone who says sunshine brings happiness has never danced in the rain.
~Author Unknown

My husband and I had just finished having dinner at a local restaurant and were enjoying strolling through the stores in an adjacent shopping center. We went into a shop that sold handcrafted items in hopes of finding a few last-minute Christmas gifts. The scent of handmade soaps and potpourri teased our noses as we walked through the door.

There was a lot to see. Every shelf and wall was loaded with different crafters' handiwork. As I walked through the store, I noticed a wooden plaque hanging unceremoniously on a wall. I turned to take a second look and remember shaking my head "yes" at the message printed on the plaque. Moving on, I enjoyed looking at other items in the store, but found myself being drawn back to the plaque.

Standing in front of the plaque, I felt a little like a child who, when digging through the sandbox, finds some unexpected treasure—a shiny quarter or a lost toy. Here among the other handmade items, I found a very simple, yet profound treasure hidden in a message. A message I needed.

"Life isn't about waiting for the storm to pass," the plaque proclaimed. "It's about learning to dance in the rain."

As I pulled my husband over and directed his attention to the plaque, I could see that he too appreciated the simple lesson the plaque shared. How often in our daily lives had we put conditions on our happiness? When we get the house paid off, then we can be happy. When things settle down with the kids, then we'll be able to do more together. There is so little joy for the here and now in the uncertainties of the whens and thens.

Looking at the plaque, I found myself thinking back to a hot and muggy day the summer before, when I unknowingly lived the plaque's message. Dark clouds had rolled in along the foothills of the Rockies, heavy with their burden of moisture. Rain began falling lightly by mid-afternoon, building to a downpour that filled the gutters with rushing water and then moved on as quickly as it had come.

Light rain continued to fall as I walked out to get my mail. Water was still running high through the gutters. I don't know what came over me, but I suddenly felt compelled to do something a little crazy for my fifty-plus years.

I slipped off my shoes and stockings and began walking barefoot through the water. It was deliciously warm, heated by the pavement that had been baked by the summer heat.

I'm sure my neighbors thought that I had lost my last vestige of sanity, but I didn't care. For in that moment, I was alive. I wasn't worried about bills, the future or any other day-to-day cares. I was experiencing a gift—a pure and simple moment of joy!

The plaque now hangs in my living room, a Christmas gift from my husband. I walk past it multiple times each day and frequently pause to ask myself, "So, am I dancing in the rain?"

I think I am. I know I try to. I'm definitely more committed to taking time to pause and recognize and be grateful for the immense blessings that are all around me—the joys that were too often going unnoticed in my rush to future happiness. I celebrate more fully my dear blessings, such as a son with special needs learning to drive alone, the love of good friends and the beauty of spring. Yes, one step at a time, I am learning to dance in the rain!

~Jeannie Lancaster

Chapter
3

READER'S CHOICE

Great Advice

Advice is like snow — the softer it falls,
the longer it dwells upon, and the deeper it sinks into the mind.

~Samuel Taylor Coleridge

Memory Lane

Memory is a way of holding onto the things you love, the things you are,
the things you never want to lose.
~From the television show The Wonder Years

was thrilled last year when Chicken Soup for the Soul chose the story I wrote about my parents to be part of *Chicken Soup for the Soul: Family Caregivers*; little did I know the real blessing would be in reading the book itself.

The piece I wrote focused on my parents' struggle to adjust to my mother's paraplegia and the commitment my father showed in taking care of his disabled wife. Around the time the book came out, my elderly mother started going downhill and within two months was placed in hospice care. My father took her home from the nursing facility where she had ended up, and hospice workers came in daily to help him care for her.

Just the word "hospice" sent my spirits plummeting. Seeing my mother, who had once been so involved in life, now noticeably withdrawn, often confused, no longer able to feed herself, and seemingly unaware of her surroundings produced a tightening in my chest that made it hard to breathe. And when the hospice nurse told us she was showing signs of dementia, it nearly broke my heart.

Reading the other stories in this book was like a lifeline. When I felt sorry for myself over my family's situation, I only had to read about families who had it so much worse to be reminded that our burden was a relatively light one. When I became saddened that the "take charge" mother I knew had disappeared, I read advice that helped me enjoy getting to know this gentler, more docile version of my mom. Other stories encouraged me to reframe the way I looked at her situation and to adjust my own behavior, while some provided helpful hints that I filed away for future use. I had thought, after twenty-five years of living with my mother's health issues, that I had learned how to deal with everything; but there were stages of my mother's life we had yet to pass through and the insights shared in this book helped prepare me for them.

So much wisdom was contained in those 101 stories that it's hard to pick one to highlight. But if I had to, I would say it was Janey Konigsberg's "Don't Take it Personally." Her advice to live in the past with the elderly patient and not try to keep them interested in the present restored my connection to my mom.

During my weekend visits with my mother, I initially tried to keep her involved in my life—telling her all about my week and asking her about hers. I thought this would entertain her and broaden her world beyond the bedroom to which she was now confined. I brought paintings I had made and showed her photographs of me with my friends. When Chicken Soup for the Soul published another of my stories, I showed her the book and read the story to her.

She smiled politely, but didn't seem very interested. There was no sign of the pride and enthusiasm she used to show for my activities and accomplishments. I was disappointed—not because I craved validation from her, but because I repeatedly failed to interest her in something that would bring her out of the shell into which she had retreated. In short, I couldn't reach her.

After reading Janey's story I resolved to try living in the past when I was with Mom. The weekend before Christmas I pulled up a chair to her hospital bed and brought her a big stack of Christmas cards my parents had received. One by one I read them to her. They represented her entire life: relatives; old friends; my parents' neighbors from when they lived in New York; and new friends from their retirement community in Maryland. I'd look at the return address, and if the name was unfamiliar to me I'd ask her, for example, "Who do you know named Elizabeth Parker that lives in Florida?" I was surprised when she answered, "Oh, that's Betty from the beauty parlor who used to do my hair. She moved to Florida when she retired." As we worked through the stack I became amazed at how much detail she remembered from years gone by.

That day Mom stayed awake the whole time I was there and was a lot more communicative than I'd seen her in the last six months. Even when she didn't say anything, her frequent smiles and the way her eyes lit up let me know that she was enjoying herself. By the end of my visit I was hoarse from reading aloud all the notes people had written. Their unique voices came through in the handwritten comments or newsletters they enclosed, and it was as if she had had a mini reunion with each of them. We both had fun reminiscing about her friendships with these people, and by prompting her with questions I learned some details about her life that I hadn't known before.

Two days later, I came back to spend Christmas Day with her. A few more cards had arrived and I read them to her. We had a good laugh over one from an Italian-American friend who signed her card, "*Buon natale e api nuier*." *Buon Natale* is Merry Christmas in Italian, but "*api nuier*" is a phonetic rendering of "Happy New Year"—with an Italian accent! My mother, who had always been a meticulous speller, found this quite amusing and seeing her sense of humor return, even for a short while, further loosened the bands that had been squeezing my heart.

At a loss for what to do once we finished with the cards, I started singing Christmas carols. Mom used to love to sing, but now she just listened. I made sure not to sing any of the newer songs—only the traditional ones. Sensitive to tiring her out or annoying her with my less-than-perfect voice, I'd stop every few songs and asked if she wanted me to continue. She always nodded her head yes. When I left at the end of the day she smiled and said, "Those were all the old songs we used to sing. Thanks for the entertainment, Sue." The sincerity in her voice conveyed her appreciation, and as I looked into her eyes I caught a glimpse of the mother I remembered.

I realize that this approach is not a panacea. Just last weekend we were having a cheery chat when my father left to do some grocery shopping. When I told her "Daddy went to the store," she thought about that and asked, "What's Daddy's last name?" But her confusion didn't sadden me the way it might have before. Even though she may have bad days or moments ahead, for the time being she still knows who I am and we are able to enjoy each other's company.

I don't know if my parents' caregiving story will help anyone else, but I'm very grateful to my fellow contributors who shared their wisdom and experiences in that book. I had no idea I'd be putting them to use so soon. Thanks to Janey's story, I found the mother I thought I'd lost on a stroll down memory lane.

~Susan Yanguas

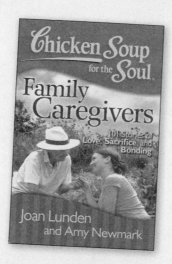

Don't Take It Personally

You can't live a perfect day without doing something for someone who will never be able to repay you.
~John Wooden

A Note from Joan

When I married my husband, Jeff Konigsberg, I married into a large loving tight-knit family that spends a lot of time together. Jeff's Grandma Rosie quickly became a favorite of mine, as she was a shining example of an eternal optimist who always looked at life through her "rose colored glasses" (this is something that my mom always suggested to me as I was growing up—in those exact words). When Rosie was in her eighties, she was still getting herself dolled up every day, never missed her hair appointment at the beauty parlor and was still going into the gym several times a week.

Despite her efforts to stay healthy, one day Rosie had chest pains and learned she needed double bypass surgery. Amazingly, at 90 they deemed her healthy enough to have this surgery, and she made it through with flying colors. However upon returning home Rosie just wasn't recovering well. Jeff and I flew down to Florida with his parents to cheer her up and get her moving again. When we got to her home, I opened up all the drapes in the house and the sliding glass doors that went to the pool area and the sunshine came streaming in on her. I knew that she liked milkshakes so we had stopped to get her a chocolate Frosty. It wasn't long before Rosie was her smiling self, looking through picture albums and laughing and reminiscing about wonderful times spent together. Our "cheer up" operation complete, we returned home.

Despite Rosie's wonderful optimistic outlook, she missed her family and she wanted to return to New York to be with them. We once again flew to Florida to scoop her up and bring her home. She literally was singing out loud on the flight home and chatting up the flight attendants like she hadn't had a chance to talk to strangers in ages. We moved her into a beautiful senior assisted home where she had a lovely one-bedroom apartment and was surrounded by old family friends from her younger days and of course all of her children, grandchildren and great-grandchildren. She was once again coming to every family function, holiday gatherings and birthdays, dressing up to the nines and smiling ear to ear.

We all felt comforted by the fact that we had given Rosie a renewed happiness, a loving secure last chapter. My mother-in-law Janey visited Rosie daily, and took care of her every need and desire. While moving Rosie back home made Rosie's quality of life much better, it unfortunately did not necessarily do the same for her loving daughter Janey. They had always had an extremely close and loving relationship, but Rosie was becoming more demanding as she grew older and it seemed like Janey could never do enough for her. I have heard about this happening often — sometimes the elderly turn on the family members who are closest to them. It can be very hurtful and it is hard to put in perspective and not take personally.

As the family was planning Rosie's 100th birthday, she developed pneumonia and in less than two weeks she passed away. Janey has since struggled with the guilt of the sometimes tense final days together. As someone who watched the whole situation unfold, I know that my mother-in-law Janey was a wonderful daughter to her mother, who at times could really be tough on her. I admire Janey for her fortitude and her willingness to hang in there anyway. I interviewed Janey for this book, and as you will see below, she is still being hard on herself.

Joan: Janey, what was your relationship like with your mother in the early years?

Janey: Extraordinary! So extraordinary, that unless you were there, you almost wouldn't believe it. We had THE MOST fun relationship. We never had the mother/daughter tension that many people experience. We went shopping together, we went out to lunch together, we laughed together, and I was the envy of all my friends. In that time, most mothers looked like "mothers" who stayed at home with their aprons. My mother was young and beautiful, she played golf and bridge and loved her friends, and many of my friends were jealous of our relationship.

Joan: Your father passed away when you were pregnant with Jeff, which I know was unbelievably difficult for both you and your mother. Your mother eventually remarried. Was that hard for you to accept?

Janey: After my father passed away my mother had an extremely difficult time. She was 50 years old, vibrant, beautiful, the matriarch of her family, and was now alone. She had no interest in dating and was in a very tough place for a while. It took her a long time before she was ready to date again. Then, when her friends introduced her to Bill, a member at their club, she got swooped up and married him within two months. While Bill was enamored with Rosie, he was less taken with her family and he soon after moved the two of them to Florida.

Joan: About five years ago, the day came when you moved Rosie from Florida, back to New York, where she was again able to spend her days surrounded by her children, grandchildren, and great-grandchildren. How did you feel about finally being able to bring her back up to live in your town?

Janey: I was ecstatic to have her back! I thought that it would be just like it used to be. I knew she had limitations now; she could walk, but with a walker for longer distances and a wheelchair for even longer distances, but for general day to day… she could still walk! (Even when she got to be 99 she could still wake up in the middle of the night and get to the bathroom with a little nightlight!) She was still as fashionable as ever—she had pants in every color, one to go with each of her happy, colorful printed tops, and of course perfectly matching jewelry, make-up, and accessories. I thought she was still the same old mom. But when she got back, the complaining started immediately.

I wanted to create the perfect environment for her. I looked at 12 different assisted living facilities before I finally decided on the place I thought would be perfect. It was beautiful, bright, and happy and it didn't feel like an "old people's home," which I knew she wouldn't stand for. I was so excited to show her what I picked… the perfect Rosie place. When I brought her in, she looked around and just said, "I'll think about it." That was the beginning of what it was going to be like having my mother back.

Mom was thrilled to have left Florida, but she wasn't doing so well at adjusting to her new life. She complained about everything: the food, the care aides, the food shopping, everything. I would walk in with five bags of things for her and I would leave with a list.

She was always out of something! It wasn't enough that she had a container of oatmeal. And it wasn't enough to have a backup container of oatmeal. She had to have a backup to the backup container of oatmeal. (The big joke was that she had us buy her toilet paper. I would always bring her the toilet paper and the aides would say "but this senior center provides toilet paper!" But Rosie didn't like the quality, so she stockpiled her own!) I think that when she became dependent on others for her household items, she developed a fear of running out of things. Now in retrospect, I can understand that.

Joan: Your relationship with Rosie became strained, was there a tipping point for you?

Janey: My family and my grandchildren are my life, I love love love being with them and watching them grow and experience their lives. But I do know that they will soon be uninterested in us as grandparents. Kids grow up, they have their own lives, they become teenagers, and I get that. So I cherish this time with them, while they are still young. I started to feel like Rosie was taking a lot of this time away from me. I also wanted to tell her everything that was going on with the kids because I thought she would so appreciate it, but I felt that she became very self-absorbed. I would tell her about something one of the grandkids said, or about a soccer game that morning, and she would just say, "That's nice…" I got no validation from her. Now, she probably took that story or anecdote and shared it with all her friends at dinner that night, bragging about her great-grandchildren. But never to me. It was very frustrating because I wanted her to care so badly the way that I do. That was hard for me.

Joan: I think there's a natural tendency to want to live in the present, and have our elderly parents also live in the present with us and frankly be like they used to be. But sometimes older people have a hard time connecting with what is going on now; however they have a great ability to connect with the past.

Janey: I wish I had realized that then. But I wanted her to be there with me in the here and now… she had just moved all the way up from Florida to be with us! But she wasn't the same person who I remembered and she just didn't really connect with me the same. I think I might have felt scared to bring up the past because my brother had died and I thought it might upset her.

Joan: Did you ever resent her or lose your temper with her?

Janey: I never lost it with her. There were a few things that ticked me off. Like when she thought I wasn't telling her things—keeping things from her—and I felt accused of lying. She thought the doctor would tell me things about her health and I wasn't telling her. One time she found a wrinkle on her face and told me that she *knew* she had had a stroke and I just wasn't telling her. I felt like saying, "Mom, you're almost 100, you might have a wrinkle!" but I didn't, because I didn't want to make her feel bad.

There was one day when my husband Donnie and I were driving in the car with her and she turned and yelled at me, speaking to me like I had never heard her speak before. When Donnie tried to defend me, she snapped at him too. We had never spoken to each other like that in our whole lives. I thought that when she came back up here to New York it was going to be just like it used to be. I thought we would go to the deli and get her favorite sandwich and we would have fun. But there was a tension there that we had never ever had before.

It became uncomfortable to be together and I am so sorry about that. It wasn't pleasant for me and so I didn't go just to hang out. I went when I had a reason to be there, something to bring her or somewhere to go with her. I'm very grateful that I didn't lose it with her, but I also didn't run to see her if I had an hour free here or there. When she had lived in Florida, I used to send my mom little things to her house for no reason. I would send cards, pillows with sweet sayings, just little things to make her smile. And there I was, living right around the corner from her, not looking forward to spending extra time with her because I knew how she would behave and how hurtful it would be for me. How could this have happened?

Even when you and Jeffrey would invite her over for Sunday night dinner, while I loved that she would be with the family, I knew what it meant for me. Jeff was amazing to do that, but I knew on those nights that she would miss the scheduled aide to put her to bed and that it would fall on me. And that was really a tough job. Besides having to get her make-up off, make the change into pajamas, get her into bed, etc... there were her preferences, everything had to be a certain way. The blanket like this, the chair like that, the water filled a certain amount—those late nights were difficult.

Joan: We all knew how hard it was on you and that she really loved you deeply. You did a great job caring for her despite how difficult it was for you. We were all amazed at how healthy Rosie remained, and we were all planning a 100th birthday bash for her in a few months, but one day she complained that she was feeling sick. Tell me about that.

Janey: Rosie really wanted to make it to 100 so badly—she had her outfit all picked out and was excited for her party and all the attention. And it seemed like she was going to make it. If there was one thing Rosie had till the end, it was her health! She really was in great health, but she always thought something was wrong. She would complain about her eyesight all the time even when the doctor told her that her eyes were better than many 80-year-olds! (Rose was 99!) However one day she complained about her breathing so I took her right over to the doctor. She was diagnosed with bronchitis but the doctor told me that he didn't want to put her into the hospital because he was afraid that if he did, she might become dependent and exhausted and never come out as is common with many elderly people. He put her on a massive dose of antibiotics but told me that "this might be it," which totally shocked me.

Joan: But about a week later, she was taken to the hospital in the middle of the night. After only a few days in the hospital Rosie succumbed to the pneumonia. After her death, you were feeling very sad about how strained the relationship had become in the final months and it seems like you are still wrestling with unresolved emotions. Tell me about how you felt and how you are dealing with it.

Janey: I felt grief stricken about her death, and about our relationship at the end. And I still am. I remember watching a video at your house that you and Jeff had made of her in her final months talking to the camera. At one point you guys are talking about how great it is that she is back up living near her family and how "you get to see your daughter every day!" She responded with, "…well, not every day…." That killed me. I did see her probably every other day… but I was not there with her every day the way I felt I should have been. I know everyone says I am being hard on myself, but I can't help how I feel.

I feel that I shouldn't have only gone there when I needed to, and I shouldn't have TRIED to talk so much about the current things that were going on in our lives. I should have gone and talked to her about the past—about all the wonderful stories she had to tell and all the wonderful times we had shared together.

Joan: But Janey, that's with a lot of reflection, and most people don't know this before they have gone through it.

Janey: Yes, I know. And with reflection Donnie and I have also come to realize that some of the things we rolled our eyes at with her, she might have been right about! We laugh that as we get older we now understand some of what she would say. We'd say, "Rosie, you should go to lunch with your friends," or, "Rosie, you love reading the paper; go downstairs to the daily talk about current events." She would respond, "You don't know what it's like to be 99." Well, she was right! As you get older, you get tired from things that you used to do unfazed. Not to mention, she wanted to take her time to pick out her outfit, put on her make-up, get her jewelry on, and all of this took time and energy! She also thought that some of the other women didn't need walkers, and she did. Those things can make a person feel bad, and with some time and reflection we now understand that.

Joan: So how are you dealing with these reflections and regrets?

Janey: I can't say that even after two years that I feel much better about things with my mom. I wake up in the middle of the night thinking about it. I went to the cemetery to talk to her to try to tell her. I just feel that I could have been a better daughter at the end.

Joan: But you brought her back to be with her family and many people grow old all alone, without the loving care of their families!

Janey: Not in our kind of family. You are supposed to be there for each other. I was there for her physically, I did her chores and took her where she needed to go, but I don't think I nourished her enough emotionally.

Joan: But aren't you coming to that conclusion in retrospect?

Janey: I don't want you to think this totally consumes my life. It doesn't. I am grateful for all the wonderful years we had together. I have so many happy things in my life, and I am grateful and happy. But I do think about this every day. I do wake up in the morning and wish that I could turn back the time and have a chance to do it over.

Joan: If you were going to give our readers one piece of advice about caregiving, what would it be?

Janey: I would say talk about the past. You tend to want to have the elderly person you are caring for live in the now... You know, fawn over the grandchildren, and talk about current events. But long-term memory is usually their greatest attribute, so keep talking about the past and all the joyful times you shared together, and just the things that bring them pleasure. I tried to focus on the present, but in the present, Rosie wasn't really herself. Now I realize that I could have talked about other things that she probably would have connected with more and taken her mind off of herself.

Also, there are so many things I wish I had asked. There are so many things that I don't know about her life. I wish I had asked her about when she first met my dad and about their first date. Things like that that I will never get to know about now.

In retrospect, yes, I am dealing with more guilt than I could have ever imagined. But I am also grateful for the unbelievably wonderful years that I spent with my mother. I've thought about it a lot since her death and I understand a lot more now. I just wish I could have had this insight when it mattered most.

Joan: Janey, thank you for sharing such valuable insight with our readers. I think your story will be able to help thousands of other adult children of elderly parents who are dealing with their changing relationships, and learn not to take some of the negative changes so personally. Unfortunately they seem to be a fact of life in many end-of-life relationships.

~Janey Konigsberg

Healthy Changes Ahead

Enough is as good as a feast.
~English Proverb

I've always viewed my mother as my mentor. She taught me how to be a woman. She showed me how to be a wife and a mom. She encouraged me to laugh, love, and have faith. Now that I've read "The Tiny Waist of the Fifties" in *Chicken Soup for the Soul: Say Hello to a Better Body!* I realize my mother also taught me something about healthy eating. For years though, I ignored her lessons just as I ignored this book.

I admit it: I didn't immediately open *Chicken Soup for the Soul: Say Hello to a Better Body!* after I received it. The book sat on my office shelves for months, its pleasant green title reminding me of things I should be doing.

Then came weeks of abdominal problems followed by weeks of medical tests. The tests confirmed my doctor's guess: my gallbladder wasn't functioning. I needed to have it removed.

One week later, I was home recuperating from surgery. That's when I reached for my copy of *Chicken Soup for the Soul: Say Hello to a Better Body!* I needed some encouraging words.

I had researched my post-surgery diet and lifestyle at various online sites. Though the medical information provided was straight-forward and helpful, the comment sections were often filled with horror stories. Well, maybe not horror stories, but definitely bleak predictions of what I would be able to eat in the future. Especially troubling were some predictions that I'd never again be able to eat certain beloved foods or regular-size portions. I would be confined to eating small portions and small meals forever. That was not what I wanted to hear when I was in pain.

Then I found Carole Bell's list of lessons learned from her mom. Carole's childhood experiences matched my own. My mother too served portions considered small by today's standards. We all survived. My mother also filled the plate with simple, unprocessed foods, refusing to let her daughters become picky eaters who wouldn't touch green vegetables. She encouraged us to enjoy many types of foods, and she never posted a calorie count by our plates.

When I finished reading Carole's story, I didn't move on to the next one in the book. Instead I lingered on her question: "What is in my future?" I knew my future habits might need to change, but change could be good. If I needed to eat smaller portions for the sake of my health, I could do it. Like Carole, all I needed to do was remember my mom's tiny waistline and my childhood dinner table.

Two years ago I volunteered to proofread a graduate student's research paper on the childhood obesity epidemic. The facts and figures in his review were sobering. I wondered how our country let this happen. When did giant dinner plates, super-sized meals, and endless soda refills win the day? Now I know it happened after the demise of the little belted housedress.

When Carole Bell compared eating and exercise habits in the fifties to those in the twenty-first century, she decided to make changes in her lifestyle. She didn't resent the need for change. Why should I? Rather than resisting a different way of eating, I could embrace the adjustments thrust upon me.

Today I'm grateful a revised diet and smaller portions are part of my future. I want to offer healthier meals to my family and friends, and I'd like to maintain my lower post-surgery weight. And thanks to Carole, I realize my mother already taught me how to do it.

Yes, my self-discipline might weaken on occasion, but I know what to do when that happens. I simply picture my mom and those tiny waists of the fifties. Then I forge ahead—June Cleaver house-dress not required.

~Donna Finlay Savage

The Tiny Waist
of the Fifties

Be moderate in order to taste the joys of life in abundance.
~Epicurus

She looked like June Cleaver except for her red hair. Like many young mothers in the fifties, mine often did housework in what she called a "housedress." It was nothing like the slouchy sweats I wear today to tackle the toilet bowl, the kitchen floor, and the cobwebs in the corners.

The housedresses our mothers wore then were unique. They were cotton and had to be ironed. They buttoned down the front to about six inches below the waist or nearly to the hem. The waistline of that dress still amazes me after all these years. Mom's waist could not have been more than twenty-two inches. The dress always had a belt that defined her tiny waistline.

That housedress, with its tiny belt-covered waist, represents an era when people didn't discuss or worry about weight control. It was something that happened due to lifestyle. Diet programs and books were much less prevalent.

Most of my adult life, I fought to keep my weight under control. It was a struggle at which I had varying degrees of success. I tried fad diets as well as healthy diets. The struggle occupied too much of my time and thought, almost to the point of obsession.

About three years ago, the image of my mom's belted house-dress began to flit across my mind frequently enough that I deemed it important. I decided to evaluate her lifestyle compared to mine. Surely there was something about how her generation lived that kept most of them trim even into their later years.

Here is what I found:

- We never ate more than one thin pork chop each. When Mom opened a can of vegetables, it was shared by four of us. Our hamburgers were probably about a sixth of a pound. Weekday breakfasts were a piece of toast, milk, and juice. Yet, I never remember passing out from hunger. Conclusion: If we eat smaller portions, we will survive until the next meal.

- We ate a wide variety of fruits and vegetables. Living in an agricultural community, we had access to fresh produce, which Mom canned. Although we had meat at most meals, produce dominated our plates. We always had some type of starch with our meals. Conclusion: Starch is not bad. Meat is not bad. The idea is to use them as additions to our meals rather than the mainstay.

- We ate food close to its source. We did not have packaged food until I was in high school. About that time, the infa-mous frozen potpie arrived. It was totally disgusting, so we seldom ate it. Conclusion: There's something about real food that promotes good health.

- Neither of my parents ever obsessed about food. If we had homemade ice cream, we all enjoyed it. I suspect Mom's bowl was smaller than Dad's, but she never mentioned the fact. We all enjoyed the ice cream guilt-free. I think my mom's idea was that if she could get enough veggies into us during the meal, there wouldn't be a lot of room for dessert. Besides, most of our desserts came from the fruit bowl. Conclusion: No food is bad. And, it may be that spending too much time analyzing one's diet causes problems.

- Mom and Dad did all their own work. Mom did the shopping, cleaning, laundry, cooking, sewing, and childcare. Dad did the yard and repair work. They raised chickens and put them in the freezer to enjoy through the year. Together, they painted and papered walls, waxed floors, and cleaned rugs. Conclusion: There was no need for a gym membership when there was so much to do at home.

- Television and computers didn't dominate our lives. Even after we bought a TV, we chose to be active. Although we weren't jogging or working out on a piece of machinery, we were moving most of the time. Even our winter taffy pulls burned more calories than sitting in front of a screen. Conclusion: An active lifestyle is conducive to trim waists and good health.

- We ate supper at six o'clock and had nothing else to eat until breakfast. That gave us about a twelve-hour fast each night. Conclusion: Bodies do well not having a continual inflow of food.

After I looked at how a family of the fifties lived, it was apparent that our twenty-first-century lifestyle was responsible for the differences in our waistlines. I decided to make some changes.

I knew any modifications needed to be gradual so I could fully embrace them. Drastic changes usually end in failure.

I set up these guidelines, knowing it would take time to totally adopt them:

- Decrease portion sizes drastically. Picture the one-fourth-can serving size of my youth.

- Plan for my plate to be two-thirds plant-based food, light on white starches.

- Quit talking and thinking about food and diets.

- Increase the amount of work I do in the house and yard. Include regular gym-type exercise because I use work-saving devices not available fifty years ago.

- Decrease screen time.

- Eat supper early and then fast until breakfast.

Has it worked? It has been three years. During that time, I have very gradually lost fifteen pounds. That is not the "fifteen pounds in two weeks" many fad diets advertise. But slow is okay, because I know I am changing.

I changed how I think about food. I know that I will not fall over if I eat a light meal. It's okay to leave food on my plate. I learned that a meal heavy on meat makes me feel sluggish, so I look for ways to get more vegetables on my plate. I eat my larger meal at noon and try to have a light supper early.

I changed how I feel about exercise. It is now like the air I breathe—necessary for my wellbeing, rather than something I force on myself. I do some weight training and yoga. I walk outside if the weather is nice, or I watch the news while I'm on the treadmill. I have a shelf for my computer in front of the treadmill, allowing me to watch inspiring or educational videos.

What is in my future? I may never totally adhere to my guidelines.

I sometimes eat too much. There are times when I eat late. I don't think about food and diets as much as I once did, but here I am writing about them now.

However, I don't believe I will ever again have an issue with weight. I expect to slowly lose a few more pounds until I am where I should be. I doubt I will wear housedresses with belted waists even if they do come back in style. It is enough to be strong and healthy, and to have more pleasant things on my mind than the number of calories in a food or whether or not it is "on my diet."

~Carole A. Bell

World Traveler

Travel and change of place impart new vigor to the mind.
~Seneca

The story in *A 2nd Helping of Chicken Soup for the Soul* entitled "The Window" touched my heart in an amazing way. The story speaks of two men who were sharing a room in a hospital. One man, bedridden, was on his back on the far side of the room. He was somewhat envious that the other man was on the side with the window.

The man by the window shared everything he saw with the man on the other side of the room. He elaborated and explained every detail to the point that his friend could see everything he saw. When the man on the other side of the room was eventually moved to the bed by the window he was surprised to discover that the window looked out on a blank wall.

I was devastated when my father became terminally ill. He was diagnosed with Parkinson's and Alzheimer's disease. The last thing he asked for before he was admitted to a long-term care facility was to go on one more vacation. I talked with the doctors about the possibility and learned that it wasn't possible. So like the man at the window who tried to encourage his friend on the other side of the room, I decided to pretend we were traveling right there in the nursing home.

The man in the story brought the outside world (the park, the people, the lake) to his friend. I decided that I could bring many famous vacations spots to my father. I got on the Internet and asked my online friends to send me pictures or postcards from their hometowns. The nicest people who I had never met began mailing me packages of pictures, cards, souvenirs and keepsakes from the festivals and other events in their hometowns. Many not only sent pictures and postcards but wrote long, descriptive letters to a dying man they had never met.

Then the oddest thing began to happen. We started getting memorabilia from places all over the world. My friends told their friends and their friends told their friends. There were days I would go to the post office and find boxes filled with exciting stuff from all over the world. My daddy became a world traveler in his nursing home room. And he didn't even have to buy an airline ticket. My online friends knew Daddy couldn't go out and see the world, so they sent their world to him.

I'll never forget the trips we took, the conversations we had and the smiles on Daddy's face as I shared all the tourist attractions with him. I received more and more stuff for weeks on end. And about the time Daddy no longer knew who he was or who I was, the packages ceased to arrive. His vacation was over, but the memories will last forever for me.

"The Window" taught me to step out and do the best I could, that life could be a joyful event. Sometimes we must use our imagination and stretch ourselves to bring joy to someone else.

The man in the story, looking at the wall, made a difference in my father's life even after he was gone. His story touched me in a way that caused me to exercise my faith and stretch my imagination. I was able to fulfill my father's dying request.

After Daddy died, in an attempt to heal my own grief, I would often pull out the pictures, the cards and the souvenirs and travel around the world once again.

It's been thirteen years since my father died, but when I think of our traveling days together, I still shed a few tears of joy and hope.

~Nancy B. Gibbs

The Window

And life is what we make it, always has been, always will be.
~Grandma Moses

There were once two men, both seriously ill, sharing a small room in a great hospital. It had one window looking out on the world. One of the men, as part of his treatment, was allowed to sit up in bed for an hour in the afternoon (something to do with draining the fluid from his lungs). His bed was next to the window. But the other man had to spend all his time flat on his back.

Every afternoon, when the man next to the window was propped up for his hour, he would pass the time by describing what he could see outside. The window apparently overlooked a park where there was a lake. There were ducks and swans in the lake, and children came to throw them bread and sail model boats. Young lovers walked hand in hand beneath the trees, and there were flowers and stretches of grass and games of softball. And at the back, behind the fringe of trees, was a fine view of the city skyline.

The man on his back would listen to the other man describe all of this, enjoying every minute. He heard how a child nearly fell into the lake, and how beautiful the girls were in their summer dresses.

His friend's descriptions eventually made him feel he could almost see what was happening outside.

Then one fine afternoon, the thought struck him: Why should the man next to the window have all the pleasure of seeing what was going on? Why shouldn't he get the chance? He felt ashamed, but the more he tried not to think like that, the worse he wanted a change. He'd do anything! One night as he stared at the ceiling, the other man suddenly woke up, coughing and choking, his hands groping for the button that would bring the nurse running. But the man watched without moving—even when the sound of breathing stopped. In the morning, the nurse found the other man dead, and quietly took his body away.

As soon as it seemed decent, the man asked if he could be switched to the bed next to the window. So they moved him, tucked him in, and made him quite comfortable. The minute they left, he propped himself up on one elbow, painfully and laboriously, and looked out the window. It faced a blank wall.

~George Target

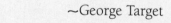

Lawn Chair Living

Reflect upon your present blessings, of which every man has plenty, not on
your past misfortunes, of which all men have some.
~Charles Dickens

Burn out. It happens to everyone—even writers. Thirteen years ago, I was a freelance executive speechwriter and advertising copywriter and my busy season ran from January to April. In that four-month period, I would write twelve to fourteen hours a day, six days a week to hit my deadlines for ads, brochures, speeches, newsletters, magazine articles, and annual reports. By the first week of May, I was comatose. My energy level was zero, my creativity was shot and my brain was mush.

That's when Gregg Levoy delivered just what the doctor ordered, a cup of *Chicken Soup for the Writer's Soul*, in his story entitled, "Power Lounging." In it, Levoy describes his extended sabbatical designed to revive his spirit, and he leaves us with a vital message not just for writers, but for any profession: rest brings restoration.

Levoy reminded me that I need to rest more and he inspired me by the ways in which he found rest and renewal in ordinary things and in simple pleasures. In his words: "I succumbed to the lazy lure of a spring afternoon spent in my own backyard, watching the shadows of clouds bend in the folds of the hills, the hawks and vultures sweep into view on long, slow arcs, the tomcats stalk birds in the low branches of the fig. And for a brief spell I was released from being pinned to the ground by the gravity of my endeavors.

"Over the next three months, as the days flicked by like white lines on the freeway, I took great long walks by the sea and in the forests, lost myself in epic novels, wrote poetry again, traveled, and stopped postponing jury duty. I went surfing, joined a men's group, got to know my friends better…"

His article not only motivated me, it changed me. I not only learned how to optimize rest and relaxation, I took it a step further. I inserted pauses into my routine to better appreciate the most meaningful moments of life. Some pauses were only a few minutes long, others hours, some days. I call it "Lawn Chair Living." Here is how it works for me.

Several years ago, I inserted a long pause into my day by grabbing a lawn chair and heading to the beach. I planted myself under a shade tree overlooking a bay. I was there for one reason. From the comfort of the lawn chair and the beauty of the idyllic setting, I was mentally preparing myself for another major transition in my life.

In the next few weeks, my father, a widower of forty years, would be moved into an assisted living center because Alzheimer's was robbing him of his memory. Soon, I would lose daily contact with one of the most significant people in my life.

What troubled me though was that the chaotic pace of my life could easily cause me to overlook the implications of this life change. Thus, from a lawn chair, I would pause, refocus, and quietly reflect on my changing role as a son.

As the gulls circled overhead and sailboats glided across the bay, I asked myself if I was the son I could have been. Should I have been more helpful forty years ago as he struggled to raise six children alone following my mother's premature death from cancer? What could I, as an eleven-year-old, have done to support him more? Did he know how much I emulated him as a child? Did I say the things I should have said before Alzheimer's systematically fragmented his memory? Did I ever tell him what he taught me about commitment in marriage?

As I sat in that lawn chair and surveyed my father's life, I realized when my mother died, a piece of my father died too. Perhaps that's why he never gave himself permission to marry again.

I remember preparing for my wedding fifteen years after my mother's death. I noticed my father never lectured me on the importance of commitment. He never pointed to himself as an example to follow, although I've never seen a better one. He just quietly lived a life committed to his children and their mother's memory, and his life spoke volumes.

Shortly after I was married I stopped by to visit him. As we chatted about my job, I slid my wedding ring off my finger.

"What did you just do?" he asked abruptly.

Surprised, I said, "Nothing. I just slid my wedding ring off my finger."

"Why did you do that?" he pressed.

"What do you mean, Dad?"

"Do you take your wedding ring off often?"

"No. Why?"

Then I realized my father was about to take me to a sacred place — his heart.

"I told your mother at our wedding that when she placed the ring on my finger, it would never pass the end of my finger again as long as she lived," he said quietly, looking down at his hands.

I knew the rest of the story. Seven years after my mother died, a jeweler had to cut his wedding ring off his finger because it was so tight it affected his circulation. For twenty-five years his wedding ring had never passed the end of his finger.

As I looked out at the horizon, I realized today was like many days I've spent in a lawn chair over the years. The locations have changed but the mission has remained the same. Pause and reflect. By inserting pauses into my life and taking time to reflect, the events of my life have paraded before my eyes again, providing a second chance to appreciate them fully.

By pausing in a lawn chair, I wrestled through the decisions to have my then four-year-old son undergo three surgeries. From a lawn chair, I made the decision to leave corporate America and become a freelance writer so I could be home more and watch my children grow up. From a lawn chair, I helped my sons sort through their college choices. And from a lawn chair, I planned the best way to move my father out of his home of forty years and into an assisted living center.

Today, I believe that a simple lawn chair, placed in a beautiful setting, has become a sacred place for me. A place to recall my past. A place to pause. And a place to reflect on the things that matter most in life.

And to think, it all began with some friendly advice from Gregg Levoy and a hot cup of *Chicken Soup for the Soul*.

~James C. Magruder

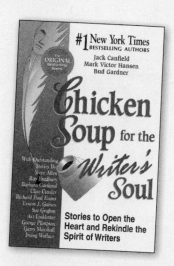

With Outstanding
Stories By
Steve Allen
Ray Bradbury
Barbara Cartland
Clive Cussler
Richard Paul Evans
Ernest J. Gaines
Sue Grafton
Art Linkletter
George Plimpton
Garry Marshall
Irving Wallace

Stories to Open the
Heart and Rekindle the
Spirit of Writers

Power Lounging

Take rest; a field that has rested gives a bountiful crop.
~Ovid

I used to think of Sisyphus as the patron saint of workaholics, one of whom I provisionally consider myself to be, though more out of economic necessity than compulsion. That is, freelance writing is a heavy stone, and demands a steady labor to keep it rolling.

Lately, though, I feel I've been overlooking the true instruction of Sisyphus's life, which is that each time his great grindstone rolls to the bottom of the mountain, he is granted a rest while he walks back down to retrieve it. Though he must work for all time, according to the myth, he does not work all the time.

Nor, I decided recently, should I.

Having completed a book that took me fifteen months of twelve-hour days, I suddenly hit a wall I had never hit as a working man and a freelance writer—burnout. The thought of doing another day's work on anything even remotely related to the machinations of career-building, income-producing or generally "getting ahead" was nearly enough to buckle me at the knees. As it was, in the waning days of the book project, I pulled myself up to my desk each morning as if to a chin-up bar.

After such an intemperance of work, no trip seemed too extravagant or protracted, no binge too vulgar, no amount of goofing off too unreasonable.

So I decided to take a break. In fact, I decided to extend the spirit of Sabbath to outlandish proportions—by taking four months off, living off savings and for a brief period here in the middle of my work life, seeing what it would feel like to simply not work, to make time for the kind of creative idleness that an acquaintance of mine calls "power lounging." For someone who had just finished a book about how to survive as a freelancer, taking a break of such duration seemed contrary to my own advice, but I simply had to do it.

Toward the end of the book project, in fact, I discovered that writers have their own patron saint, Saint Francis de Sales, who exhorts his flock to practice "simplicity, simplicity, simplicity." And I felt that when the disparity between my work ethic and my desire for simplicity and balance grows too large, as it had during that year spent writing the book, then I begin to feel like a man with one foot on the dock and other foot on a boat that is slowly drifting out to sea.

What I needed was what people so obliquely refer to as space, a distance from what was pressing in on me, a penetrating quiet inside. And I needed to hold that silence up to my ears, like an empty shell, and listen to the roar of my own life. I needed time to reacquaint myself with some non-work modes of expression, to open myself to some of the things that gave me joy as a child, to savor the benediction of play, to read a novel again—and to await further instructions.

And I wanted time, unencumbered by economic concerns, to experiment with my writing—a luxury I rarely grant myself when on the treadmill of earning a living—and by doing so to make out what direction my writing wanted to take next, and where I was willing to be led.

When I told a colleague what I planned to do now that the book was done, he asked, "What are you, rich?"

"No," I replied. "Desperate."

The first phase of my vocational celibacy was marked by the postpartum depression that followed the delivery of the book. A big project, to say nothing of a lifetime of working, generates a tremendous momentum that doesn't end just because the work ends. It's a bit like a head-on collision. The car stops, but the passenger doesn't.

This seemed to set the tone for my entire sabbatical: a delicious and bewildering freedom marked by a maddening restlessness that routinely propelled me back into my office as if in a trance, despite my policy statements to the contrary. There I would sit for sometimes hours, twisting slowly back and forth on my chair and pulling anxiously at my lower lip, listening to the blathering traffic of noises in my head, while my legs vibrated like tuning forks.

"This is what it must be like when men retire," my partner Robin declared after a morning of watching me pace around the house aimlessly, opening the refrigerator half a dozen times.

The pull of work, the rhythm of the nine-to-five world, exerts a force that is nearly tidal in its irresistibility. Cut off from it, I felt adrift. This was exacerbated by being in a profession in which there is such a thin, porous line between life and work. Simply to be a writer is to always be at work. Vacations turn into assignments, lunches with friends become interviews. I study movies instead of just enjoying them, and my office is at home. As a writer, to be is to do, and without a clear sense of where one leaves off and the other begins, it is almost impossible to punch out.

Thus, unconsciously and instinctively, I began reestablishing order, ebb and flow, routine. Before I knew it, I had managed to fill half my time with busyness that looked suspiciously like business: sending manuscripts out to magazines, doing market research, feeling behind, worrying about what would happen when the four months were up. I felt as though I were cheating on a fast, or taking my briefcase with me on vacation.

What I began to realize with crackling clarity is that I come from a long line of doers, starting with a workaholic family that hardwired me to excel, to stay on top of things, to expect that hard work and material wealth would put me in line to receive the key to the cosmic washroom. On his deathbed, my grandfather asked my mother what day it was. "Tuesday," she said.

"Pay the gardener," he instructed her.

His obituary was like most others, betraying the compulsive preoccupation with work, and helping me to understand why I had such a devil of a time not working. Obituaries are little more than posthumous résumés, lists of accomplishments: books authored, titles held, military ranks attained, degrees earned. They are summary statements of our lives, testaments to what we hold in esteem, and there are no hallelujahs for idleness, for time spent with family, for afternoons given over to long, dreamy walks.

Droning away in the boiler room of the culture is a juggernaut of a machine, one that heaves out a message strong enough to pump cement through my veins: Work! Value adheres to what I produce, so I'm constantly doing. And when I'm busy doing, I don't have to be busy feeling—feeling that maybe I'm burned out, that I need a change, or that my work, which normally offers me a sense of control over my life, has instead made my life feel like a parody of being in control, like I'm frantically trying to shovel coal into a furnace that's burning it up faster and faster.

About a month into my leave of absence from writing, I had a dream that was to prove pivotal. A Zen monk gave me a large block of wood to sand down to nothing. As I neared the end, and began to look forward to the project's completion, the monk came back and took my sandpaper away, telling me to use only my fingernails. The point, he said, was the process, not the goal. Every life ends the same way, I understood him to be implying—the hero always dies—so why be in such a hurry to get to the finish line.

With that dream, something shifted inside me, and I became determined to not only take the full time off, but to use it well—to return the free to freelancing. Although it was a tremendous discipline to not be disciplined and goal-oriented, to stop looking for work, to stop feeling like I was wasting time (when really it is time that is wasting me), I slowly began immersing myself in the kind of activities I had originally intended for my sabbatical.

The day after the dream, I succumbed to the lazy lure of a spring afternoon spent in my own backyard, watching the shadows of clouds bend in the folds of the hills, the hawks and vultures sweep into view on long, slow arcs, the tomcats stalk birds in the low branches of the fig. And for a brief spell I was released from being pinned to the ground by the gravity of my endeavors.

Over the next three months, as the days flicked by like white lines on the freeway, I took great long walks by the sea and in the forests, lost myself in epic novels, wrote poetry again, traveled, and stopped postponing jury duty. I went surfing, joined a men's group, got to know my friends better, and even did my exercises with greater observance, not so grimly and perfunctorily. I felt expansive and that life was full of possibilities.

I not only discovered that I can stop work for months at a time and my life doesn't crumble, but that having my nose to the grindstone, my ear to the ground, and my shoulder to the wheel is, for long periods of time, not the most comfortable position. Sometimes lying in the bathtub is.

As my time off drew to a close, and I prepared to reenter the world of work, to start writing in earnest again, I felt as I usually do at the end of vacations: not ready to come back, but renewed nonetheless. And though I saw that I'm not quite the master of my fate that I claim to be, I also realized that my life utterly belongs to me, and that it is meant to be savored and not just worked at.

~Gregg Levoy

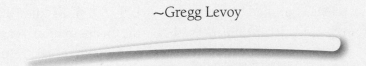

How I Learned to Read a *Chicken Soup for the Soul* Book

You learn something every day if you pay attention.
~Ray LeBlond

I am an avid reader. My mother said that as a child I always had my nose "stuck in a book." I have been a fan of *Chicken Soup for the Soul* books since the very first one was published.

I already had about 100 *Chicken Soup for the Soul* books in my collection when my first story was accepted, for *Chicken Soup for the Soul: Thanks Mom*. The day the book arrived I read the first story, by Brad Meltzer, entitled "What My Mother Gave Me Before She Died." Brad's bio was in the back of the book in a section called "Meet Our Contributors." As soon as I read his story I flipped to the bio section. I had never heard of Brad Meltzer, but I already felt like I knew him a bit from his story. I imagined Brad talking to his mother on the phone. She wanted to know if he was taking his vitamins and getting enough fresh air and exercise. I visualized a small lady with a tall son. She was worried he was writing too much and not getting out. He needed his vitamin D.

After letting my imagination run amok, I went to his website and immediately recognized the names of the bestsellers he had written. I had a new author to read!

Brad Meltzer's story was a great contribution to me personally. It was an "a-ha!" moment in my own life when I realized that as each mother is bound to her child, they also bind us together as authors who all owe something to our mothers. It was also an "a-ha" moment because I realized that I had been missing out on a crucial element of the *Chicken Soup for the Soul* experience. Now I look up the author's bio after I read each story. I am in awe of the lineup of authors and I am humbled that I am one of them! These people are all so very special.

The author list is as long and as varied as the stories in each *Chicken Soup for the Soul* book. Now I need to re-read each of the 140 *Chicken Soup for the Soul* books I own so that I can meet the contributors.

I didn't know how to properly read a *Chicken Soup for the Soul* book when I first started. You see… I only read the stories. I missed the endings… the part about the authors. To me, they are the most important part.

~Linda A. Lohman

What My Mother Gave Me Before She Died

God could not be everywhere, so he created mothers.
~Jewish Proverb

She's the kind of woman who would say, "Ucch, what a depressing funeral." And so the obvious thing to say is that I want to celebrate my mom. But what I really want to do is share my mom. Not the person who was here the past few months, but the woman who was here the past sixty-three years.

My mother fought to have me. She tried for three years to get pregnant. And I think that struggle always left her feeling thankful for what she had. It is, to this moment, the only rational way to explain the never-ending love she gave to me.

As I entered grade school, my father, who breathes baseball, signed me up for Little League. I lasted one year. But it wasn't until a few months ago that I finally found out just who saved me from year two. *Stewie, don't make him play if he doesn't want to play.* Even back then, she knew me. And for all of childhood, she nurtured me, growing my little artsy side and always making sure that I could find my own adventure. And she fed it with one of the greatest seeds of imagination: Television.

This will sound silly and trite, but in my mother's honor, I'm not apologizing for it. One of my clearest memories of childhood is sitting at the side of my mom's bed—the side that faced the TV—and watching show after show with her. To be clear, TV wasn't something that watched me—she didn't put it on just so she could go do something else. My mother watched *with* me. Or rather, I watched with her. Old movies like *Auntie Mame*, and modern classics like *Taxi*, *Soap*, *MASH* and, of course, our favorite for every Wednesday night, *Dynasty*. (Please, what else are you gonna do with a son who doesn't play baseball?) Some mothers and sons never find anything they can truly share. But my mom always treated me like an adult, always let me stay up late to watch the good stuff, and in those moments, she did one of the best things any parent can do: She shared what she loved with me.

When I was thirteen, my mom faced the worst tragedy of her life—the death of her father. My Poppy. Poppy would do anything for my mother, and when he died, I remember being at his funeral. My mom was screaming and yelling wildly because the funeral home had neglected to shave him and she wanted him to look just right. It was a ferocity she saved for people messing with her family—something I had never seen before and would never see again. And I know she put that one in me, too.

When I think of my mom—more than anything else—I think of the pure, immeasurable, almost crazy love she had for me. I remember the first time I gave her *The Tenth Justice*. It was my first published novel, my first time ever putting real work out for anyone to see. I was terrified when she said she'd finished it. And then she looked right at me and said, "Bradley, I know I'm your mother, but I have to be honest with you. This book… *is the greatest book of all time!*"

When someone was recounting the story to me a few days ago, he called my mother the queen of hyperbole. But as I think about it, he had it wrong. Hyperbole is a deliberate exaggeration. My mother never used hyperbole. My mother actually *believed* it. In her eyes, I really did write the greatest book of all time.

A few years ago, I went to the headquarters of Borders Books up in Ann Arbor. And when I was there the main buyer for Borders said to me, "Guess where your books sell more than anywhere else? Straight sales, not even per capita." So of course I said, "New York." That's eight million New Yorkers in one city.

"No."

"Washington, D.C.? I write about D.C."

"No."

"Chicago, the flagship superstore?"

"No."

The number one place my books sell was the Boca Raton Borders, two miles from the furniture store where my mother worked. That means my mother *single-handedly* beat eight million New Yorkers. Messing with the power of a Jewish mother is one thing, but never ever mess with the power that was Teri Meltzer.

Of course, what made my mom *my mom* was the fact that that love—that love that burned in her brighter than fifty suns—was there even when times were bad. When *The First Counsel* was published, *USA Today* gave me a ruthless review. It was the kind of review that just felt like a public humiliation. The headline was: "Make First Your Last." But when my mother saw it, she said to me, "Don't worry. No one reads that paper anyway." It's the number one paper in the entire country!

And when the second novel had bombed and I was wracked with fear, I'll never forget my mom on the phone—she said to me, "I'd love you if you were a garbage man." And to this day, EVERY day that I sit down to write these books, I say those words to myself—"I'd love you if you were a garbage man." I don't care where she is—my mother is *always* there for me.

Let me be clear: All our strength, confidence, any success my sister and I have been blessed enough to receive, those were all watered and nurtured by the strength of the love that my mother showered on us. When I found out the last book had hit the top spot on the bestseller list, the first person I called was my mother. And of course my mom started crying hysterically. She was so proud. And when I heard her crying, I of course started crying. And in the midst of this tear-fest, I said to her, "Where are you now?" And through her sobs, she said to me, "I'm at Marshall's."

Of course she's at Marshall's, still trying to buy irregular socks for two dollars. It was my mother's greatest lesson: Never, ever, ever, ever change for anyone. And her second greatest lesson: That Marshall's just may be the greatest store on Earth.

In the end, my mother died the same way she lived. She laughed and smiled and enjoyed everything she could get from life, most of all, her grandchildren. They were the second great love of her life. When each of my children was born, my mother said to me, "Now you'll understand how I love you."

She was right. And it was the first time I got to see life through my mom's eyes.

I don't miss particular moments with my mother. I can always remember those moments. What I miss is my mother, and her reactions, and how she never hesitated to tell you whom she hated or what she thought, and most of all, how she loved me and my family with more love than one person should be able to muster.

She once said to me, "I'd saw off my own arm for you." Again, not an exaggeration. Just Teri Meltzer being Teri Meltzer.

That love my mom gave me is my strength. It never. Ever. Wavered. It's like the hum of an airplane engine—it's there and it never lets up and it never stops—and you get so used to it, it just becomes part of the ride. But you'd know the second it was gone. My mother's love for us never stopped.

It was a constant.

A foundation.

A law.

It is the pillar that has carried me everywhere and holds me up right now. Her love is a gift that she gave me. And it is the part of her that I hope I carry with me every time my child or grandchild shows me a picture they colored, every time I say thank you to the valet who parks my car, and damn well every time I drive past Marshall's.

I miss you, Mom. And I thank you. I thank you for teaching me how a parent is supposed to love their child. And I hope you know that, in that and so much else, you live on forever.

~Brad Meltzer

A Smart Choice

If fifty million people say a foolish thing, it is still a foolish thing.
~Anatole France

was in fifth grade when my mom bought me *Chicken Soup for the Teenage Soul* at my school's book fair. Despite being a few years shy of being deemed a "teenager" I was eager to read the book. With all the different stories I couldn't decide where to start so I began flipping through it. One story I landed on has stuck with me over all these years.

"Just One Drink" by Chris Laddish describes the devastating loss of a brother who rode with a friend who drove after only having one drink. The grief of suddenly losing a loved one, especially in a tragic accident, is unbelievably sad. Aside from the sorrow I felt in reading this story, the fact that it could happen to anyone also made the story stick with me. I had known adults who would have more than one drink and then drive, and it made me see that this story could easily be about them.

This story had a tremendous impact on me. We had been taught about drugs and alcohol in school, that they were bad, and that some really terrible things can happen because of them. Combining that message with this story made me realize that even one drink could do some serious damage, the one drink that we were taught wouldn't seem like a big deal, but was huge. Learning about alcohol and then reading this story made me fully understand the possible repercussions and consequences of drinking alcohol, which unfortunately for Michael, Chris's brother, did happen. I read the story and decided at that moment I would not drink and drive nor would I get into a car with a friend who had been drinking, even if it was "only" one drink.

That decision came into play some years later when I was at a party and my first opportunity for underage drinking came about.

"Do you want one?" a friend asked, gesturing at a can of beer.

"No, thanks," I replied.

I knew my rights and wrongs. I wasn't going to stop my friends from doing what they wanted to do, but I didn't want to take part in it. Underage drinking was commonplace, but it wasn't for me.

Later that night they wanted to go get food.

"I'll drive," I quickly volunteered.

I wasn't willing to let any of them drive, even though they had only had one drink. I remembered the story "Just One Drink" as we were walking out to my car. I was a little surprised that the promise I made to myself all those years before, after reading the story, still stood strong, but was grateful because it also made me remember the impact that just one drink could have. It put a small smile on my face to know I resisted the temptation to have just one drink and then stood firm on being the sober driver.

This story has popped into my head randomly over the years and each time it does I think of how much it has shaped my decisions when it comes to drinking and driving. Chris Laddish wrote: "The only thing that helps is telling my story, hoping you will remember it if you are tempted to get into a car with someone who has had a drink—even just one drink" and I have remembered it. I am very thankful Chris shared his story. I am twenty-five years old now and still stand by the choice I made when I was ten after reading "Just One Drink."

Thank you, Chris.

~Sarah Winkler

New York Times BESTSELLER

Chicken Soup for the Teenage Soul

Stories of
Life, Love and
Learning

Jack Canfield, Mark Victor Hansen
and Kimberly Kirberger

Just One Drink

Drinking and driving: there are stupider things, but it's a very short list.
~Author Unknown

There's a small cross by the side of Highway 128, near the town of Boonville. If this cross could talk, it would tell you this sad story:

Seven years ago, my brother Michael was at a friend's ranch. They decided to go out for dinner. Joe arrived and volunteered to drive—after just one drink.

Lightheartedly, the four friends traveled the winding road. They didn't know where it would end—nobody did. Suddenly, they swerved into the opposite lane, colliding with an oncoming car.

Back home we were watching *E.T.* on video in front of a warm fire. Then we went to bed. At 2:00 a.m. a police officer woke my mom with the devastating news. Michael had been killed.

In the morning, I found my mother and sister crying. I stood there bewildered. "What's wrong?" I asked, rubbing my sleepy eyes.

Mom took a deep breath. "Come here..."

Thus began a grueling journey through grief, where all roads lead to nowhere. It still hurts to remember that day.

The only thing that helps is telling my story, hoping you will remember it if you are tempted to get into a car with someone who has had a drink—even just one drink.

Joe chose the road to nowhere. He was convicted of manslaughter and served time. However, the real punishment is living with the consequences of his actions. He left us with an ache in our hearts that will never go away, a nightmare that will haunt him—and us—for the rest of our lives. And a small cross by the side of Highway 128.

~Chris Laddish, age 13

Dedicated with love to the memory of Michael Laddish

Just One More Minute, Mommy

We've had bad luck with our kids — they've all grown up.
~Christopher Morley

I was a nervous and uncertain new mom, the perfect target audience for the recently released *Chicken Soup for the New Mom's Soul* that I received as a gift from my husband. I read it cover to cover within two days and dog-eared my favorite stories. They would continue to inspire me on the days when I needed reassurance that I wasn't the first to tackle the challenges of being in this new role. One story in particular, "Be Careful What You Wish For," stuck with me for some reason. I remember thinking how I couldn't wait until my baby girl, Priya, was potty trained. I couldn't wait until we were past the baby stage, then the toddler stage, and most definitely could not wait until we were through the terrible-twos.

Well, we made it through all of those first years with Priya and I was blessed with another pregnancy. It was time to move Priya into a big girl bed and start getting things ready for baby number two. In those early days of the transition to the new bed, we had to lie beside Priya to convince her to stay in her room and resist the temptation to explore her new nighttime independence. It became a nightly chore and my husband and I would begrudgingly take turns every other night lying in that little twin bed trying to get her to fall asleep. After lying silently beside her, pretending to be asleep for five, ten, sometimes fifteen minutes, I would ever so quietly try to roll off the bed without waking her. But without fail, night after night, Priya would whisper, "Just one more minute, Mommy?" I was certain that some nights she actually spoke those words in her sleep.

But that bedtime routine stuck, and here I am years later, still lying beside Priya each and every night as she goes to sleep. Through all of these years, the last thing she says every night as I try to make my quiet exit is the same, asking for "just one more minute." She still has that same twin bed, but a lot has changed within the walls of that bedroom. Priya is almost six now and is nearing the end of kindergarten. She is growing up way too quickly with her talk of boys and music, and sometimes an attitude that I thought wouldn't arrive for another ten years at least. Over the past few months it has really hit me that my baby girl is growing into a big girl much faster than I expected. I am not ready for her to stop believing in princesses. Or to stop holding my hand in public. Or to call me "Mom" instead of "Mommy."

In the past few months my son, Keegan, has become fully potty trained and is now sleeping in a big-boy bed of his own. I think back to that story I read years ago and realize that I am in the very same position as the woman who wrote that story. I realize completely now what she meant when she said "Be Careful What You Wish For." Our bedtime conversations have now changed and there is a little less room for me in that twin bed, but I still lie with Priya as she falls asleep each night. I realize that these days are numbered and soon the time will come when she won't even want me in her room at all.

So tonight when she whispers "Just one more minute, Mommy?" I know there is no other place in the world I would rather be. I will snuggle her close, give her a kiss on the head and tell her, "Yes Priya. Just one more minute."

~Ritu Shannon

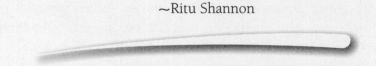

Chicken Soup for the **New Mom's Soul**

Touching Stories About the
Miracles of Motherhood

Jack Canfield, Mark Victor Hansen,
and Patty Aubery

Be Careful
What You Wish For

*Enjoy the little things, for one day you may look back
and realize they were the big things.*
~Robert Brault

B
e careful what you wish for. You just might get it. As my two-year-old sits astride the potty grinning from ear to ear over his first "success," I can feel a lump growing in my throat. This is what I wanted, right? For my youngest child to be potty-wise? No more diapers. No more paying those diaper prices. No more making sure I have an ample supply before leaving the house. No more feeling guilty because I opted for the convenience of disposable over the environmentally responsible cloth ones. No more clipping diaper coupons, which I never remembered to use. This is the day I've been dreaming about? Isn't it?

But with the end of the diaper era, I see the beginning of the end of a most meaningful chapter of my life. My mind flashes back to the insecure, nervous parent I was, just seven years ago, when I brought Haley home from the hospital. I remember smiling at the nurses as

David wheeled me out of the New Family Center while inside I was screaming *Are you people crazy? I don't know how to take care of this baby!* I think about the sleepless nights I spent, not because Haley kept me awake, but because I had to jump up every few minutes to make sure she was still breathing.

I remember the overwrought, inept mother I was when just twenty months later, I brought little Molly home and attempted to balance myself between a demanding toddler and a premature newborn, while trying to figure out how my marriage figured into all of this, not to mention any chance for a life of my own.

Next came three years of wrestling over whether to have a third, ending with a very pleasant surprise — the birth of my perfect baby boy. The day we brought Hewson home from the hospital, the five of us spent the morning on the bed just snuggling and falling in love with each other. *This is a family!* I thought. *I feel sorry for anyone who's not a part of it.*

Has so much time passed since that day? When did my baby get this big? With Haley and Molly I tried to speed along each phase of their baby and toddlerhood. "I wonder if she'll be sitting by Christmas?" "I hope she's walking by summer." I pushed them into learning their colors, their numbers, their alphabet. Now, I wish I could slam on the brakes. I just want to drop to my knees right here on the bathroom floor and beg him to let me put him back in a diaper, a little gingham romper, and high-top shoes. Maybe we'll tackle the potty next year.

To think of all the times over the past seven years when I've longed for a life of my own, to have time to pamper myself, to read like I used to, to have an uninterrupted phone conversation or bath. Suddenly all of that seems superfluous when compared with the feeling of knowing exactly who I am. I am this mom, wife, writer, teacher, storyteller, gardener, baker, volunteer person. I've loved that feeling of knowing beyond a shadow of a doubt that I'm in the right place at the right time. Whenever I feel overwhelmed with things I'm not getting done, I can stop, read a book with one of my children, and know, beyond a shadow of a doubt, that there's nothing more important, more monumental, more future-building than what I am doing at that moment.

I wonder who I'll be when all of that's taken from me. I wonder how I'll pass my days when I finally have the freedom for which I've longed. What will it be like to crawl into bed without first tucking three warm, little bodies under their own covers? How will I spend my mornings when I'm not drinking my coffee with the expectation of sleepy little feet shuffling my way for that first morning hug?

I close my eyes and make a pledge not to take any of it for granted, to enjoy every hectic, exhausting, demanding moment I have left in this chapter of my life. I pledge not to take a single snuggle or fish kiss or phonetically spelled love note for granted. Hewson is staring up at me. I know it's time to lift him off the potty and run to the phone to tell his dad the "good news." I wonder what his reaction will be.

~Mimi Greenwood Knight

Messages of Love

When someone you love becomes a memory, the memory becomes a treasure.
~Author Unknown

nspiration jumped off the page and into my heart when I read the story, "To Read When You're Alone," from the book *Chicken Soup for the Mother's Soul*. I felt encouraged and motivated to write notes to my three children and husband after reading the story about a mother who put letters under her son's pillow. Because of this story, writing little notes became a common practice in my family. I stashed notes under pillows, in backpacks, lunch bags, briefcases, and jacket pockets. It was fun to think of sneaky ways to hide my messages of love as I sent my family off to school or work.

I didn't realize how valuable the note writing practice had become until years later, when my husband Ben, forty years old, was stricken with a rare liver disease and was told he would not survive without a liver transplant. Our children, Amanda, Benjamin, and Jordan, were ages twelve, ten, and eight at the time, too young to understand the full ramifications of his diagnosis. We chose not to tell them the seriousness of Ben's condition to protect them as long as we could. They knew their dad was sick, but their worrying would not help their dad, and we wanted their world to stay as normal as possible, to continue with their sports, time with friends, and school activities.

Ben eventually had to take a leave from work to go on short-term disability, and eventually long-term disability, as he was spending more of his time sleeping. Frequently, Ben would find little notes hand scrawled in children's writing hidden under his pillow: "I love you, Daddy. God bless you, Daddy, and have a fun day! You're the best dad in the whole wide world!"

Many times Ben woke to find one or more stuffed animals beside him that one of the kids had brought him while he was sleeping, along with a note saying, "My friends will keep you company today. I love you, Daddy!"

Ben would often leave me notes under my pillow telling me how much he loved me, and what a great job I was doing with the kids. His words of encouragement kept me going, especially when his health deteriorated and he was in the hospital more than he was out. When he was put in the hospital full-time to wait for a liver transplant before Christmas, there was no more hiding the severity of his condition from the children.

On one of our visits we planned a family movie night. We brought microwave popcorn and we piled onto Ben's hospital bed with him to watch the movie. It was great fun. "Now you kids get your homework done and listen to your mother." Ben instructed all three kids from his hospital bed before we gave him hugs goodbye.

"We will, Daddy," all three said in unison.

"God bless you and I love you," Ben said, drawing a cross on their foreheads with his thumb before giving each one a goodnight hug.

"Oh, I have one more thing for you, Daddy," Benjamin said, taking a folded envelope from his coat pocket. Handwritten on the outside it said, "To Dad. Open when we leave." "Something for you to keep under your pillow."

"Well thank you, Benjamin. I will keep it in a special spot," Ben said, holding the letter to his chest.

"God bless and I love you too," I said, bending over to draw a cross on Ben's forehead, as he did the same for me, followed by a warm embrace in his arms. I longed to climb up beside him to stay and not let go, but I had to get the kids home to bed. They had school the next day, and I had work.

Arriving home late from our visit to the hospital, I rushed

through our bedtime routine, tucked the kids into bed, and said bedtime prayers with each of them. Exhausted, I fell into my own bed and began to sob. I cried out, "Dear Lord, what can I do to hold my family together? What can I do to bring encouragement, comfort, and peace to Ben? Please God, I need your help."

I slipped my hand under my pillow and was surprised to bump into something. It was a little plastic flower and a note from my younger son Jordan: "Dear Mom, I know you're tired. Just relax and don't fold all the laundry on your bed. I will help you fold it tomorrow. Go to sleep and rest. I love you. Love, Jordan."

The next morning I woke with an important plan. I needed to take Ben some stationery and envelopes for him to write a letter to each of the kids. In my heart I knew he would not be coming home for Christmas, as much as I didn't want to accept the reality.

Christmas Eve, with Ben still in the hospital, I carefully placed the bright red envelopes containing Ben's letters to each of us on our Christmas tree. Of all the gifts given and exchanged that year, the letters from Ben were the favorites for all of us.

Ben lost his battle and passed away that January. Our world had been ripped apart. For all three of my children, the letter they received from their dad that Christmas is among their most prized possessions. And I have a treasure box with letters and note cards that Ben left under my pillow.

One night a few months after Ben passed away, as I was tucking Jordan into bed, I saw the familiar corner of a red envelope peeking out from underneath his pillow. It was the letter from his dad. It warmed my heart to see Ben's letter there still helping Jordan.

All three kids are grown now, but they still treasure the letter from their dad, with its special message of love for each of them. For me, I still slip my hand under my pillow at night sometimes and remember the sweet memories of finding my own special messages of love under my pillow handwritten from Ben.

~Patricia Gallegos

To Read
When You're Alone

The heart of a mother is a deep abyss at the bottom of which
you will always find forgiveness.
~Honoré de Balzac

was thirteen years old. My family had moved to Southern California from North Florida a year before. I hit adolescence with a vengeance. I was angry and rebellious, with little regard for anything my parents had to say, particularly if it had to do with me. Like so many teenagers, I struggled to escape from anything that didn't agree with my picture of the world. A "brilliant without need of guidance" kid, I rejected any overt offering of love. In fact, I got angry at the mention of the word love.

One night, after a particularly difficult day, I stormed into my room, shut the door and got into bed. As I lay down in the privacy of my bed, my hands slipped under my pillow. There was an envelope. I pulled it out and on the envelope it said, "To read when you're alone."

Since I was alone, no one would know whether I read it or not, so I opened it. It said "Mike, I know life is hard right now, I know you are frustrated and I know we don't do everything right. I also know that I love you completely and nothing you do or say will ever change that. I am here for you if you ever need to talk, and if you don't, that's okay. Just know that no matter where you go or what you do in your life, I will always love you and be proud that you are my son. I'm here for you and I love you — that will never change. Love, Mom."

That was the first of several "To read when you're alone" letters. They were never mentioned until I was an adult.

Today I travel the world helping people. I was in Sarasota, Florida, teaching a seminar when, at the end of the day, a lady came up to me and shared the difficulty she was having with her son. We walked out to the beach, and I told her of my mom's undying love and about the "To read when you're alone" letters. Several weeks later, I got a card that said she had written her first letter and left it for her son.

That night, as I went to bed, I put my hands under my pillow and remembered the relief I felt every time I got a letter. In the midst of my turbulent teen years, the letters were the calm assurance that I could be loved in spite of me, not because of me. Just before I fell asleep I thanked God that my mom knew what I, an angry teenager, needed. Today when the seas of life get stormy, I know that just under my pillow there is that calm assurance that love — consistent, abiding, unconditional love — changes lives.

~Mike Staver

Chicken Soup
to the Rescue

Wherever you go, no matter what the weather,
always bring your own sunshine.
~Anthony J. D'Angelo

Plans had been made weeks in advance for the upcoming Valentine's high school dance. I had two teenagers and one younger child in elementary school. Both of the older ones had dates for this very special occasion. Suits and dresses were chosen with all the accessories needed to complete everyone's wardrobe. It was a draining experience for my energy and my budget. Flowers were ordered; it looked like it would be a wonderful evening for both of them. Our youngest was happily anticipating the class party that would be held on that day at his grammar school. Our house was full of emotion, excitement, and a bit of nerves.

Things began to change on February 11th as I was watching the nightly weather report. A crippling ice storm was headed our way and due to arrive the night of the 13th. We live just outside Dallas, Texas and when an ice storm hits here, the entire city shuts down. There is just not enough equipment or manpower to make the roads quite as safe as they do up north. I decided not to say anything to the three kids about what I had seen on TV, but I kept a close watch on the weather over the next few days.

The weathermen were certain it was coming and it was going to be a bad one. A thick coat of ice would blanket the city and six inches of snow would follow. I decided to prepare for the worst. I knew I needed to pull a rabbit out of my hat to make this Valentine's a special one for my three children, who were in for a major disappointment.

Just a few weeks earlier I had read a story by Kathleene Baker in *Chicken Soup for the Soul: Thanks Dad*. It was called "Valentine's Day Ambush." It gave me some great ideas for how I might be able to pull off a great and memorable Valentine's Day for my family. The more I thought, the more enthusiastic I became. I made a list of everything I needed to prepare.

I began shopping. I bought gifts for everyone, including two bouquets of beautiful fresh pink and red roses. I even bought several heart shaped pans and had all the groceries on hand for a wonderful feast, just in case there was no dance and no party. I made sure that the menu would include a favorite dish for each member of the family.

February 13th arrived. With my cup of coffee I sat down to listen to what the weather station had to say yet again. Every channel agreed the storm was coming. "Batten down the hatches; get ready, it's on the way." I was prepared for everything except the tears and sad faces I would encounter once my three excited kids heard the news. I kept busy that day baking and cooking everything that I could do in advance. As I was pulling a lovely heart-shaped cake from the oven, I heard something strange. I put the cake on the counter to cool and walked toward the noise, peeking out the window I observed ice slivers falling from the sky. The older kids arrived home shortly after that and came bursting into the house in an all-out teenage panic. "Mom," they shouted in unison. "They may have to cancel the dance; we're going to have an ice storm!" I assured them that it would be okay. "I am positive the school will reschedule the dance once the weather clears." I tried to reassure them. That statement seemed to be of no comfort, especially to my daughter as I watched her eyes fill with tears. The youngest had been playing with his toy cars and overheard the conversation; he began to wail as if his heart would break.

The next day when I awoke, I glanced outside and the streets looked like an ice skating rink. Trees and bushes drooped, glistening with a heavy layer of ice. Schools and most businesses were closed. The newscasters were telling everyone to stay home. Most people heeded their advice, including us.

I allowed the kids to sleep late as I began to prepare the wonderful feast in celebration of Valentine's Day. I kept thinking that if Kathleene's dad could pull it off, I could too. He was my inspiration.

That evening the table looked beautiful, with red dishes and fresh flowers. Festive gifts were placed on each plate. Food filled every inch of space on the table and many things were heart-shaped. I told everyone to put on their best outfits and come into the dining room. I wore a gold and beige evening gown that had been hidden away in the back of my closet. My husband donned his blue suit and the two teens wore the new outfits they had chosen for the dance. Our youngest dressed himself; he looked so cute, with his church pants and a sweater three sizes too big.

Soon smiles and laughter filled the room; we enjoyed a Valentine dinner fit for the royal family, with seconds on dessert! Neither the dance nor the school party was mentioned the entire evening; everyone was wrapped up in all of the festivities. Before everyone went to bed that evening I received praises and hugs from them all.

We were stuck indoors several days before the roads were safe to travel again. Just as I had predicted, the dance was rescheduled for the next weekend and the elementary school party would be held the following day.

Had it not been for that inspirational story in *Chicken Soup for the Soul: Thanks Dad*, I doubt I'd have thought to conjure up something to salvage the day for three disappointed children. "Chicken Soup" came to my rescue, but this time it was not for a cold.

~Carol Commons-Brosowske

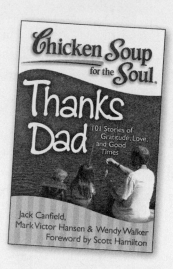

Valentine's Day Ambush

The beauty of fragrance is that it speaks to your heart...
and hopefully someone else's.
~Elizabeth Taylor

Valentine dinners with my parents became a thing of the past once I was old enough to date. Still, before heading out for the evening, I always received a sweet card and possibly a small gift. Upon returning home later, I indulged in my fair share of whatever homemade, mouth-watering dessert Mom had prepared for the occasion. Typically, it was a layered cake baked in heart-shaped pans, a scrumptious treat she served each year.

During my senior year of high school, Kansas was under siege on Valentine's Day, with a winter storm blasting its way across the plains. School was dismissed early and "puppy love" dates were cancelled. For the first time in a few years, I'd be celebrating with my parents. Amazingly, it made a real impression on me.

Mother had prepared Dad's favorite meal for dinner, but as the storm intensified she began to watch the clock and pace the floor.

"I'm really getting worried. With this weather I knew your dad would be a little late getting home, but not this late!" She busied herself keeping dinner warm, determined not to burn anything, but continued her march to and fro, glancing out the windows for headlights.

As a self-absorbed teenager, I continued with my phone conversation until I heard the door open and Mother wailing, "Oh, where have you been? I've just been worried sick!"

I rounded the corner to see Dad with his arms full of flowers and a box of chocolates. He smiled, "Happy Valentine's Day, honey!" Mom threw her arms around him causing him to juggled gifts while trying graciously to accept Mom's embrace.

The bouquet of flowers took center stage on the table as we seated ourselves for dinner.

I reached for my napkin and spied a small package by my plate that had seemingly appeared out of nowhere. "What's this?" I asked, filled with excitement and surprise.

"Just open it!" Dad's brilliant blue eyes sparkled with mischief.

I ripped the package open and could barely speak; it was a new bottle of Ambush cologne, quite a popular and affordable scent for teenagers at that time.

"Dad! Did you buy this all by yourself?" I squealed.

"Well, just kind of. It took some help from the clerk—actually it took a lot of help!"

I was stunned beyond belief. A Valentine gift purchased by Dad. I gave him a bear hug and a big kiss!

"You know I've seen that perfume around here forever and figured I could remember the name if I thought about Western movies. You know how they're always ambushing one another. Well, everything was fine until the clerk asked me what brand... I told her Apache."

"Apache!" I giggled until I had tears rolling down my cheeks.

Dad informed me it really wasn't that funny at all. The clerk insisted there was no such cologne, while he swore there was. They went back and forth until he decided maybe he had forgotten the name—but made it clear he would recognize the smell his daughter obviously bathed in. That's when the "misting marathon" began.

"It wasn't long until I started to sneeze non-stop. My nose began to run, and I almost got sick from so many smells. Just when I thought I'd have to take a break outside in the fresh air before continuing, the clerk suddenly hit on it!"

Dad said he smiled at the clerk through the sneezing. "That's it, that's it! Thank you for your time ma'am." Then he charged out the door toward his car through an all-out blizzard.

Never once have I asked Dad what possessed him to buy me a gift that year. I suspect it had something to do with the realization that my days under his roof were quickly coming to an end.

Roses, teddy bears, and cupids abound each February, creating fond memories. As for me, I have comical but precious memories of my Valentine's Day Ambush! They reside in a special niche in my heart.

~Kathleene S. Baker

Losing Boomer

Dogs' lives are too short. Their only fault, really.
~Agnes Sligh Turnbull

We recently had our fifteen-year-old Chihuahua put to sleep. Boomer was not my dog. He belonged to my late wife, Linda. Still, I found myself pretty choked-up the day my daughter, Emily, and I took him to the vet.

At times, Boomer was not an easy animal to live with. He barked at strangers, turned up his nose at dry dog food, and relieved himself on the floor instead of going outside. A difficult dog, yes, but since his death it's become even more difficult to live without him.

Boomer wasn't my dog, but he was an excellent running partner. When I was training for marathons seven days a week, Boomer accompanied me as I ran in the mountains behind our home. I'm not talking a short jog in the forest, here. It was ten, sometimes twenty miles. How could a small dog run that far? I'm not sure. He must have had a special running gene other Chihuahuas didn't have. Together we slogged through mud, wind, heat, and hailstorm. We scampered up mountains so steep they would make a Kenyan distance runner cry uncle. The little guy didn't have an ounce of quit in him.

Boomer was treated like a king around our house. Lots of food, a warm bed, and oodles of affection. Linda and I pampered him more than a four-star hotel concierge. When he wasn't sneaking scraps from the table or snatching a cookie from the hand of an unsuspecting child, he was eating steak, ham, and turkey dinners. Begging for tasty tidbits was Boomer's favorite pastime.

When Linda died of cancer, it was a very difficult time for our family. Boomer mourned right along with us. He lay in his bed and (shockingly) refused to eat, no matter what kind of yummy morsel I placed in front of him.

Emily headed off to college a few years later, and the relationship between man and Chihuahua continued to grow (although I still refused to call him "my" dog). Boomer was always there for me, through good times and bad. I took him for walks, gave him treats, talked to him and caressed him. In return, his love was unconditional.

But then he had a stroke and his health quickly began to fade. Walking became a problem, and his appetite began to diminish. Before long he completely stopped eating. Emily and I decided it was time to put him down. It was a tough thing to do. Boomer had been with us for a long time. He was also our last living memory of Linda.

It was going to be another heartbreaking hurdle for our family to overcome.

I had read a story by Bobbie Jensen Lippman titled "When It's Time to Say Goodbye" in *Chicken Soup for the Soul: What I Learned from the Dog*. The story had a big impact on me, and I drew some strength from it. Bobbie had let her beloved dog go when the time came and I felt like she was talking me through the process now.

A storm blew in the morning we took Boomer to the vet's office. Rain was coming down in buckets. I was grumpy and out of sorts that day, and I foolishly snapped at the poor receptionist who asked me to fill out a few forms.

"Dad, you sound like a cranky old man," Emily whispered. I apologized and confessed that the thought of watching Boomer die was just too agonizing. I'd been through the death of a loved one before. I wasn't sure I could handle the grief again, that period leading up to the last exhale that is so excruciating, so unbearable. Grief. One small word. One short syllable. But there is nothing small or short about it. Emily understood.

The vet came in to administer the anesthetic. I massaged Boomer's head one last time and stepped out of the room, leaving my daughter to shoulder the burden. I was glad she had the strength to be there with Boomer in those final moments, to ease his passage. I was proud of her.

On the ride home I thought about how much happiness Boomer had brought to our family. I also thought about what Bobbie Lippman said about losing her dog, Czar, in the final paragraphs of her story. The line I remembered was "…unless we expose ourselves to the painful lows in life, how can we ever experience the happy highs?"

The tears came when I reflected on what a gift Boomer had been to us. I finally understood that Boomer had been my dog all along. I'd just failed to realize it.

~Timothy Martin

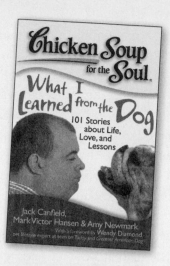

When It's Time to Say Goodbye

There are things that we don't want to happen but have to accept,
things we don't want to know but have to learn, and those we can't live
without but have to let go.
~Author Unknown

People with old or ailing animals often ask, "How do you know when it's time to let them go?" I once heard a veterinarian answer, "You just know."

The other morning our dog, Czar, let me know it was time. There was no mistaking the look in those big, brown eyes. Eyes that said, "I'm old and there is no longer any quality or dignity to my life. It's time."

After a long walk on the beach, trying to prolong the decision, I came home knowing there was no choice.

To make it easier for Czar, our veterinarian agreed to come on his lunch hour. I spent the morning sitting next to the old dog as he lay on his blanket, his head in my lap.

My thoughts drifted back to the day Czar came into my life. He was owned by people who perhaps shouldn't have had a dog as big as a Russian Wolfhound—or Borzoi—which is the official name of this breed.

Czar was never allowed in the house and I was told he spent much of the time standing outside, looking mournfully at the humans through the window. One day, the family maid said, "I'm sick and tired of washing nose prints off the glass. Either that dog goes or I do." Apparently good maids are harder to find than a good dog, and Czar was soon on his way to the animal shelter.

It was love at first sight when this tall hound and I discovered each other. He stood up on his hind legs, planted his front paws on my shoulders and greeted me with a big kiss.

When I was a little girl, we always had dogs, but usually of the small mixed-breed sort. I distinctly remember a series of vodka advertisements showing a pair of tall, elegant, snow-white Russian Wolfhounds. I dreamed of someday owning one, but honestly believed only the wealthy could afford such a beautiful animal. Finding a dog like Czar at the shelter was indeed a dream come true for me.

After several months of adjusting to each other, I put Czar through a ten-week dog obedience course. When you spend a great deal of time training an animal, you seem to bond with him ever more closely. On "Commencement Night" several friends came to watch, bringing "doggy" gifts for the new graduate. Czar gave the exercises his enthusiastic all and received the first place trophy.

Not long after that, my brother, Daniel, came for a visit, and after unpacking sat down in the living room. Five minutes later Czar carefully carried in a sweater from the guest room, depositing it in my brother's lap. Daniel is still wondering if perhaps Czar was trying to say, "You look cold, here's your sweater," or maybe, "I think you've stayed long enough. You can go home now."

I took Czar everywhere with me. One day while sitting on a grassy bank watching a tennis tournament, a small boy circled, and then finally approached. He stared at Czar for quite some time, then finally asked, "What do you s'pose a dog like that costs anyhow?"

"Oh," I answered absently, "probably about $500."

"Well," said the boy, "you certainly got your money's worth!"

While spending the final hours with Czar, I thought of this thing called grief and remembered the time when I stopped by the vet's office to pick up some medicine for a sick cat. The only others in the waiting room were an elderly man and woman, who were standing by some plastic plants in the corner, their backs to me. I sat there, watching, with curiosity. Just then the vet came out and said to them, "I'm very sorry. I was hoping surgery would help, but your Laddie was just too old. He didn't make it."

I will never forget the sight of that elderly couple, walking slowly toward their car, shoulders bent in grief.

In the old man's hand was a frayed, red dog collar.

When I started thinking about all my long walks on the beach with Czar—and how there would be no more—my tears fell down onto his muzzle, his tail wagged feebly, and he looked up at me as if to say, "Please don't cry. Just remember all the good years we've had together."

I sat with Czar, thinking about what animals bring to us. Some are trouble, especially in the early days of training them to fit into our lifestyles. But eventually they almost always give back total loyalty and love.

The last hours with this grand old dog went by too fast. Soon Dr. Brown arrived and moments later it was done… with the exception of tears and a deep gratitude for the quiet dignity of euthanasia.

There are people who avoid having pets because it hurts too much to lose them. But unless we expose ourselves to the painful lows in life, how can we ever experience the happy highs?

Before the day was over, friends dropped by. Some came just to hug. Some brought bunches of flowers. And today another note arrived from the local animal shelter saying a donation had been made in Czar's name so that other animals might live. (If you care about someone who has lost a pet, this is a wonderful idea.)

Czar had a long, good life and gave so much. The least I could give to him was a kind and gentle death.

~Bobbie Jensen Lippman

It Wasn't My Fault

The worth of a book is to be measured by what you can carry away from it.
~James Bryce

I can clearly remember those last few days of middle school when I was absolutely miserable. Recalling what happened that day at school still sends shivers through my body.

At the age of thirteen, I met a guy named Brandon. He was actually friends with my best friend Jonalynn, which is probably the reason why we saw each other every day. Overall he was quite charming. I had a huge crush on him.

One day I was sitting at an empty lunch table waiting to meet a teacher. I had my headphones on and I was listening to a track by Taylor Swift. I felt someone grab my waist and then touch a part of my body that should not be felt without permission. That's when I heard a very familiar voice... Brandon.

I knew that I should go tell an adult about this. But for some reason, I couldn't find the strength. I was scared.

For the next couple of days, I constantly blamed myself for what happened. After all, it was me who had a huge crush on him. I was the girl who constantly walked by his locker. I felt suffocated because I decided that I couldn't tell this to my strict parents. I had no friends to confide in.

At school, whenever I saw him, I felt alarmed. I wouldn't dare make eye contact with him. In order to go to classes I would take longer routes so I wouldn't pass him. Basically, I was isolating myself from everyone.

One day when I was walking by the lunchroom, I was surprised to see him sitting at my normal lunch table. As I passed by him, he called my name and said, "Yo Maisha, come here so I can feel you." Instead of standing up for myself, I panicked and walked away. There was only a month of school left but I couldn't find the courage to talk to anyone. And I started wondering if I had given him the wrong idea all those times I talked to him.

A couple of days later, I was cleaning my bookshelf when I came across *Chicken Soup for the Girl's Soul*. My sixteen-year-old cousin had given it to me and told me to treat it like the Bible. As I skimmed through the book, I came across a story by Hattie Frost called "It's Never Your Fault." I read the story over and over again; I analyzed every single word and was surprised to see how many similarities there were between the storyteller and me.

Hattie had written "it's never the victim's fault" and that rang in my ears. I decided that I had to talk to someone and I decided to call the cousin who gave me the book. She told me that she was proud of me for telling someone what happened. She said she gave me the book so I would be prepared for something like this. I have kept this book ever since.

~Maisha C., age 15

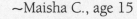

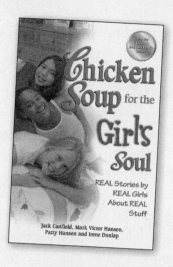

REAL Stories by
REAL Girls
About REAL
Stuff

Jack Canfield, Mark Victor Hansen,
Patty Hansen and Irene Dunlap

It's Never Your Fault

Yesterday I dared to struggle, today I dare to win.
~Bernadette Devlin

I sat there with my body trembling from head to toe, wondering what was happening to me and what would happen next. I knew that what was occurring was not right, but I didn't know how to stop it. I wanted with all my might to push his dark soul away from me, but being about three feet tall and only weighing around forty-five pounds, I didn't have the physical capability.

I was four, and my parents were busy with work and social lives, so they began looking for babysitters near our house who could watch my sister and me at night. They found two guys who lived down the street who were more than willing to be our babysitters. Although they looked a little scary when I first saw them, my parents assured me that everything would be okay and that I should be on my best behavior. I still had a feeling of insecurity running through my veins. I didn't know why, but I thought the men weren't good people.

After they were there for a couple of hours, I needed to go to the bathroom, so I went upstairs and shut the door. Shortly after, the door opened and in came the older of the two. I thought at first that maybe he just thought I needed some help since I was so young, but then he just stayed there and watched me. As I was getting up to leave, he started feeling me in places that aren't meant to be seen by other people. I didn't do anything to stop it. I was so small, and he was so big. Eventually he stopped, probably so my sister wouldn't become suspicious. He told me not to tell anyone what had happened and that it was to be kept a secret.

Having an older sister, I knew what secrets were and I knew that they were meant to be kept, so I never said a word to anyone. Each time he came over to babysit, the same pattern would occur, and I began to feel really uncomfortable and violated; but he was starting to get more threatening and I was beginning to fear losing my life if I told, so I remained quiet.

In elementary school, visitors from child abuse organizations would come and talk to us. That's when I learned that what was happening to me was called sexual molestation and that it's never the victim's fault. Up to that point, I had been blaming it on myself. They also said that it is very important to tell someone as soon as it happens to you and that telling is the most important thing to do. I really wanted to say something after hearing this, but I still didn't have the courage. I feared that he might come after me if the cops came after him.

The summer before sixth grade, I was walking back to my house after swim team practice. Normally, I walked back with my best friend, but she was staying at the pool all day, so I walked back on my own. As I headed up the long hill, a car started passing by very slowly, and the guys in the car were watching me. I could only make out one person—my former babysitter—and I started to run. I ran in between houses and went through back yards. I did everything possible to avoid getting into that car. After a half hour of that car chasing me, I made it into my house. I told my sister what had happened, and she called my mom at work, but she said that we should just lock the doors and watch for the car. I never saw that car again.

My junior year, I was on my high school's dance team. We had just finished performing our half-time routine and were in the process of heading back to the bleachers, where we had our bags, when someone who looked kind of familiar spit at me from over the fence and cursed at me. I wasn't sure at the time where I knew the face from, but I got extremely scared. A senior member on the team overheard what had happened and took me to the coaches. She explained to them what had happened, and my coach was about ready to jump over the fence and punch the guy's lights out, but I knew that wouldn't solve anything. That would only make me seem weak and would show that I let his hostility get to me. I wanted to be stronger than that and not give in, so I asked my coach if we could just forget about what happened and just enjoy the rest of the game.

Although I wanted to forget what had happened, I couldn't. I started having panic attacks and nightmares with flashbacks from that football game. I lost my appetite and became really depressed. After a couple of months of not being able to eat much at all, my family and friends became very worried and wanted to help in any way that they could. However, I wasn't ready to admit the fact that I had a problem.

One night, after a dance practice, I got these intense pains in my side, and my mom rushed me to the hospital. I was given many tests, but they couldn't figure out what was wrong with me. I wasn't too sure myself. Finally, they took me back for a question-and-answer session, and a psychologist started asking me a ton of questions and had me respond to them. He asked me if I had ever had sexual contact. I wasn't quite sure how to answer that because I never had any willingly, but it did happen, so I told him the whole story. He was shocked to hear me say it so quickly and was glad that I did—and so was I. He asked why it had taken me so many years to tell, and I answered that I had been worried that I would be hunted down if I ever told. He found that quite understandable and contacted some social workers and legal offices to see if anything could be done about the sexual molester. Since I had waited so long and didn't have a witness, there really wasn't anything that could be done except that I should start seeing a psychologist regularly and that would help all the physical pain my body had been enduring.

I'm telling this story not to get sympathy, but because it was an important lesson that I learned. If something happens to you that you suspect isn't right, tell someone right away. It will only help. Your life will become more tranquil. I used to have nightmares any time my eyes would shut, but after telling someone, I can now sleep peacefully. My only regret is not having told earlier.

~Hattie Frost, age 18

Chapter 4

READER'S CHOICE

Motivation

The important thing is to strive towards a goal which is not immediately visible. That goal is not the concern of the mind, but of the spirit.

~Antoine de Saint-Exupéry, Flight to Arras

Matters of the Mind and Heart

What the teacher is, is more important than what he teaches.
~Karl Menninger

looked out at a sea of anxious, expectant faces, thirty to be exact, and wondered if I was up to the test. It was my first day back teaching high school Biology in sixteen years. The classroom was large, filled with equipment: microscopes, test tubes, video projectors and computers. Lab tables served as desks. I had the curriculum, grade book, textbooks, lab supplies, sharpened pencils and plans. I had all the "things" I needed to teach but then there were the faces: thirty this hour, thirty the next hour, thirty the hour after that until 150 would pass through my door every day.

I knew I could teach them Biology. The question was: could I reach them? Could I find a way in a school of 2,000 teenagers to convince each of those faces they were unique, wonderful and worth the effort? I knew teenagers—you have to win their hearts before you can win their minds. I had to find a way to reach into the souls of the students behind those faces and make them believe they were capable. *Chicken Soup for the Soul* became my gateway.

On Friday of the first week of school I casually sat on the lab table in front of the room and chatted with the students. "Today we are going to take a few minutes to do something apart from Biology that I hope will give us a chance to know each other better," I began. "Because we spend so much time working hard, I think it's important that we also spend some time sharing with each other.

"So we are going to start writing what I call Mind Matters, because what you have on your mind matters to me. Every Friday at the beginning of class, I will read you a story from the *Chicken Soup for the Soul* series. Then you'll have five minutes to write a short note and tell me how you feel about the story or the topic it represents. You don't have to write about the story. You can tell me about anything else that is on your mind but the story will give you a good place to start."

The thirty faces watched me skeptically.

"If you write a Mind Matter, sign it, and turn it in, you'll get one extra credit point. I won't share what you write with anyone else unless you tell me you plan to harm yourself or that someone has harmed you. I will always read your Mind Matter. I will always write back and then return the Mind Matter to you alone."

Now the thirty faces looked intrigued.

The school I taught in was located about twenty-five miles outside Washington, D.C. It was a pressure cooker community of upwardly mobile parents and high expectations. At first the students were skeptical about writing Mind Matters. But the concept of taking ten minutes off task, and earning extra credit in addition, was very appealing. It didn't take them long to warm to the idea.

I always started the year with the story "Follow Your Dream" by Jack Canfield. This story consistently had a huge impact on the students. They were appalled by the idea a teacher would reject a student's dream outright. Some of them were astounded the student would take an "F" rather than rewrite his paper for the sake of his GPA, while others considered him a hero because he believed in himself and stood up to his teacher. Most were amazed by the twist at the end when the teacher visited the student on his dream ranch years later and apologized for not believing in him.

This story helped mold my relationship with my students in many ways. First it let them know I was interested in their dreams and goals whether or not they involved Biology. Some of my students had a real fear of science so it took the pressure off them thinking they had to love the subject to be successful in my class. Second, it let them know I am a person who thinks it's okay to challenge an idea if you don't agree with it. After all, questioning the "known" is the entire basis of scientific inquiry. The story also let them know I felt it was important for them to believe in themselves and for me to believe in them. This helped create a safe and supportive atmosphere in my classroom. Finally, the story let them know everyone makes mistakes, even teachers. Making a mistake isn't the end of something; it's the beginning of a deeper understanding.

After reading the story, I would tell the students their assignment was to tell me their dreams. And dream they did! It was as if a dam had burst. As promised, I read every single Mind Matter that was turned in. I wrote comments like "Wow, this is an awesome dream!" or "Can I have your autograph now before you become famous?" or "Will you bring some of your artwork by so I can see it?" Every time, the students were anxious to have their notes returned so they could read my comments. I was humbled by how much they longed for the positive feedback.

Allowing the students to share their dreams in a supportive atmosphere set the stage for the rest of the year. We built a bridge of trust and respect because the story allowed us to begin to know and accept each other as people, not just student and teacher. The story "Follow Your Dream" kept me mindful that words are potent stimuli in a person's image of themselves. It made me acutely aware of the chance I had to influence a child's life for the better. As a result I was more generous with my praise and judicious with my corrections. I came to school every day looking for ways to help. I visualized each student as a dream about to happen.

Every Friday a new story was read. Every time the bond and understanding we shared deepened. I read over 50,000 Mind Matters in ten years. The things students wrote about ranged from the mundane, like what they had for breakfast, to the crucial: some were being bullied at school, abused at home or feeling suicidal. Whether the information was humorous or heart-wrenching, it gave them a chance to reach out and me a chance to interact or intervene.

A teacher touches the dreams of thousands of students in the course of a career. What an incredible responsibility! What an awesome opportunity. Comments like the following kept my dream of making a difference alive:

"I really appreciated how hard you worked to make each student feel special and accepted." Gracy O.

"I thought my parents were giving up on me and I even began to give up on myself, but you wouldn't let go. I love you." A

"I'm sorry that this is my last Mind Matters. Your caring, understanding, attitude about the troubles in teenage life helped me immensely. Thank you!" Carrie J.

I trust they learned some Biology along the way as well.

~Liz Graf

Follow Your Dream

Put your future in good hands — your own.
~Author Unknown

I have a friend named Monty Roberts who owns a horse ranch in San Ysidro. He has let me use his house to put on fundraising events to raise money for youth at risk programs.

The last time I was there he introduced me by saying, "I want to tell you why I let Jack use my house. It all goes back to a story about a young man who was the son of an itinerant horse trainer who would go from stable to stable, race track to race track, farm to farm and ranch to ranch, training horses. As a result, the boy's high school career was continually interrupted. When he was a senior, he was asked to write a paper about what he wanted to be and do when he grew up.

"That night he wrote a seven-page paper describing his goal of someday owning a horse ranch. He wrote about his dream in great detail and he even drew a diagram of a 200-acre ranch, showing the location of all the buildings, the stables and the track. Then he drew a detailed floor plan for a 4,000-square-foot house that would sit on the 200-acre dream ranch.

"He put a great deal of his heart into the project and the next day he handed it in to his teacher. Two days later he received his paper back. On the front page was a large red F with a note that read, 'See me after class.'

"The boy with the dream went to see the teacher after class and asked, 'Why did I receive an F?'

"The teacher said, 'This is an unrealistic dream for a young boy like you. You have no money. You come from an itinerant family. You have no resources. Owning a horse ranch requires a lot of money. You have to buy the land. You have to pay for the original breeding stock and later you'll have to pay large stud fees. There's no way you could ever do it.' Then the teacher added, 'If you will rewrite this paper with a more realistic goal, I will reconsider your grade.'

"The boy went home and thought about it long and hard. He asked his father what he should do. His father said, 'Look, son, you have to make up your own mind on this. However, I think it is a very important decision for you.'

"Finally, after sitting with it for a week, the boy turned in the same paper, making no changes at all. He stated, 'You can keep the F and I'll keep my dream.'"

Monty then turned to the assembled group and said, "I tell you this story because you are sitting in my 4,000-square-foot house in the middle of my 200-acre horse ranch. I still have that school paper framed over the fireplace." He added, "The best part of the story is that two summers ago that same schoolteacher brought thirty kids to camp out on my ranch for a week. When the teacher was leaving, he said, 'Look, Monty, I can tell you this now. When I was your teacher, I was something of a dream stealer. During those years I stole a lot of kids' dreams. Fortunately you had enough gumption not to give up on yours.'"

Don't let anyone steal your dreams. Follow your heart, no matter what.

~Jack Canfield

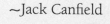

My Own Goal Board

Only those who will risk going too far can possibly find out
how far one can go.
~T.S. Eliot

I n 1988, I was the editor-in-chief of my high school newspaper, *Skyline*. I had big dreams of becoming a globetrotting, investigative journalist, but I also had big dreams for *Skyline*. I had three main goals: have *Skyline* join three new scholastic journalism organizations, have *Skyline* win the prestigious All-KEMPA newspaper award, and take my hardworking staff to New York City for the Columbia University high school journalism conference.

I had no idea how I was going to achieve these goals, but I believed they were possible. In fact, after reading my mom's copy of *Chicken Soup for the Soul*, I figured out how I was going to do it. The story, "Glenna's Goal Book" gave me the blueprint. Her principle: I x V = R, which is short for Imagination mixed with Vividness becomes Reality, spoke to me.

I, like Glenna, believed that God gives us "the desires of our heart," and my *Skyline* goals were written on my personal prayer list. But what I didn't have were pictures of my goals to help me actualize them. So, I started cutting photos out of magazines and newsletters. For the first goal, I cut out the names of the journalism associations I wanted *Skyline* to join. For the second, I cut out a picture of the All-KEMPA award, and above it, I printed out the words, in big capital letters. For the third, I cut out photos of New York's gorgeous skyline and a photo of a previous conference.

Since these goals weren't just for me—they were for my entire newsroom—I didn't put them in a photo album. Instead, I tacked them all up on the bulletin board in our office. There, every day, when we made phone calls, wrote stories or worked on layout, we'd see the pictures of our goals, and it wouldn't be just me seeing them.

The first goal was the easiest to achieve. I simply talked to our newspaper advisor, Miss Miller, and she approved a budget item that would allow us to join three scholastic journalism organizations. I was pretty impressed with how well the IVR principle was working, but most of my fellow editors and reporters were not as wowed.

However, not a month after pushing all the tacks into the corkboard, our second big goal was realized. Our entire staff took an all-day field trip to the All-KEMPA journalism conference. Everyone gasped when Willowbrook High School's *Skyline* was named the All-KEMPA newspaper of the year. It was surprising, but we had worked really hard for the last two years so some of my co-editors were not willing to ascribe the win to my goal board.

The last goal—getting our staff to New York City—seemed completely impossible. But I refused to give up. I knew we could get there. I researched how other newspapers funded conferences, approached local businesses for sponsorships, tried to drum up extra revenue for the paper, and even wrote a grant proposal that I sent to the school district office.

It was to no avail. No grants. No sponsorships. Not even our advertising budget would budge. Still, I maintained to myself, and I proclaimed to my staff, that we would be going to New York. Not going was not an option. Finally, the week before I was scheduled to fly out to Washington, D.C. to participate in Presidential Classroom (one of my own personal dreams that I had achieved), I sat down with my staff of eleven, and I asked them, "Who stands with me to go to New York City?" My best friend Venetia immediately said yes, but only three other members of our staff—Tom, Glenn and Ali—agreed. The rest, including my assistant editor, had excuses.

"Jeanette, don't get your hopes up," or "Jeanette, this just isn't a realistic idea," or, my favorite, "I just don't think I want to go."

So I wrote a revised proposal changing the budget from eleven students to five, and I sent the proposal back to the district office. While I was in D.C., Venetia called me. "You'll never believe it — but someone in the district office likes us. They were impressed with all the awards our paper has won so they're completely funding our trip!"

And what a trip it was. We got limo rides to and from the airport because Miss Miller and the five of us couldn't fit into a single cab. We stayed in a plush Manhattan hotel. We saw *Les Miserables* — from front-row seats! We looked out from the top of the Empire State Building, dined in Chinatown and Little Italy, and learned so much about journalism and writing. For the six of us, including Miss Miller, it was the trip of a lifetime!

I've since made dozens of other goal boards, with goals as whimsical as swimming with dolphins and as serious as finding my soul mate. I did become an investigative newspaper reporter, and I've traversed the globe, including a visit with dolphins. I'm now an award-winning food and travel author, I'm married to an amazing man, and we have a wonderful son. I've even started doing corkboards for him, and he's just three years old.

The most curious thing about my very first goal board is what happened after the school district decided to fund my dream. As soon as we got the go-ahead, the six naysayers on staff decided they, too, wanted to go to New York. It was too late, however; my revised — and accepted — proposal only budgeted for five believers.

So, you see, it's not just picking out images that speak to your dreams and aspirations, It's really believing in your goals, really convincing yourself that they are attainable, and really knowing that you deserve to have them come true. There's no such thing as an impossible dream, but there are people who are afraid to dream. Dare to dream big. And get some tacks for your corkboard.

~Jeanette Hurt

Glenna's Goal Book

Success isn't a result of spontaneous combustion.
You must set yourself on fire.
~Arnold H. Glasow

I n 1977 I was a single mother with three young daughters, a house payment, a car payment and a need to rekindle some dreams.

One evening I attended a seminar and heard a man speak about the I x V = R Principle. (Imagination mixed with Vividness becomes Reality.) The speaker pointed out that the mind thinks in pictures, not in words. And as we vividly picture in our mind what we desire, it will become a reality.

This concept struck a chord in my heart. I knew the Biblical truth that the Lord gives us "the desires of our heart" (Psalms 37:4) and that "as a man thinketh in his heart, so is he" (Proverbs 23:7). I was determined to take my written prayer list and turn it into pictures. I began cutting up old magazines and gathering pictures that depicted the "desires of my heart." I arranged them in a photo album and waited expectantly.

I was very specific with my pictures. They included:

1. A good-looking man
2. A woman in a wedding gown and a man in a tuxedo
3. Bouquets of flowers (I'm a romantic)
4. Beautiful diamond jewelry (I rationalized that God loved David and Solomon and they were two of the richest men who ever lived)
5. An island in the sparkling blue Caribbean
6. A lovely home
7. New furniture
8. A woman who had recently become vice president of a large corporation. (I was working for a company that had no female officers. I wanted to be the first woman vice president in that company.)

About eight weeks later, I was driving down a California freeway, minding my own business at 10:30 in the morning. Suddenly a gorgeous red-and-white Cadillac passed me. I looked at the car because it was beautiful. The driver looked at me and smiled, and I smiled back because I always smile. Now I was in deep trouble. Have you ever done that? I tried to pretend that I hadn't looked. "Who me? I didn't look at you!" He followed me for the next fifteen miles. Scared me to death! I drove a few miles, he drove a few miles. I parked, he parked.... And eventually I married him!

On the first day after our first date, Jim sent me a dozen roses. Then I found out that he had a hobby. His hobby was collecting diamonds. Big ones! And he was looking for somebody to decorate. I volunteered! We dated for about two years and every Monday morning I received a long-stemmed red rose and a love note from him.

About three months before we were getting married, Jim said to me, "I have found the perfect place to go on our honeymoon. We will go to St. John's down in the Caribbean." I laughingly said, "I never would have thought of that!"

I did not confess the truth about my picture book until Jim and I had been married for almost a year. It was then that we were moving into our gorgeous new home and furnishing it with the elegant furniture that I had pictured. (Jim turned out to be the West Coast wholesale distributor for one of the finest East Coast furniture manufacturers.)

By the way, the wedding was in Laguna Beach, California, and included the gown and tuxedo as realities. Eight months after I created my dream book, I became the vice president of human resources in the company where I worked.

In some sense this sounds like a fairy tale, but it is absolutely true. Jim and I have made many "picture books" since we have been married. God has filled our lives with the demonstration of these powerful principles of faith at work.

Decide what it is that you want in every area of your life. Imagine it vividly. Then act on your desires by actually constructing your personal goal book. Convert your ideas into concrete realities through this simple exercise. There are no impossible dreams.

~Glenna Salsbury

Treasured Time

Waking up this morning, I smile. Twenty-four brand new hours are before me. I vow to live fully in each moment.
~Thich Nhất Hạnh

"Just think! We won't ever have to set our alarm clock again now that you are retired, too," my husband said as I watched the hand on the clock move to the exact time my retirement would begin. Now I hoped to keep "normal hours." For me, this meant going to bed and getting up when I felt like it. I looked forward to spending quality time together doing all the things we had been unable to do when we were young and we were busy raising a family and holding down full-time jobs. On the other hand, it was scary.

Doing research about retired people, I learned that divorce rates for couples in retirement were skyrocketing. Though many causes have been given, some of the reasons point to the difficulties couples have adjusting to being together too much. In time, they can become bored with each other. I wondered if this would happen to my husband and me.

At first, my fear was unfounded. We traveled to Ireland, took a barging trip around Texas, and attended our favorite concerts. For a while, I felt we were honeymooners. But just as the honeymoon wears off, so did our retirement bliss. I found I needed some space to be by myself. And even though my husband and I were communicating more with each other, I felt depressed at the end of the day because I had accomplished nothing.

I remembered my career days when my days were fulfilling and filled full. At my job as a high school teacher, I felt I had accomplished something every day as I helped my students to create a fresh piece of writing, add a new word to their vocabulary, or put geographic locations on a map. In turn, I learned something from my students, too.

My to-do list was finished on the weekend. The thoughts of doing something for me were out of the question. I always wanted to learn to play a musical instrument, listen to music, or become a published author.

But when I finally had the time as a retiree, I caved in to all the vices of late risers—sleeping late and staying in my nightgown as I glued my eyes to the television till noon over endless cups of coffee. I was getting further behind every day; many jobs had to be done in the evening or left undone. I began to feel useless. And frankly, I became bored with watching my husband sit around all day watching me.

About this time, I purchased a copy of the book *Chicken Soup for the Soul: My Resolution*. I read it from cover to cover, and all the stories touched my heart; but there was one story that stood out above all the others: "Confessions of a Morning Person" by Mimi Greenwood Knight.

That story began to change my life by altering my daily schedule at the most opportune time. Mimi Greenwood Knight relates how she kept early morning hours by getting up as much as four hours before dawn, as quiet as a cat burglar. And her secret—she enjoyed it. I thought, "If it worked for her, why I couldn't make it work for me?"

Instead of getting up at 7:00 with my husband, I started my day a few minutes earlier. Then I started getting up at 6:00, then 5:00 and finally 4:00. Our fourteen-year-old cat became my alarm clock as she grew accustomed to the earlier feedings. Her meow let me know if I were even a few minutes late.

I could hear the sounds of the house as I sat at the table in the kitchen sipping tea and writing for at least twenty minutes. I listened closely to the rhythm of the second hand on the clock and the gurgling sounds of the refrigerator.

I came to love these early morning hours. I found I was my best self in the morning. That special story changed my lifestyle permanently.

I signed up to take piano lessons. With the aid of my headphones plugged into the keyboard, I started practicing my music during these early morning hours without waking my husband. I found I was more alert then and could concentrate better. In the same manner, I listened to my favorite singers, playing a favorite song three times in a row with no one to get tired of hearing it. I exercised with a DVD, and it gave me energy to tackle my chores all day long. I attended writing seminars and took an online writing course, and recently I had the honor of publishing two stories in *Chicken Soup for the Soul* books.

As the morning wore on and the dawn came, I observed the birds at the feeder on the deck and learned to identify them by name. For the first time, I looked through my kitchen window to see a downy woodpecker with the rising sun as a backdrop. I wondered if heaven could be more beautiful. As Terri Guillemets says, "I used to love night best, but the older I get the more treasures and hopes and joys I find in mornings."

One morning my husband greeted me with "What are you doing up so early this morning?" as he poured his first cup of coffee. It was 7:30.

"I am well into my day," I answered as I rattled off a few of my activities. He didn't know I had tiptoed out of bed in order not to disturb him and started my day three hours earlier.

"When you finish your coffee, let's go out and smell the dawn," I told him.

His eyebrows furrowed as he said, "How can you be so cheerful at this hour?"

I forgot about our encounter until a few weeks later when my husband came to the kitchen smiling and said to me, "Do you still want to walk? I haven't smelled the dawn since I was a young boy."

I relaxed, as I had already done my routine chores for the day. We walked out into the early morning sunlight hand in hand. I knew I had no worries about boredom.

~Janet N. Miracle

101 Stories...
Great Ideas for
Your Mind,
Body, and
...Wallet

Jack Canfield,
Mark Victor Hansen,
D'ette Corona & Barbara LoMonaco

Confessions of a
Morning Person

I love the sweet smell of dawn—
our unique daily opportunity to smell time,
to smell opportunity—
each morning being, a new beginning.
~Emme Woodhull-Bäche

It happened again today. I found myself apologizing to someone for being too perky in the morning. It wasn't even that early. I called a client at 9:00 a.m.—after watching the clock until precisely 8:59 and 59 seconds, which I figured was late enough to make a business call. I jumped into the conversation with a bit too much enthusiasm, I suppose, because my client responded with, "Whoa, you are WAY too awake for this time of morning."

I didn't tell her I'd been up for five hours and had already run two miles, answered a bunch of e-mail, studied my Bible, got four kids up, fed, dressed and off to school, done a batch of wash and weeded my herb garden. I especially didn't tell her I got up that early because I wanted to.

That hasn't always been the case. Motherhood did this to me. When my husband and I were first married, he was much more coherent in the wee hours. I'd force myself out of bed after the fifth assault of the alarm clock and relocate to the cold, hard bathroom floor desperate for a few seconds more sleep but knowing I'd be miserable enough on the floor to relent and stagger toward the shower.

Then we brought home that first little squalling bundle and my sleep habits were rearranged. We'd wanted a baby for so long that each time I heard the glorious sound of Haley O'Hara crying for another feeding, I was determined to respond with an eager, happy face no matter how sleep deprived I was.

I never wanted her or the three babies who followed to feel that they were disturbing me or were a burden at whatever hour they decided was morning. I determined I'd be 100% Mom as soon as they called me into action.

But the real metamorphosis didn't occur until I stumbled upon a secret.

Because I was lucky enough to make raising my kids a full-time gig, our routine tended to be pretty loosey goosey. We got up when we felt like it (okay, when they felt like it) and went to bed when we were tired of being awake.

We woke up together. We went to bed together. We grocery-shopped, ran errands, ate, played and bathed together. We did everything together. Life was grand.

Then one day I realized that if I could only make myself get up an hour before my kids, I could have sixty minutes alone in my own home — something I hadn't experienced in years.

The first day was intoxicating. I could serve myself a cup of coffee and drink it while it was still hot. I could write a letter and keep my mind on what I wanted to say. Most of my letters at that time consisted of disconnected thoughts written with two or three different pens whenever I could grab a minute, usually perched on the edge of the sandbox or sitting on the floor beside the bathtub where the kids were temporarily distracted by bubbles.

But in my stolen hour, I could read a book, exercise, listen to grown-up music and eat a leisurely breakfast. I could coax one of the cats to snuggle in my lap rather than hunker by the food bowl with one eye on whichever preschooler might decide he'd enjoy some dress-up clothes.

Even if I used my time to do laundry or wash dishes, it felt indulgent to be doing it in complete solitude. I could begin a task and see it through to completion without stopping and starting it fifteen times. I could sneak in a bath all by myself without an audience or running commentary. I bought myself grown-up bath products and adult breakfast foods—aromatherapy and English muffins, hot oil treatments and lemon curd.

I had no idea how starved I'd become for my own company and quickly honed skills that will serve me well if I ever decide to become a cat burglar. I can do anything soundlessly if it means I get to do it alone. Of course, before long, an hour wasn't enough, so I got up two hours earlier, then three and sometimes four.

More than a decade has passed since that epiphany. The kids are teenagers now and having their own morning wrangle with the snooze alarm. But I've kept my early hours to myself. I've changed my title from stay-at-home mom to work-at-home mom (from SAHM to WAHM) but that first hour or two of the morning is still my favorite time. Most days I accomplish more between 4:00 a.m. and 6:00 a.m.—when the kids wake up to sing a few bars of Mom, I need... Mom, I want... and Mom, I gotta have...—than I do between 6:00 and bedtime.

Even though they're taller than I am, I still like the idea of my kids waking up to a pleasant mama. And after a brisk run with the dogs, some quality time with the cats, my daily Bible study, a little e-mail interaction and as much coffee as I care to drink, I'm far more chipper than my husband or kids—or my clients—would like me to be.

So that's it. That's my dirty little secret. I get up early and I like it. Besides if I ever consider a career change, I'd make one heck of a good cat burglar.

~Mimi Greenwood Knight

Redemption of a Hack

*Ideals are like stars: you will not succeed in touching them with your hands,
but like the seafaring man on the desert of waters, you choose them as your
guides, and following them you reach your destiny.*
~Carl Schurz

Somewhere during journalism school many years ago, it was drilled into my mind that journalists were the moral watchdogs of society. They wrote the truth, the whole truth and nothing but the truth, regardless of social or political pressure. The world had the right to know the truth and journalists were the only trustworthy professionals who would deliver it. With ideals such as these, we aspiring journalists yearned for those big headlines and bylines that would change the world.

I once dreamed of being a foreign correspondent. I would be multilingual, travel the world and write about gripping human stories that inspired global change. My work would appear in *Time* magazine and *National Geographic*. But that was many years ago, and sometime during my life, the line between journalistic integrity and commercialism blurred. It was probably during the same time that I got married and had children with chronic medical conditions. There was a fork in my road, and I chose my children—with no regrets.

The effect on my writing was clear. With less time or energy for research, reading and practice, my writing never improved and was marginal at best. Hard news stories were replaced by easy-to-spit-out features, essays, one-shots, fillers and whatever would sell to the local newspapers. Nothing newsworthy. Fluff, it was called in newspaper lingo, and I wrote it. I even wrote those dreaded advertorials which are advertising pieces masked as real news content. I had become the most disrespected type of writer: a hack. *Webster's Dictionary* defines a hack as "one who produces banal and mediocre work in the hope of gaining commercial success in the arts."

So there I was, feeling demoralized and ashamed of what I had become: a dishonorable, talentless writer with the irrepressible desire to keep writing. Maybe I should, as Stephen King wrote in his *On Writing* book, do us all a favor and pick up another hobby. But suppressing the urge to communicate is like trying to stop the flow of a mountain spring, or in my case, an old hose with an irreparable leak.

And then I read Ava Pennington's "Writing My Story" in *Chicken Soup for the Soul: Inspiration for the Young at Heart.* Her second life ambition to write made me realize that it wasn't too late for me to realize my own writing dreams. In her words, rejection felt "as if I had shown my baby to people who said, 'Boy, is she ugly!'" and that was exactly how I felt, too. I knew then that all writers are kindred souls, afraid to present their babies for society's approval. My pieces were my babies. I loved them regardless of how anyone might pass judgment. Like Ava, I had written short stories, a novel, and children's stories that were precious to me; but unlike Ava, I was a negligent mother who failed to nurture her work and let it go forth into the world.

Ava's efforts humbled me. For years, she braved those rejection letters while I, after getting one, would stuff my manuscript into a drawer and sulk. I was a whining writing wimp (with a deplorable penchant for alliteration, I might add). I felt ashamed again, not because I had "sold out" to commercialism, but because I missed the point of written expression entirely.

Yes, there is an art to expressing yourself on paper. It doesn't have to win a Pulitzer or Nobel Peace Prize to have merit. The joy and reward is in the writing, and if there is just one reader who might give his time to reading your work, count yourself worthy of writing. If you can help one reader learn something or better yet, feel something, you have done no small thing.

Ava's publishing success was the natural outcome of her unbridled persistence and passion. That is what I had left behind a long time ago. Persistence and passion. There were still truths to be revealed through my writing. Ava's piece reminded me that everyone is a story. There are lives and stories to be told, and I need not be a foreign correspondent to write a story that can change the world.

Ava's story changed mine. She gave me the courage to resurrect my babies, dust them off and send them out with pride and positive expectations. It might not be a story about war and famine that touches my readers, but the simple, everyday stories about my own life. That is all I have to offer, and people seem to like those best.

I credit Ava's story for returning me to the writing world a bit braver and nobler. For persistence and passion turned a hack into a writer once again.

~Lori Phillips

Writing My Story

And by the way, everything in life is writable about if you have the
outgoing guts to do it, and the imagination to improvise.
The worst enemy to creativity is self-doubt.
~Sylvia Plath

I opened the local newspaper, eagerly searching the pages. Did they publish my tribute to my mother? They did! The article was the first thing I had ever published. I wasn't paid for the work, since it was featured in a weekly human interest column. Still, it was encouraging to realize someone thought enough of my writing to publish it for public consumption.

Work, family, and a mortgage crowded out any further thoughts of writing. After completing an MBA degree, I enjoyed a twenty-year career as a Human Resources Director for multinational financial services firms. Although I worked on Wall Street in New York City, global responsibilities enabled me to travel across North and South America and even to Europe.

One of my coworkers had a dream of her own. She was in the middle of writing the "Great American Novel." As we worked together over a period of several years, she would write a chapter and I would provide feedback. Her book was good, and against all odds for an unknown author, it was represented by the first agent she contacted and published by a major New York publisher.

Holding her book in my hand was almost as encouraging for me as it was for her. It validated her effort to follow her dream, and it gave me hope for my dream, too. She honored me by including my name in the book's acknowledgments as one who encouraged her not to give up during the long, and frequently lonely, process of birthing her book.

It was about this time that my husband retired and I left the corporate world. We relocated to another state to begin the second half of our lives. It was finally time for me to start writing. But what to write?

I noticed a small newspaper article announcing that the famous *Chicken Soup for the Soul* series was inviting submissions for its upcoming book, *Chicken Soup for the Working Woman's Soul*. Perfect!

I put pen to paper, or more accurately, fingers to keyboard. I wrote about an experience that happened to me during a morning commute, and submitted "Not Just Another Rat." Of course, I thought they would immediately agree that it was an enthralling and wonderfully written story. I eagerly and naively awaited the letter notifying me of its acceptance for publication.

I waited and waited and waited… for more than a year! I later learned that more than 5,000 submissions were received from all over the world, but my story was chosen!

Wow, I thought, this writing stuff isn't so hard. My friend was published on her first try. My first newspaper article was published. My first anthology submission was published. Maybe all those horror stories about how difficult it is to get published were nothing more than just stories. After all, my experience proved otherwise. Surely an agent or editor would soon recognize the quality of my writing and offer me a book contract.

After I finished patting myself on the back and celebrating publication of my story, I continued to submit short stories to anthologies. No takers. I wrote an inspirational non-fiction book and submitted it to agents and publishers. No interest. I wrote a novel. No interest in that one, either.

In fact, no one was interested in my work for the next two years. The rejection letters kept on coming. It was a discouraging cycle: write, submit, rejection, write, submit, rejection. Or write, submit, then silence. I'm not sure what was worse: rejections or silence. At least with the rejections, I knew where I stood!

I had two choices. I could turn off my computer and quit, or I could grow a thick skin and keep trying despite the painful rejections. Each one felt as if I had shown my new baby to people who said, "Boy, is she ugly!"

One thing that kept me going was learning the history of Chicken Soup for the Soul. The first book in the series was published in 1993 after being rejected more than 100 times. That book went on to sell more than eight million copies and the series is one of the most successful in publishing history.

So I kept plugging away. I joined a writers' critique group and began attending writers' conferences. I had much to learn about writing and publishing. I began writing articles for magazines and continued to submit short stories to Chicken Soup for the Soul and other anthology publishers.

Then, in 2005, I submitted to *Chicken Soup for the Recovering Soul: Daily Inspirations*. I sent in six submissions and three were chosen for publication. A few weeks later I was notified that the *Chicken Soup for the Soul Healthy Living* series would include a piece I had written on diabetes. By the third *Chicken Soup for the Soul* book, I went from wishing *someone* would publish me to wishing someone *else* would publish me! My husband put it in perspective when he reminded me of the days when I would have been thrilled if anyone published me!

Since 2003, I have been published in twenty anthologies, including fourteen *Chicken Soup for the Soul* books. Additionally, I have published more than thirty magazine articles with more submissions in the pipeline.

Best of all, I published my first solo book in 2010 with a

traditional publisher, and I've co-authored two children's picture books published by another traditional publisher in 2011!

My corporate career was successful, but I'm having much more fun following my dream. My desire is to use my writing, both fiction and non-fiction, to encourage others. That's my passion. I refuse to be discouraged by obstacles, rejections, or the naysayers who told me I was too old to start a second career. The publication of my story in *Chicken Soup for the Working Woman's Soul* encouraged me to keep persevering, to continue networking with other writers, and to continue learning as much as I could about the publishing industry.

Overnight successes in publishing are rare. For me, the path to success consisted of a series of small steps: membership in writers' groups, attendance at writers' conferences, writing magazine articles and short stories, co-authoring a children's book, and finally, authoring my own book. In the process, I'm becoming a better writer as I find the lessons—and the humor—in daily life.

I don't know how many more of my books will be published. Whether it's one or ten, I'm enjoying the journey!

~Ava Pennington

What Saralee Said

No, really, just do it. You have some kind of weird reasons that are okay.
~Paul Thomas Anderson

There have been many Chicken Soup for the Soul stories through the years that have warmed my heart and renewed my spirit, but one story I think about nearly every day is Saralee Perel's "Just Show Up," featured in *Chicken Soup for the Soul: Think Positive.* Saralee's suggestion, to "just show up," instead of fretting over every little step that it might take to accomplish a certain task, has helped me change my tendency to become overwhelmed by my various responsibilities. With four children, a brand new grandson, chronic pain from a long-ago facial injury, and caring for my elderly mother, I'm often stretched pretty thin, but Saralee's story inspired me the moment I read it. That Saralee lives with paralysis, yet touches her readers with such positivity, humor, and grace, is a testament to her courage and strength of character.

"Just Show Up" is an account of how Saralee met a man named Morris while walking in the woods near her Cape Cod home and of the three magical words Morris taught her. "Here's how I understand it," she later told her husband, Bob, when he asked what Morris meant. "When the thought enters my brain, 'I should go exercise,' I instantly start thinking about every single step it takes to get around to doing it. First I have to shower. Then I have to find something to wear. Then I have to find everything I need for safety. Then I have to—blah, blah, blah. I think what Morris meant was to scrap all of those thoughts. In other words, I should replace talking-myself-out-of-it thinking with the words: 'Just show up.'"

Priceless, I decided. I could do that too.

In the beginning, it felt like a miracle cure. "Need to clean the house today?" I'd ask myself, and then, instead of talking my way out of the job by concentrating on all of those mind-boggling little steps (first I'd have to de-clutter, then I'd have to attack the dust-bunnies camped out on my kitchen floor, then I'd have to vacuum...), I'd think: "Remember what Saralee said: 'Just show up.'" "Need to take Mom out for errands, respond to e-mails dating back to prehistoric times? No more step-by-stepping, girl! 'Just show up!'" I applied the miracle cure to my writing too, particularly regarding first drafts, since staring at a blank screen can scare the creative flow right out of me. All those little craft details are what I freak over (narrative here, dialogue there, how to connect these two passages—yikes!), but by changing the way I viewed the process and "just showing up" at my computer, I could relax enough to write the draft on the first try.

My husband calls this "meets minimum" thinking, that for any given task, if you begin with the minimum amount of things you need to do to accomplish it, well, you're halfway home. But I like Saralee's motto better, because, to me, "meets minimum" implies that you're making very little effort, when sometimes "just showing up" requires the greatest effort of all.

I discovered the importance of that whole effort thing this past summer, when one of my twin daughters, Holly, got married. Implementing Saralee's approach was working well for me, but preparing for a wedding really put the theory to its test. There was so much to do that Holly and I scarcely knew where to start. We needed to figure out the dress, the venue, the centerpieces, the cake... and on and on. We found ourselves texting/calling/meeting multiple times a day.

"I had no idea there'd be so much," I told Holly one evening as we gulped down dinner, a casserole I'd made that was her favorite. Neither of us even tasted the meal, however, wedged as it was between corsage crafting and vow drafting. "I don't know how we'll ever get it done."

Holly looked as tired as I felt.

Where was Saralee's advice now? It appeared to have lost its verve. And just when it seemed that I couldn't possibly add one more thing to my already packed to-do list, another commitment arose.

It happened by way of a phone call, one from my older son, Dave. "Hey, Mom," he said when I answered. "Can you babysit Sawyer two days a week? My work schedule has changed."

"You mean just this week?" I asked.

"Um... no," he hedged. "All summer."

My brain went instantly into overdrive. I'd have to get up extra early. Then I'd have to check on Mom early too. Then I'd have the forty-minute drive in rush-hour traffic. What about my writing projects, not to mention the ongoing wedding plans? It wasn't that I didn't want to keep my precious little eight-month-old grandson, but how could I fit it all in?

Suddenly, amidst all this dithering, Saralee spoke right to me—and I bet you can guess what she said.

So I followed her advice yet again. I "just showed up." And somehow, it all got done. My writing got submitted. My beautiful daughter got married. My mom's chores got finished. My house got cleaned (more or less!). Not to say that it all went perfectly or easily. Of course, few things ever do.

But you know what? Those two days a week were what got me through last summer. I could relax on those days. I could breathe on those days. Sawyer was just learning to walk and would squeal with delight when we played "Where's Nana?" and chased each other around the living room. One morning a hummingbird came to call at the feeder outside our open window. Its wings made tiny buzzing noises, which I mimicked, and Sawyer laughed. His big blue eyes locked with mine as I fed him his bottle, and when he fell asleep in my arms, I inhaled his sweet baby scent, feeling very close to heaven.

That was when it dawned on me. If I hadn't "just shown up," I would have missed those tranquil summer days. I would have missed my grandson's gorgeous blue eyes and that pretty hummingbird outside. I finally, completely, saw the true meaning of what Saralee said—and I was grateful.

Which doesn't mean my schedule's not still sometimes mind-boggling. There are still dust-bunnies camped out on my kitchen floor and e-mails time-stamped "Jurassic Period." But I've heard it said that worrying is simply lack of faith, and I'm attempting to live by that truth.

I've never met or even emailed Saralee, yet her words have changed my life. That is the power of connection, of story. Happy 20th Anniversary, Chicken Soup for the Soul. That is the power of you!

~Theresa Sanders

Just Show Up

Courage is being afraid but going on anyhow.
~Dan Rather

While walking in the woods near our home on Cape Cod, I met a man who taught me a three-word lesson that has altered my life.

His name was Morris and he seemed to be in his seventies or eighties. He told me, "I walk here every day, rain or shine."

Noticing that I was wearing a neck brace and holding onto a tree with one hand and my cane with the other, he said, "So, is it hard for you to get around here?"

"Sometimes."

He nodded in understanding and remarked, "But you still do it." We seemed to form an unusually special bond on that day in the woods as we both spoke from our hearts.

"Frankly," I said. "It's harder for me to get here than it is to walk here. And that has nothing to do with needing a brace or a cane. It has to do with my thinking."

"You get caught in maybe-I-will, maybe-I-won't land. That's the problem."

"Yes!" I laughed at how perfectly he put that. "And that one second of debate is enough of a time gap for me to come up with a perfect excuse to talk myself out of it and press the button on the TV remote instead."

Then he said the three magical words I now say to myself nearly every day: "Just show up."

Later my husband, Bob, asked me what Morris meant.

"Well, here's how I understand it. When the thought enters my brain, 'I should go exercise,' I instantly start thinking about every single step it takes to get around to doing it. First I have to shower. Then I have to find something to wear. Then I have to find everything I need for safety. Then I have to—blah, blah, blah. I think what Morris meant was to scrap all of those thoughts. In other words, I should replace talking-myself-out-of-it thinking with the words: 'Just show up.'"

Bob started practicing Morris's philosophy and it's working for a lot of things. "I get overwhelmed at the computer with all the details I have to do," he told me. "Sometimes I just avoid it, but that's crazy. So instead of thinking about the big picture, I say, 'Just show up,' and I do."

Now, this new way of approaching things was working fine and dandy until a fellow named Kelvin and his wife, Amy, contacted me. They organize and operate the Cape Cod Challenger Club. They've read many of my newspaper columns. My topics often include disabilities. That's why they got in touch.

Kelvin e-mailed, "We provide year-round athletic, recreational and social activities for physically and developmentally disabled youth on the Cape."

He continued, "We pack the park with hundreds of people every Sunday during our baseball season. We would be honored if you would be our opening day speaker and throw out the first pitch."

I held my head in my hands. Public speaking is my number one phobia. But I couldn't say no. So I instantly had the altruistic and benevolent thought, "I hate you, Kelvin."

The next day Bob went with me to meet Kelvin at Dunkin'

Donuts. "Please don't make me give a speech," I pleaded with this delightful young man who had the crazy notion that since I write stories, somehow that implied that I could form words—out loud.

"Just a few sentences?" he said.

I was able to buy time by licking the cream cheese off my bagel. Bob kept kicking my leg and touching his mustache, which I found out way too much later meant that I had a huge wad of cream cheese on my upper lip.

I reluctantly agreed.

In the middle of the night before my speech, I shook Bob awake. "What if I can't talk and just hiccup for ten syllables instead of saying words?" (That did happen at our wedding.) "What if I can't walk that day? What if I have a panic attack? What if..." And Bob sweetly silenced me.

He said, "You know there's only one thing that matters."

I knew.

And so, I decided to "just show up" for the opening game.

It went beautifully. And by that I do not mean I did a good job giving my speech. It means that I faltered and stammered and even went blank twice. Should I have been embarrassed? Of course not. All I had to do was look around at the children and their parents, teachers, volunteers—and the beautiful expectant looks on everyone's faces. They were seeing someone disabled, like them, who simply got up there and tried.

I did the weirdest thing for my speech. I told the truth. Here's what I said:

"I am so excited to be here today with you wonderful people of the Cape Cod Challenger Club. I'm honored that Kelvin and Amy invited me.

And... I'm also scared to be talking in front of such a large group. But I'll tell you—I'm scared of a lot of stuff and I try to do it anyway.

So my message to you is this:

Winning doesn't matter.

Being scared doesn't matter.

The only thing that matters... is that we try!!

Now, who's going to help me toss the first pitch?"

Many children, all disabled, raised their hands. "I will! I will!" They excitedly came running over to help me. I was very wobbly. My crew of helpers kept me from falling. I had the children hold onto my arm and the ball so that they also felt they were tossing the first pitch. And when we did, we all yelled, "PLAY BALL!"

Then someone handed me a huge bouquet of flowers.

You know, I found out that it wouldn't have mattered if I lost my balance. It wouldn't have mattered if I suddenly had trouble talking or any of the bad things that sometimes happen to me.

The only thing that mattered was that I just showed up—for the children's sake—for the caregivers' sake—and for mine.

Thank God I had that chance encounter in the woods that day with Morris. Although he told me he walked there every day, I haven't seen him since.

And even though I know over forty people who walk that same path in the woods, not one of them has ever seen Morris. Kind of makes you wonder.

~Saralee Perel

Good Morning, Birdie

Why not go out on a limb? That's where the fruit is.
~Mark Twain

I am a devoted Innkeeper at The Channel Road Inn and The Inn At Playa del Rey, which are two beautiful bed and breakfast hotels in Los Angeles. I truly adore the women I work with, so I always look forward to our annual Christmas party. Prior to the party, we all draw "Secret Santa" names for our gift exchange. Two Christmases ago, I noticed my fellow Innkeeper and true friend, Rebecca Hill, was particularly antsy to start the "Secret Santa" game. I was excited, for she is a very thoughtful gift-giver. She handed me a beautifully wrapped present and inside was a book called *Chicken Soup for the Soul: Food and Love.*

I was touched by this gift as I've always loved the *Chicken Soup for the Soul* series. I especially loved the topic of this book because I do feel food and love are intrinsically intertwined. Showing love to people through the food I make for them is very important to me so I knew I would enjoy the stories.

As I began glancing through the book, I noticed a bookmark. Curious, I flipped to the page and soon realized Rebecca had written a story about my "Morning Bird Granola." I was completely overwhelmed! I knew Rebecca loved my homemade granola, but I'd never had someone support it so fully—and in print!

Seeing written accolades about my special homemade granola

made me begin to realize that my hidden dream of creating yummy baked goods on a professional level could actually come true. It made me feel that my little "Morning Bird Granola" was something truly special to the outside world. It was already special to me because I named it in honor of my late father, who always called me Birdie and would call out "Morning, Birdie!" to me every morning in his booming voice when I was a child playing outside.

When Rebecca held a book signing for *Chicken Soup for the Soul: Food and Love* she asked me to be by her side to hand out samples of my granola. This was the first time I'd presented my granola outside of the Inns so I was delighted when it was well received. As a dreamer, you don't always find the courage to try to make your dreams become a reality for fear that the reality will fall short of the dream. Therefore, it's emotionally daunting to take that first important step. But when people complimented my granola at the book signing and began asking where they could buy it, I felt encouraged that Morning Bird Granola could become a "real product" that I should share on a broader level.

As I drove home from the book signing, I reflected on my life. By age six I already knew that I wanted to be a professional ballerina. I remembered traveling the world feeling it was such a privilege to tell stories through my dancing. I felt at home being able to express my emotions so thoroughly through artistic movement to gorgeous music. I was living my dream come true. Being a dancer was what I was born to do. It was shocking to have my dreams taken away from me one day through injury. For many years, I mourned the loss of my dream and felt hollow inside. Luckily, I eventually found a way to dance again, just not as part of a professional travelling company any longer.

Searching for something else to devote myself to, I discovered that the art of innkeeping made me feel somewhat like myself again. Being rooted in kindness, it is a wonderful form of offering a sanctuary to strangers. I worked in the Virgin Islands and Boston; then, one day I had the fortuitous luck of being hired as an innkeeper at The Channel Road Inn. As I began baking, I felt my artistic soul awakening in ways it hadn't since my world fell apart. For the first time in a long time I felt I had a brand new way to express my artistic self and touch others again. I soon discovered that I derived great satisfaction from creating my own recipes. As with my dancing, I search for harmony, light and balance in my recipes and of course I am elated when "the curtain goes up" and I can present the food I've made for others to enjoy.

It was a wonderful feeling in my heart to see Rebecca and so many guests at the Inns having such a positive reaction to my granola, and even more exciting when I started receiving e-mails requesting it. It was deeply gratifying knowing that I'd connected with others in this way, as it is my intent to positively nourish those I come in contact with in my life. As I do it through my dancing, I now also do with my baking....

When Chicken Soup for the Soul published Rebecca's story—"Cereal Killer"—it encouraged me to take that leap of faith and try to bring a dream of mine to live again. I began saving money so I could afford packaging and product labels. I was also given permission to sell my granola at the Inn at Playa del Rey and I've even had a few people order my granola by mail!

I hope one day to have my own bed and breakfast where I can sell all my homemade baked goods. My bed and breakfast will be somewhere nestled in nature—a sanctuary where people can come to rest, relax and restore their souls. I'd like to have a café on the ground floor as well, and rooms upstairs for guests to stay the night. I, of course, dream of having my granola sold in supermarkets too, but I never want to lose touch with the day-to-day contact I have with the people who eat the treats I create. The symbiotic relationship between myself and those I nourish is essential to me. From where I stand at this moment, this seems like a very big dream but thanks in large part to the courage I gathered from my granola being so lovingly supported in *Chicken Soup for the Soul: Food and Love*, I find myself ready to leap again.

~Dominique Young

Cereal Killer

There is no sincerer love than the love of food.
~George Bernard Shaw

My friend Dominique and I are innkeepers at Channel Road Inn. Working at a bed and breakfast hotel is fun! We take reservations, help guests with their dinner plans and we bake homemade cookies, breakfast cakes and goodies from scratch every day for our guests.

Dominique and I have been friends for a while now. We've shared secrets, lots of laughs and even a few tears, but lately something has come between us... it's her granola recipe. She won't tell me (or anyone!) how it's made.

Dominique's granola is the best thing I've ever tasted. Sure I love the homemade banana bread and blueberry cakes we bake at the Inn. Our scones, egg soufflés and French toast are amazing and our homemade chocolate chip cookies are to die for but nothing—NOTHING!—can top Dominique's granola.

When you ask Dominique what's in the granola she pretends to tell you. "Oh, it's simple—just your basic granola but I add in some fruit and I sweeten it with coconut and honey," she says (while not looking you in the eye). But she must be leaving something out of her description because I have never tasted granola (or anything) that tastes as good as this. I cannot even hear, much less talk, when I'm eating this granola. The whole world stops moving and all I can hear is the crunching of the granola in my mouth. I can't hear the phones or the doorbell ring and even when people talk to me, I can see their lips moving but their voices sound like they are in slow motion. In that sense, Dominique's granola is an occupational hazard for me, so I try to eat it only after my shift has ended.

I am known to get overly exuberant about certain things, so I took a sample of Dominique's granola to one of my girlfriends at Curves so she could tell me if she found it as amazing as I do. By the time I drove home, there was already an e-mail from my girlfriend saying, "Wow, you were not kidding! That stuff is addictive! Yum, yum, yum! I'm thinking Dominique should start small and go to farmers' markets, fairs, etc... and just sell locally... word will spread!"

And word has spread! Though Dominique has not had time to go to farmers' markets or fairs yet, we do have guests e-mailing and calling to ask for the recipe for Dominique's homemade granola. Over the past twenty-three years all of the innkeepers at Channel Road Inn have been open and generous with our recipes. We freely and willingly give them to our guests and we'll even let them watch us bake the cakes or prepare the egg soufflés and French toast so they can replicate them at home. Dominique's granola is the only recipe they cannot have. Their response is always the same. They laugh and say, "I always knew you innkeepers had a few tricks up your sleeves," and then they add, "No problem. But can I buy some of that granola? Could you mail it to me? I keep thinking about it."

I like these phone calls and e-mails because they reassure me that I have not lost my mind. This granola is that good! I think about it every day and always hope Dominique has had a chance to make it when I come into work. I've even been known to call down to the Inn on my days off just to see if, by chance, Domi has made any granola. I scour the freezer at the Inn looking for leftovers and hidden stashes, but I rarely find any because the guests eat it by the heaping spoonfuls. On the days Dominique's granola gets served, our home-made cakes are barely touched. People are nuts for this stuff.

My girlfriend from Curves asks me on a weekly basis how she can get more of Dominique's granola. Though she has an apartment nearby, she's considering booking a room at Channel Road Inn just so she can come to breakfast and eat granola. It's that bad — this granola is ruining the lives of everyone who eats it. We all become addicts and start devoting our lives to finding out how and when we can get more granola.

And all the while, Dominique sits in the kitchen feigning surprise that everyone is rabidly searching for more granola. She's like the Master of the Universe — the one who holds the key to our happiness. When she knows I'm having a hard week, she definitely makes granola. One time she even went out and bought coconut herself because the Inn was out of it and she knew I wanted and needed (yes, actually needed) her homemade granola that day.

We have a repeat guest at Channel Road Inn who has stayed at the Inn several times a year for the past ten years. She's crazy about Dominique's granola too! Like me, she has begged for the recipe and then finally settled for just eating a bowl of granola once she realized that Dominique's vague description of "fruit, coconut and honey" is just a dodge. We all adore this guest — from her Missouri drawl to her darling grandchildren and impeccable manners, she is the most charming woman in the world.

Under normal circumstances, there's nothing I would deny this guest, but when she checked in last week and immediately asked if "Dominique had made any granola" I had to think fast. The technical answer was, "No, Domi has not had time to make granola today." But the underlying truth, the one that troubled my heart, was: "Domi has not had time to make granola today... but she did give me a small bag of it last week. I have it hidden in the back of the freezer with my name on it and I have been rationing it out to myself half a cup at a time."

I stared at our loyal guest, wondering if I should share my secret stash with her. I love this guest... but I also love Dominique's granola.

I adore this guest... but I also adore Dominique's granola. I should have shared my granola with this guest... but I didn't. I tried to ease my conscience by offering her a cup of tea and a slice of hot vanilla streusel cake, fresh out of the oven. She politely said, "No thank you" and as I watched her walk down the hall to her room, I felt slightly bad—but not as bad as I would have felt had I given her the last of my granola.

Dominique shows her love for Channel Road Inn's guests—and employees—through her baking. She works on her recipes for weeks to perfect them and is truly delighted when the guests "ooh and ah" over her creations. She is generous with most of her recipes, except for one. And that's okay, because this granola is so good, I'm betting one day it will be available in stores, and then our charming guest from Missouri, my girlfriend from Curves, and I can all eat Domi's granola to our heart's content!

~Rebecca Hill

Good Enough to Eat

Let food be thy medicine and medicine be thy food.
~Hippocrates

The fast food wrapper crinkled as I freed my roast beef sandwich from its folds. Smoothing the wrapper flat, I placed the curly fry container upon it.

The mixed aroma of fried foods and juicy beef had garnered the attention of my brown tabby. She waddled into the kitchen and climbed onto the empty chair, nearly filling its space.

As I lifted my sandwich for a bite she meowed.

"No, MaMa. You can't eat people food."

She looked from my eyes to my curly fries and back to my eyes.

"No fries. This stuff isn't good for kitties to eat."

I pondered that statement as I shoved a seasoned fry into my mouth and chewed under MaMa's watchful gaze. It had been a long time since I had eaten fast food.

As I had been meandering through life checking off big moments like college graduation and getting married, a multiple sclerosis diagnosis had put a hitch in my plans. It was during those years of uncertainty about the future and experimenting with medicines to find the combination that would keep me active and working, when Ginny Dent Brant's story titled, "It's a Dog's Life," from *Chicken Soup for the Soul: Shaping the New You* landed in my inbox.

The story was about Ginny adopting a dog and the breeder making a specific request that she not feed it table scraps. The breeder explained that they are high in fat, calories, and processed foods, and low in nutritional value. Ginny scrutinized her eating habits and decided if they weren't good enough for the dog then they weren't good enough for her family either.

That story made me take a hard look at my diet. It was full of processed, packaged food. Was I really doing all that I could to be healthy with MS? No. I was poisoning the body I was trying to save.

There are no conclusive studies that show eating a diet rich in fruits, vegetables, complex carbs and lean protein will slow or halt the progression of MS. There are, however, hundreds of case studies that show people with MS who have changed their diets for the better and went from being disabled to enabled and ready to lead full, active lives.

I needed to get my life back on track so I started doing my research. I learned to ask questions about what was in my food, where it came from and how it was grown.

The first time my husband and I went on our bi-weekly grocery trip after we changed our strategy was our longest ever. We pushed the cart along our usual aisles perusing item after item and turning our nose up at high fructose corn syrup, red dye #40 and partially hydrogenated vegetable oils, among others. I felt empowered, like I knew a secret that the woman ahead of me didn't know as she tossed sugary breakfast treats into her cart. If we couldn't pronounce an ingredient, we didn't buy the item.

By the last aisle the bottom of our cart was still visible. We had successfully avoided the bad food, but we didn't really have anything in our cart other than frozen vegetables, a few whole grain cereals, and yogurt. Then we turned the corner and the vegetable and fruit aisle shone like a gift from heaven. We loaded up on leafy greens, potatoes, cruciferous vegetables, onions, garlic and tomatoes, and then decided that apples, kiwis, bananas and pineapple needed to go in too. We added nuts for good measure and grabbed a loaf of fresh baked bread that was preservative free.

In addition to shopping at our usual grocery store we started making regular visits to our local farmers market. There we purchased local produce that didn't travel hundreds of miles in a truck.

Our effort worked. I changed the direction my life was going and got back on track by changing careers from one where I felt imprisoned to one where the creative juices could flow. As a bonus, I was doing well with my MS and I was down six pounds.

And then I had an off day and went and bought a curly fry that MaMa couldn't eat because it was bad for kitties. I scooped up the remaining fries and tossed them into the garbage can. And then I drove to the farmers market.

~Valerie D. Benko

It's a Dog's Life

If we're not willing to settle for junk living, we certainly shouldn't settle for junk food.
~Sally Edwards

We got our precious Corgi, Reggie, when he was just a pup. The breeder made an important request of us before signing the papers.

"If I let you have this dog," he said, "I want you to promise you won't feed him table scraps."

"What's wrong with the scraps from my table?" I replied.

"They are high in fat, calories, and processed foods, and low in nutritional value."

His response puzzled me. If my scraps were good enough for my family, they must be good enough for my pet. This made me start thinking about the quality of the food I was eating. I must admit as a teenager I easily captured the title of "Junk Food Queen." I had to change my diet at age seventeen when my doctor warned me I was headed towards Type II diabetes.

This incident with my dog made me again examine my diet. I was better than the average American—wasn't I? After all, I did not smoke, drink alcohol, or chew. Added to that, I did not eat many carbs or drink caffeine. I was looking more like a health nut every day. Upon further investigation, I realized much of what Americans consume daily is exactly what this vet challenged me to avoid for my dog. If these foods were not good enough for my dog, then they were not good enough for my family.

I was beginning to see that we have inverted the food pyramid. This contributes to our problems with heart disease, blood pressure, cancer, etc. I decided to change my diet by drinking more water, eating more fresh fruits and vegetables, eating lean meats, and further limiting fast foods. It did not take me long to feel and see the difference. My blood work was looking better with every checkup. I admit it was hard to give up the desserts and fried foods that had snuck back into my lifestyle—but what a difference it made in my health. As age creeps up on me, my health means everything. And yes, I can still occasionally eat one of those savory desserts.

I was beginning to discipline my diet when my dog taught me another lesson. At age three, my dog began to have seizures. The vet said Reggie needed medication. We increased his water intake, but never gave him the medication. We had moved to an apartment while building a new home. Our dog was cooped up all day until we got home from work, so we decided to walk him several miles daily. Several months later, I took him to the vet for his checkup.

"How are Reggie's seizures?" he asked.

"Well," I pondered, "he has not had a seizure in about… five to six months." We were so busy moving and building, I neglected to notice they had stopped.

"What has changed?" he inquired.

After thinking, I responded, "We have been exercising him each day after work, and we have been giving him more water."

"Exercise and hydration have great benefits," he explained. "Dehydration can be a cause of seizures and exercise helps to regulate chemicals in the brain. It appears this new exercise and increased water may have cured Reggie's seizures."

I began to think—if all this exercise and hydration is good

enough for my dog—then surely, it is good enough for me. I researched the benefits of hydration and found this body of mine must have the right amount of water for thousands of chemical reactions to take place daily, which ensure my good health. My brain and body are comprised of 70 to 75 percent water. I was astonished to find dehydration of cells is a major cause of cancer, kidney stones, and can be a cause of seizures. Exercise also benefits the body by strengthening the heart, lungs and bones, and keeping our brains alert and healthy. We now exercise vigorously 30 to 60 minutes four to five times each week.

Reggie went to the vet for his fifteen-year checkup recently. The vet was amazed at how well he has done.

"He's almost ninety-nine years old in dog years," he marveled. "The average Corgi lives about twelve years. He's beating the averages."

Reggie can no longer walk several miles with us. In his older years, he can only walk about one mile without becoming exhausted. I am thankful Reggie has made it this long and retained his health. Exercise, water, and diet are clearly the reasons why. We have benefited, too. Our diets are filled with fresh fruits and vegetables, lean meats and seafood, and healthy omegas and oils. We count those glasses of water and squeeze a lemon or lime to add a little taste. We have even bought an elliptical machine so we can exercise when it is cold or raining.

My dog Reggie was actually not my first lesson in taking care of my body. My first lesson came in my childhood years when my dad worked for U.S. Senator Strom Thurmond. The Senator treated me as one of his own and constantly gave me lectures about food, diet and exercise. My third grade health book was also filled with this same information. Unfortunately, I didn't listen.

"Don't eat too much junk food," Senator Thurmond would always say. "Fruits and vegetables are God's way of keeping you healthy."

At age eighty, the Senator jogged five miles each day, worked sixty- to eighty-hour weeks, and kept up with his four young children. When Strom Thurmond died at age 100, the doctor signed his death certificate with these words, "Cause of Death: old age." Rarely does anyone's death certificate say that these days.

The Bible commands us to take care of our bodies. The discipline we have developed in this area has helped us to grow in mind, body, and spirit. We now look at our health in a new light. If it's good enough for my dog, it's good enough for me. Better said, I should take care of myself as least as well as I care for my dog.

~Ginny Dent Brant

The Happiness Committee

The best way to cheer yourself up is to try to cheer somebody else up.
~Mark Twain

I was happy to get out of the office. I, along with a co-worker, was taking a management course that would require us to be out of town for two days a week for a month. Our office consisted of about sixty people, many of whom had known one another for more than fifteen years. We shared one another's triumphs and sorrows. This had been a particularly difficult year. We had suffered through regulatory changes and personal challenges. The morale at work was at an all-time low.

One of the homework assignments from our class was to conduct a study, following specific guidelines, to assess the level of workplace satisfaction. I didn't need a process for that. All I had to do was spend some time in the office to see that satisfaction was low. People were unhappy and it seemed like we could not recover from one blow before another one hit.

I recalled a story that I had read in *Chicken Soup for the Soul: Think Positive* by Mandie Maass titled "First Class Attitude." It was about two women who found themselves stranded at an airport, for hours, with a gate full of tired, disgruntled people. Determined to keep a positive attitude, they did everything they could to make the other passengers feel happier. They had no power to change the situation with the planes, but they could help change attitudes. I convinced my co-worker that we should assess the happiness of our workplace, and if possible, make it a more positive place to work.

We had to finish our project in two weeks so we moved quickly. The first thing I did was get permission from one of the vice presidents to move forward. Securing that, I sent an e-mail letting everyone know what we were doing and asking them to think about what could be done to make our office a happier place to work. I gave them the parameters we had to work with so that they would understand the scope of this endeavor. These suggestions would be voiced during a series of Happiness Meetings.

We recruited people for the Happiness Committee. This committee was a small group of supervisors who understood our limitations, had authority to make decisions, and would advise on which suggestions could be executed. We also enlisted a trio of scribes to write down the suggestions during the Happiness Meetings.

The following day, one department at a time, we gave each person an opportunity to list things that they thought would brighten the workplace for them. Our scribes wrote everything down. Suggestions ranged from putting a new coat of paint on the walls, to planning some fun activities, to onsite training. I was surprised and pleased at the thought they had put into their suggestions. Up until this point, I was uncertain as to how much cooperation and enthusiasm we would get.

The work of the scribes was typed into a document, listing all of the suggestions, and reviewed by the Happiness Committee. Any items deemed inappropriate, or just beyond the scope of the Happiness Project, were eliminated. A ballot was compiled of the remaining suggestions. An e-mail was sent out to let everyone know that they would vote for their five favorite suggestions.

The next day, I got on the intercom to let each department know when to vote. When people began to line up to vote, I noticed that there was already a change. The familiar chatter was back. People were smiling. I was getting excited. Was this going to work?

After the voting, the ballots were tallied and the top twenty suggestions, by number of votes, were compiled. Once again, these were reviewed by the Happiness Committee. This time, their job was to determine what could be done about each suggestion and what the timeline was for getting it done. It was time to let everyone know.

We had thought about this and decided to use it as an opportunity to begin fulfilling the items on the list. One of the top ten items was for the office to get together, periodically, for a potluck breakfast or lunch. Just some fellowship among coworkers. We planned the Happiness Café. All employees would be invited to breakfast. They would be given menus from which they could choose and their breakfast would be prepared to order. The best part? The supervisors served as the waiters and the cooks.

Dressed in white aprons, all the supervisors lined up as the rest of the employees took their seats at the Happiness Café. Employees were delighted to have their supervisors waiting on them. Supervisors tried to outdo one another with their customer service. I was a cook and, even from the kitchen, I could hear the noise and laughter. I took a minute and peeked through the door. It did my heart good to see all the happy faces. My coworkers. My friends.

Once everyone had a chance to eat, I had announcements to make. I read the list of the top twenty suggestions and let everyone know what actions were planned and the estimated timelines. Everyone applauded. I also announced that a permanent committee had been formed, a mix of supervisors and other employees, to make sure the suggestions were carried out and the momentum of the Happiness Project continued. This new committee would be called the TEAM Committee.

To introduce the new committee, I shouted out, cheerleader style, each letter of TEAM. As I did, each member ran out holding that letter high overhead. Once all were in place, everyone applauded and cheered. What can I say? Sometimes corny works.

Not only did every item on the top-twenty list come to fruition, the TEAM Committee is still in place today. The CEO has handed out letters of commendation to the committee for its work. These are very hard to come by so they mean a lot.

My coworker and I went back to class the following week and listened as everyone reported on their projects. When it was our turn, jaws dropped. We hit it out of the park. Neither our classmates nor our teacher could believe how far we took our project.

Our work had not only increased morale in the office and caused workplace improvements, it had boosted our morale also. I learned that making other people happy is one of the best ways to make yourself happy, just like the two women in the story "First Class Attitude."

~Debbie Acklin

First Class Attitude

People are not disturbed by things, but by the view they take of them.
~Epictetus

A few years ago, looking to open an inspirational bookstore, a friend and I attended a booksellers' course in New York. After a busy few days filled with learning and sightseeing, we were ready to get home to our families. We left the convention center looking to hail a cab with what felt like plenty of time to make our flight.

No sooner than leaving the building it began to rain. "A little rain never hurt anyone," we thought. Besides we were about to embark on a business of inspiring people, so we couldn't let a little bad weather steal our joy. After a short while with no luck finding a vacant cab, it suddenly dawned on us, "It's five o'clock in New York City! This is rush hour traffic. We may never get a cab." My friend then remembered she had saved the card of the van company that had driven us in from the airport several days prior. As the rain began to pick up we scurried to a nearby awning and gave them a call. Over an hour later, our van finally arrived and shuttled us to the airport.

We arrived at the airline ticket counter with little time to spare, only to discover the airline could not locate my flight reservation. We looked at each other in disbelief yet somehow managed to maintain a smile as we worked with the attendant to find a solution. Fifteen minutes before take-off we were finally able to resolve the issue. Doubtful of making the flight, yet refusing to lose all hope, we headed through security and made a mad dash towards our flight gate.

A sigh of relief came upon us when we arrived at the gate to discover the flight had been delayed half an hour. Not only did we not miss the flight but now we had a few minutes to collect ourselves and grab a quick snack before boarding. About twenty minutes passed and we eagerly headed back toward the gate. Much to our dismay however, upon reaching the gate we discovered the delay had been extended another hour due to bad weather in another state. Although we were tired and ready to get home, we refused to end our trip on a sour note. Instead, we decided to make the most of our wait and grabbed a nearby seat on the floor to relax and chat about our trip.

We ended up sitting near a gentleman who at some point joined in on our conversation. After a bit of talking, the conversation turned to the gentleman sharing with us some struggles he was experiencing in his life. My friend and I, being women of strong faith, were then able to share some experience, strength, and hope with him that we believe influenced him in a positive way.

My friend and I talked afterward about how delays in life can be frustrating, but you never know why they may be happening. There could be some underlying purpose for them that you don't realize in the moment. Maybe it's to alter your life course for the better, maybe it's to afford you an opportunity you would not have had otherwise, maybe it's to share hope with someone in need, maybe it's to stop you from making a huge mistake, or maybe it's to protect you or someone else from harm's way.

We continued to sit and chat as announcement after announcement trickled in informing us each time that our delay had been extended. Being that we were sitting near the airline counter we also were able to hear passengers approach the airline employees and express their dissatisfaction and frustration. We were impressed with the empathy and style with which the airline handled each customer's concern. I admit, at this point, we were fighting ourselves to not let the frustration get to us, yet somehow we managed to keep smiling. This furthered our conversation on how good it felt to make the most of the situation.

Well into the middle of the night, airline employees began bringing out refreshments to the passengers. My friend hopped up and offered to help. I jumped up after her, agreeing it sounded like a good idea. We then proceeded to pour cups of juice and water and offer them to weary passengers. We found ourselves sitting and sharing stories with some, while just offering smiles and encouragement to others.

Once all the passengers were served, we sat back down and continued our conversation. We talked about how great it felt to see frowns turn into smiles and how encouraging it was to us to sit and listen to others. We were truly realizing what it meant to look at the glass half full and what can happen when you chose to make the most of every opportunity. Life is going to throw you lemons sometimes. Will you make a sour face or add a little sweetener and drink up the lemonade? Sometimes we want so badly for our reality to change. Yet what we don't realize is that sometimes in order for our reality to change our perception must change. We may not be able to control the things around us, but we can control our attitude and sometimes that makes all the difference.

As my friend and I sat and chatted some more, an airline attendant walked over to us and bent down. He thanked us for our help and told us how much the attendants had appreciated our positive attitudes. He then asked for our boarding passes, telling us the airline wanted to upgrade us to First Class! Shortly after exchanging our tickets our plane was finally ready for take-off. We boarded the plane with a new enlightened perspective on how big an impact our attitude can truly make.

~Mandie Maass

Chapter 5

READER'S CHOICE

Doing Good

Being good is commendable,
but only when it is combined with doing good is it useful.

~Author Unknown

Made a Difference to That One

Act as if what you do makes a difference. It does.
~William James

Twenty years ago—in the very first *Chicken Soup for the Soul* book ever published—I read a story by Jack Canfield and Mark Victor Hansen that changed me forever. The story was entitled "One At A Time." Its message? Just because you can't save the whole world doesn't mean you shouldn't try to make a little piece of it better.

Through the years, I was reminded of that message every time I helped a kid learn to dribble a basketball. Every time I delivered homemade oatmeal raisin cookies to a nursing home. Every time I picked up litter or took in a homeless kitten or let somebody who seemed more hurried and harried than I go ahead of me in the grocery checkout line.

But the message hit the hardest the summer Caroline came into my life.

She was standing in ninety-degree heat in the parking lot of the tiny branch library I'd just been hired to manage. "Hey," she said, as I fumbled to unlock the door. "Are you the new library lady?"

"I am," I told her. "Who are you?"

"Caroline," she said. "And I just turned ten."

Hmmmmm, I thought. Caroline was certainly the smallest ten-year-old I'd ever seen. But it was clear that she could read, for she had obviously noted the sign on the door that said: CHILDREN LESS THAN TEN YEARS MUST BE ACCOMPANIED BY A PARENT.

"Come on in here where it's cool, Caroline," I said. "Let's see if we can find you some good books."

We did. And because not one other patron entered the library for the first two hours it was open, we had plenty of time to enjoy those books. I read to Caroline for a while and then she read to me. I helped her find kid-friendly games to play on the computer. I showed her where the restroom and the water fountain were. But as morning became afternoon, my stomach began to growl. I'd brought a sack lunch—when you're running a one-person operation, there's no going out for a meal—but I hated to eat in front of Caroline.

"Don't you think you ought to head home and get some lunch?" I finally asked.

Her eyes narrowed and she shook her head. "Nobody's home at my house."

"Did your parents leave you something to eat?"

"My mom locks the door every morning when she goes to work. She won't be home till dark."

I turned away so that Caroline wouldn't see the tears welling up in my eyes. And, of course, I shared my bologna sandwich and tangerine and Little Debbie oatmeal creme pie with her. She stayed at the library all day. And as I watched her curled up in the yellow bean bag chair in the cool quiet, reading about Clifford the Big Red Dog and Horton the Elephant and Amelia Bedelia, I couldn't help but wonder how many other children there were in this little town and in this big world, locked out and lonely and left to fend for themselves.

There were millions, no doubt. Just thinking about them made me want to weep. To gnash my teeth. To wring my hands in despair. How could I possibly make a dent in such a problem? Then I remembered the story of the man walking along the beach, picking up starfish and throwing them—one at a time—back into the ocean so they wouldn't die.

Every day, that whole summer long, Caroline was waiting for me when I pulled into the library parking lot and climbed out of my car holding two sack lunches. She'd help me unlock the door and turn on the lights and fire up the computers. And then she'd plop down in the yellow beanbag chair and grin at me.

"Let's start with *Horton Hatches the Egg*," she'd say.

It's true. One library lady in one little town couldn't make a difference to every child on the mean streets of this planet. But I could make a difference to one.

~Jennie Ivey

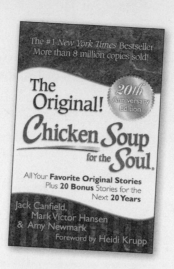

One At A Time

We ourselves feel that what we are doing is just a drop in the ocean.
But the ocean would be less because of that missing drop.
~Mother Teresa

A friend of ours was walking down a deserted Mexican beach at sunset. As he walked along, he began to see another man in the distance. As he grew nearer, he noticed that the man kept leaning down, picking something up and throwing it out into the water. Time and again he kept hurling things out into the ocean.

As our friend approached even closer, he noticed that the man was picking up starfish that had been washed up on the beach and, one at a time, he was throwing them back into the water.

Our friend was puzzled. He approached the man and said, "Good evening, friend. I was wondering what you are doing."

"I'm throwing these starfish back into the ocean. You see, it's low tide right now and all of these starfish have been washed up onto the shore. If I don't throw them back into the sea, they'll die up here from lack of oxygen."

"I understand," my friend replied, "but there must be thousands of starfish on this beach. You can't possibly get to all of them. There are simply too many. And don't you realize this is probably happening on hundreds of beaches all up and down this coast? Can't you see that you can't possibly make a difference?"

The man smiled, bent down, and picked up yet another starfish, and as he threw it back into the sea, he replied, "Made a difference to that one!"

~Jack Canfield and Mark Victor Hansen

The Little Things

What this world needs is a new kind of army — the army of the kind.
~Cleveland Amory

have always enjoyed the *Chicken Soup for the Soul* series and, in browsing through a bookstore a few years ago, I found a used copy of the *Chicken Soup for the Woman's Soul* edition. Sandy Ezrine had written a poem titled "It Couldn't Hurt" that focused on the small acts of kindness she had shown toward others.

That poem made me stop and think that opportunities to help others in the big, outstanding ways do not often come our way, but we can make a difference in the lives of other people when we focus on the little things we can do for them. I decided to put that attitude into practice and began looking for the little things I could do for the people who crossed my path each day.

Almost immediately, I began to see the difference it made not only in the lives of others, but also in my own life as I focused more on others and less on myself. The poem that follows is the result of Sandy's inspiration to me in my own personal life.

The Little Things

I baked muffins for the young man who cut a portion
of my yard and would not take any money.
He said how good they tasted.

I went to the grocery store for an older neighbor couple
during a snowstorm when they were afraid to drive.
They were grateful for the food.

I took a special pastry to the gentleman in the neighborhood
on his 90th birthday when he was not expecting it.
He smiled and said he liked sweets.

I prepared lunch for the carpet-layers as they worked in the heat
and had forgotten to bring lunch with them.
They ate like hungry children.

I took drinks to the trash men on a hot afternoon in summer heat
when they looked so exhausted from the humidity.
They drank it like men never having water.

I took homemade chicken noodle soup, crackers, and cheese
to a lady in an auto accident, temporarily confined to a wheelchair.
She liked the taste of something she had not prepared.

I sent a special card to a lady in the neighborhood
who was facing her husband's first birthday after his passing.
She thanked me for being sensitive.

I had a "thank you" lunch for the ladies who had helped with food
after my knee surgery and the following convalescence.
They had a good time of fellowship.

I baked brownies for the plumbers I always called with problems
when they did not charge me for a service call.
They appreciated the recognition.

I spent the afternoon with a friend who had lost a close
family member

when she had no one else with whom to share her hurts.
She felt the freedom to cry and felt better.

I sent a special card to a lady whom I had known for years
when she faced the first Christmas without her husband.
She knew that I truly understood her situation.

I stopped and thanked the custodian at the busy local hospital
when he was mopping the dirty footprints from the hall.
He stood up straighter and seemed so pleased.

I prepared a meal for a friend who works many long, hard hours
when she came home weary from being on her feet.
We enjoyed the meal together and talked.

I thanked the checkout lady at the grocery store cash register
when she totaled my bill and gave me change.
She was pleased that someone appreciated her.

I read a poem by Sandy Ezrine when she shared her thoughts
about not waiting to do the big things for others.
I was a better person for it.

~Carol Goodman Heizer

It Couldn't Hurt

Wherever there is a human being, there is an opportunity for a kindness.
~Seneca

Random Acts of Kindness—huh!
It couldn't hurt.

I told my husband I love him.
It couldn't hurt.

I packed a note in my son's lunch box telling him how special he is.
It couldn't hurt.

I opened the door for a lady in a wheelchair at Walgreens.
It couldn't hurt.

I left a box of cookies for the mailman.
It couldn't hurt.

I let someone go in front of me in the grocery line.
It didn't hurt.

I called my brother to tell him I miss him.
He misses me too!

I sent the Mayor a note saying what a good job he is doing.
It couldn't hurt.

I took flowers to the nursing home.
It couldn't hurt.

I cooked some chicken soup for a friend who is sick.
It couldn't hurt.

I played Candy Land with my daughter.
It was fun.

I thanked the person who bagged my groceries.
He beamed.

I gave my assistant the day off with pay.
It only hurt a little.

I played ball with my dog.
It felt good.

I invited a woman who doesn't drive to lunch and to a movie.
I enjoyed myself.

I got a massage for me.
It felt marvelous.

Random Acts of Kindness—hmmm, maybe I'll live this way all year.
It couldn't hurt.

~Sandy Ezrine

Always a Teacher

Age is only a number, a cipher for the records.
A man can't retire his experience. He must use it.
~Bernard Baruch

My hands trembled as I handed my husband the sealed, addressed envelope. "Please take this to the post office and mail it immediately. If you don't get it out of the house now, I'm apt to change my mind."

After mulling it over for weeks, I had made a decision. I would accept the Independence, Iowa school district's early-retirement offer and trudge off to that dismal world of blue-haired, early-bird-special retirees. To say I was less than enthusiastic about my pending "opportunity" would be an understatement. I was, in first grade terminology, one unhappy camper.

I taught squirming little six-year-old bundles of energy in five different school districts over a span of forty-two years, but it never felt like work. A teacher has a job; but a good teacher has a passion. I think most students, parents, colleagues and administrators regarded me as passionate. I loved the classroom and everything that went with it. Well, almost everything.

The pay was skimpy and the uncompensated overtime hours were endless. Much of the paperwork was state and/or federally mandated busywork, and staff development sessions fluctuated between boring and inane.

There were, however, many things that I would miss. I'd miss hearing the nervous little six-year-old read a five-word sentence for the first time. I wouldn't get any more precious handcrafted pictures with "I luv u" notations scribbled at the bottom. There would be no more "World's Best Teacher" ornaments for my Christmas tree. I'd never again hear the excitement in a little kid's voice as he exclaimed, "Now I get it!" I'd miss the support of parents, the leadership of administrators, and the camaraderie of colleagues. And finally, I would forever lose the satisfaction that goes with belonging to a group of people working toward a common goal.

I replayed these positives, and countless more, over and over in my mind as I struggled to make a decision about retiring. But the process always ended with the same question. What would be best for the kids?

Finally, after weeks of soul searching and more than a few tears, I knew what I had to do. Little munchkins deserve a teacher who can run and jump and climb on the monkey bars and crawl on the floor, and maintain patience — at all times. I had fulfilled that role for more than four decades, but those days were behind me. It was time to move on.

Move on? Where would I go? Retirement was a place where old people went to brag about their grandkids and complain about their aches and pains. It wasn't my idea of fun.

The following weeks evolved into a never-ending self-pity party, but without the gifts of sympathy or empathy. Parents, colleagues, friends and family members all seemed to think my elevator had gotten stuck on the way to the top. Earlier retirees told me in great detail about all the advantages they were privy to, and my younger friends whined about how much they envied my pending opportunity. Nothing helped. I was in a self-imposed funk. Fortunately, I didn't stay there long.

On my sixty-second birthday, a former student gave me a copy of *Chicken Soup for the Teacher's Soul*. I lived vicariously through all of the stories, but John Wayne Schlatter's "I Am a Teacher" was my wakeup call.

"Material wealth is not one of my goals," he wrote, "but I am a full-time treasure seeker in my quest for new opportunities..."

A-ha! There was the solution to my problem. If I wanted my retirement to be as fulfilling as my teaching career had been, I had to stop wallowing in self-pity and start looking for new opportunities. It wasn't rocket science, but it was an idea that had not occurred to me.

Shortly after the school year ended I began writing *From the Teacher's Desk*, a help-your-child-succeed book for parents. My book didn't come close to making the New York Times bestseller list, but it did open doors that I hadn't known existed.

Two years later, I founded an interactive website for educators: www.theteachersdesk.com. I update the material on six of the site's links on the first day of every month throughout the school year, and e-mail monthly newsletters to more than 1,100 subscribers. I have written countless articles for parenting magazines and academic journals, as well as single chapters for two reference texts: *Visual Literacy* and *Reading in 2010 and Beyond*. My most recent book, *If They Don't Learn the Way You Teach... Teach the Way They Learn*, was released a couple of years ago.

When I'm not on the road I try to keep up with what's new in the world of education by subbing in my local school district and picking the brains of exemplary teachers, many of whom are former colleagues. I serve on the public library board in Independence, and on the Upper Iowa University Press Advisory Council. I provide professional development training throughout the Midwest during the school year, and teach several literacy workshops each summer.

International Reading Association State Conferences are the fragrant flowers in my retirement pasture. To date I have been one of several featured speakers at seventy-two IRA conferences, with more on the docket. These stimulating and enjoyable venues have made it possible for my husband and me to visit nearly every state in the union, to participate in new activities, to try new foods and to make new friends. Ah yes, retirement is great. And no, my hair isn't blue.

Alexander Graham Bell said, "When one door closes another

door opens; but we so often look so long and so regretfully upon the closed door, that we do not see the ones which open for us."

Teacher John Wayne Schlatter illuminated my open doors through his "I Am a Teacher" story, and the memory of 1,500 former students inspired me to walk through those doors. It was a powerful lesson that has served me well.

~Jacquie McTaggart

I Am a Teacher

Teaching creates all other professions.
~Author Unknown

I am a teacher.

I was born the first moment that a question leaped from the mouth of a child.

I have been many people in many places.

I am Socrates exciting the youth of Athens to discover new ideas through the use of questions.

I am Anne Sullivan tapping out the secrets of the universe into the outstretched hand of Helen Keller.

I am Aesop and Hans Christian Andersen revealing truth through countless stories.

I am Marva Collins fighting for every child's right to an education.

I am Mary McCloud Bethune building a great college for my people, using orange crates for desks.

And I am Bel Kaufman struggling to go *Up the Down Staircase*.

The names of those who have practiced my profession ring like a hall of fame for humanity… Booker T. Washington, Buddha, John Dewey, Leo Buscaglia, Moses and Jesus.

I am also those whose names and faces have long been forgotten but whose lessons and character will always be remembered in the accomplishments of their students.

I have wept for joy at the weddings of former students, laughed with glee at the birth of their children, and stood with head bowed in grief and confusion by graves dug too soon for bodies far too young.

Throughout the course of a day, I have been called upon to be an actor, friend, nurse and doctor, coach, finder of lost articles, money-lender, taxi driver, psychologist, substitute parent, salesman, politician, and a keeper of the faith.

Despite the maps, charts, formulas, verbs, stories and books, I have really had nothing to teach, for my students really have only themselves to learn, and I know it takes the whole world to tell you who you are.

I am a paradox. I speak loudest when I listen the most. My greatest gifts are in what I am willing to appreciatively receive from my students.

Material wealth is not one of my goals, but I am a full-time treasure seeker in my quest for new opportunities for my students to use their talents and in my constant search for those talents that sometimes lie buried in self-defeat.

I am the most fortunate of all who labor.

A doctor is allowed to usher life into the world in one magic moment. I am allowed to see that life is reborn each day with new questions, ideas and friendships.

An architect knows that if he builds with care, his structure may stand for centuries. A teacher knows that if he builds with love and truth, what he builds will last forever.

I am a warrior, daily doing battle against peer pressure, negativity, fear, conformity, prejudice, ignorance and apathy. But I have great allies: intelligence, curiosity, parental support, individuals, creativity, faith, love and laughter all rush to my banner with indomitable support.

And who do I have to thank for this wonderful life I am so fortunate to experience, but you the public, the parents. For you have done me the great honor to entrust me with your greatest contribution to eternity, your children.

And so I have a past that is rich in memories. I have a present that is challenging, adventurous and fun because I am allowed to spend my days with the future.

I am a teacher… and I thank God for it every day.

~John Wayne Schlatter

Knowing They Are Loved

Children make your life important.
~Erma Bombeck

"Hey Grandma, what can I do to help?" My four adopted grandchildren burst through the door. This was the first holiday that we were celebrating with them. My daughter had been trying for almost three years to jump through the hoops required by the Department of Social Services, so she and her husband could rescue their nieces and nephews from foster care and group homes and add them to their family.

Although from the beginning I harbored serious doubts about this endeavor, I knew how important these children were to my daughter and her husband. The birthmother of the children was my son-in-law's sister. Every contact with her, his parents and his other siblings had been disastrous for him and for my daughter. I worried that contact with the children meant increased contact with the rest of that family. Bits and pieces of information about the abuse the children had endured merely added to my conviction that the plan to adopt them was fraught with problems.

Of course I hated what these poor innocent children had suffered, but I worried that intervention would not be successful, especially for the older ones. I almost didn't write the letter of support that my daughter needed as part of her paperwork.

Then I read a vignette in the very first *Chicken Soup for the Soul* book. It was called "I Like Myself Now." That convinced me that our love for these kids might help them believe in themselves helped. I wrote the letter for my daughter.

What these delightful children, ranging in age from nine to sixteen had endured in their lives prior to their rescue, still makes my heart ache. Their birthmother, who used drugs and consistently exposed them to the abusive men in her life, had never provided a safe and stable home. After her parental rights had been taken away, the children seemed stuck in limbo.

During the waiting period, Sarah and her husband, Rob, visited the children frequently, celebrating birthdays and holidays, bringing gifts and love. Although we had never met them, my husband and I began to shop for gifts and send them with Sarah for those visits.

Listening to Sarah's stories about what the kids had endured was painful. But she tempered these stories with delightful anecdotes about their quirks and foibles. Their startlingly different personalities began to emerge in those stories. Without planning it, we began to love them long before we met them.

Finally Sarah and Rob became guardians and the children moved into their small house. The weekend after the kids came "home," my husband and I went to meet them.

To give the children some distance, we decided our first meeting would take place at a local family-friendly restaurant. Sarah and Rob are always prompt and as often happened, my husband and I were a few minutes late. As we pulled into the parking lot, the two boys, nine and twelve, erupted from the restaurant lobby with "Uncle Rob" in tow, and ran toward our moving vehicle.

We quickly exited the car, only to see that the boys had suddenly turned shy. Their eyes were huge and questioning. I could almost hear the question, "Can you love us?" hanging in the winter air. It seems likely, given their past, that they wondered if they would measure up to our standards. The minute we pulled them into a hug, the boys' tense bodies relaxed. They couldn't stop smiling.

The girls, fourteen and sixteen, more reserved than their brothers, were waiting just inside the restaurant door. The older one dazzled us with a wide and engaging smile, while the younger one accepted our hugs but held back.

Two years later, the oldest of the four and the one who had assumed the role of protector and mother, told us that she couldn't understand why we loved her, that she had been "such a brat."

Can you imagine the conviction she held that she could never measure up and we would reject her as everyone else in her life had done? For months after her arrival, she was frequently angry and out of control. Patience and love and her slow realization that her new family would love her regardless of what she did pulled her through those difficult times.

Since that first meeting my husband and I count our blessings that these children have become part of our family and are finding new pathways for themselves with the love and support that all of us willingly give them. Although they continue to struggle with the residue of those early years, I am convinced the progress they have made directly relates to the knowledge that they are loved.

~Judythe Guarnera

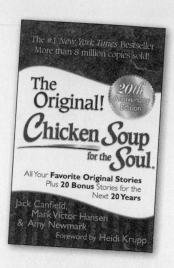

I Like Myself Now

Once you see a child's self-image begin to improve, you will see significant gains in achievement areas, but even more important, you will see a child who is beginning to enjoy life more.
~Wayne Dyer

I had a great feeling of relief when I began to understand that a youngster needs more than just subject matter. I know mathematics well, and I teach it well. I used to think that was all I needed to do.

Now I teach children, not math. I accept the fact that I can only succeed partially with some of them.

When I don't have to know all the answers, I seem to have more answers than when I tried to be the expert. The youngster who really made me understand this was Eddie. I asked him one day why he thought he was doing so much better than last year. He gave meaning to my whole new orientation: "It's because I like myself now when I'm with you," he said.

~A teacher quoted by Everett Shostrum in *Man, The Manipulator*

Worship Together

The test of courage comes when we are in the minority.
The test of tolerance comes when we are in the majority.
~Ralph W. Sockman

A story in *Chicken Soup for the Christian Family Soul* entitled, "A Guy Named Bill" made a big impact on my life. Bill was a college student dressed like a hippie. He didn't look like the other members of the middle-class church he visited one day. There was no place to sit, so Bill sat down on the carpet near the pulpit. An elderly deacon stood up and made his way to the young man. Everyone in the church expected him to take care of the situation by asking him to leave. They were surprised by the deacon's action. He dropped his cane and plopped down on the floor beside Bill and worshipped alongside him.

As a pastor's wife, I've served in many churches, both large and small. I've seen people who want to handpick the members who worship with them. Too many church members want people who look like them, think like them and act like them. They want to pick and choose those who attend "their" church. Of course, not all churches are like that; neither are all members. But some certainly are and they need to be taught that the church doesn't belong to them, but to God.

After reading "A Guy Named Bill," I was moved to tears. I knew of a small church where the congregation split because someone inside the church invited some people who were considered undesirable to attend. Let's just say the visitors didn't resemble the rest of the congregation.

When I heard of this situation, I decided that I would stand firm and insist that all people who want to worship in a church should be welcome. The authority of the church is neither with the pastor nor with the deacons. The church should not be run by committees of people. Charter members should have no say as to who can worship in the church. The authority of the church is God and God alone.

When God opens the door to a church, He opens it to all who want to come. I remember standing up inside a church one Sunday evening several years ago and saying, "If we have a welcome sign outside, we must welcome anyone who wants to worship. This is God's house and all people are welcome."

This boldness came after I read "A Guy Named Bill." If we want to join a social club that allows a select few to become members that is one thing. But nobody has the right to restrict anyone from coming to God's house to worship.

Today, I often speak at women's events—banquets, teas and conferences. I see a variety of ladies as I stand before them and share God's precious word with them. God does not show favoritism. Every time I look out over the audience, I see the people God loves.

It is my heart's desire that I will always demonstrate the same kind of love as the elderly deacon who met Bill at the front of the church. I will always welcome those who come with open arms. And I just might go and plop down beside them if they find a place on the floor.... Or better yet, I will offer them my seat, welcoming them in the same way God would welcome them. I will do unto others as I would have them to do unto me. I will show kindness.

~Nancy B. Gibbs

A Guy Named Bill

I'd rather see a sermon than hear one any day.
~Edgar A. Guest

His name was Bill. He had wild hair, wore a T-shirt with holes in it, blue jeans and no shoes. In the entire time I knew him I never once saw Bill wear a pair of shoes. Rain, sleet or snow, Bill was barefoot. This was literally his wardrobe for his whole four years of college.

He was brilliant and looked like he was always pondering the esoteric. He became a Christian while attending college. Across the street from the campus was a church full of well-dressed, middle-class people. They wanted to develop a ministry to the college students, but they were not sure how to go about it.

One day, Bill decided to worship there. He walked into the church, complete with wild hair, T-shirt, blue jeans and bare feet. The church was completely packed, and the service had already begun. Bill started down the aisle to find a place to sit. By now the people were looking a bit uncomfortable, but no one said anything.

As Bill moved closer and closer to the pulpit, he realized there were no empty seats. So he squatted and sat down on the carpet right up front. (Although such behavior would have been perfectly acceptable at a college fellowship, this was a scenario this particular congregation had never witnessed before!) By now, the people seemed uptight, and the tension in the air was thickening.

Right about the time Bill took his "seat," a deacon began slowly making his way down the aisle from the back of the sanctuary. The deacon was in his eighties, had silver-gray hair, a three-piece suit and a pocket watch. He was a godly man—very elegant, dignified and courtly. He walked with a cane and, as he neared the boy, church members thought, *You can't blame him for what he's going to do. How can you expect a man of his age and background to understand some college kid on the floor?*

It took a long time for the man to reach the boy. The church was utterly silent except for the clicking of his cane. You couldn't even hear anyone breathing. All eyes were on the deacon.

But then they saw the elderly man drop his cane on the floor. With great difficulty, he sat down on the floor next to Bill and worshipped with him. Everyone in the congregation choked up with emotion. When the minister gained control, he told the people, "What I am about to preach, you will never remember. What you've just seen, you will never forget."

~Rebecca Manley Pippert

Really Growing Up

The only way to make a man trustworthy is to trust him.
~Henry L. Stimson

I grew up in a small city in Connecticut and had everything going for me: great parents, two older brothers who watched out for me, and a good set of friends. But when I turned fifteen, I felt that I was being smothered by my family's rules and the rules at school.

Who were they to tell me what was best for me? I was smarter than any of those uptight rule makers! I skipped my sports practices and starting skipping class when I got into high school. I started smoking cigarettes, having a few beers, and smoked some pot with the "cool kids" on the path behind the school. I felt like I had finally figured out life and was having some real fun with my new friends, hot girls, and the coolest parties for the first time. By the time I was sixteen I had already experimented with some harsher drugs such as LSD and cocaine. I took Excedrin during the school day just to get the caffeine to make it through until lunch. Deep down I knew I was running down the wrong path but I didn't care.

During my sophomore year I started school with a new career selling pot. I was saving up for my first car, a Mitsubishi Conquest. I thought I would have the world at my fingertips once I didn't have to rely on my brothers and friends to drive me around. I trusted my new friends and thought they would stay by my side no matter what. Turns out one of my friends was getting "pinched" and set me up to sell to an undercover cop. I sold the cop some drugs a couple of times and a week later my home was raided. I was busted!

They surrounded my parents' house, ran in the back yard and attacked my older brother Dennis while he was cooking on the grill, pushed my mom onto the couch, and made my brother Chris come upstairs to join us on the couch in his boxers, which was a funny sight since he had been innocently listening to music in his room. Two cops yelled at me to "freeze and drop the weapon." I replied "It's ChapStick!" They tackled me and then a policewoman kept checking my back pockets and was getting frustrated because I didn't have a belt on and my pants kept falling down.

They only found a few joints in the house but with the cop's testimony I knew I was going away for a long time. They had four felonies on me and I could be spending the next twelve years in jail. I knew at that moment I had to start making better choices.

My parents got me a good lawyer and I got the break of a lifetime. I was sentenced to one year at Manson's Youth Institute and would have the chance to be home in six months if I demonstrated good behavior. I was never so scared in my life as when they brought me to an adult prison in New Haven to be processed. I will never forget that long ride in the "ice cream truck" as they called it.

Within the first week I was being bullied by the older inmates until I won my first fight and got the new nickname of "Baby Gerber" since I looked so innocent. The first two weeks were like being in hell because of all of the withdrawal symptoms. The corrections officers were amazing and gave me a bunch of sugar packets to combat the symptoms.

About a month or so into my stay my mom brought me a copy of *Chicken Soup for the Teenage Soul* from my aunt who couldn't come up to visit me. I never liked reading much and never even read any of the books I was supposed to in school but I read this book over and over every night. One of the stories that made a big impression on me was called "Broken Wing" and it was about a kid who had a long arrest record and was the biggest juvenile delinquent in his school. An adult decided to trust him, and actually put him in charge of a big charity program, and the kid turned out to be a born leader who earned everyone's respect and did a great job.

The book was like my escape. I read every story and related to each of them in some way or another. I started to write poetry for my girlfriend, jokes to do some stand up comedy to my friends, and songs for my new band once I got out. I started to realize that I had a choice as to how my life was going to go. I felt clearheaded for the first time in a long time. I knew that somehow I would be able to help others, just as this simple book was helping me. I was showing such progress and good behavior that I was going to be released six months early. My cellmate kept borrowing the book from me, so before I left I wrote a note on the back cover that said, "Don't judge a book by the cover—read it, if it helps you let me know. Here's my address…"

I am thirty-two years old now and I have a beautiful wife, two wonderful kids, a great family, and true friends. I have learned from my mistakes and I live a great life. Every once in a while I still get a letter from a kid in jail thanking me for leaving the book behind. As I walked out of that correctional facility many years ago the correctional officer told me "never look back or you'll be back." I took that advice seriously and have always looked ahead and appreciate that one-way ticket out of jail and trouble. I know that every day is a learning experience. We all make mistakes, but recognizing that once is a mistake and twice is a habit will help us to overcome any obstacle in life.

~Kevin Michael Nastu

Broken Wing

You were born with wings. Why prefer to crawl through life?
~Rumi

Some people are just doomed to be failures. That's the way some adults look at troubled kids. Maybe you've heard the saying, "A bird with a broken wing will never fly as high." I'm sure that T. J. Ware was made to feel this way almost every day in school.

By high school, T. J. was the most celebrated troublemaker in his town. Teachers literally cringed when they saw his name posted on their classroom lists for the next semester. He wasn't very talkative, didn't answer questions and got into lots of fights. He had flunked almost every class by the time he entered his senior year, yet was being passed on each year to a higher grade level. Teachers didn't want to have him again the following year. T. J. was moving on, but definitely not moving up.

I met T. J. for the first time at a weekend leadership retreat. All the students at school had been invited to sign up for ACE training, a program designed to have students become more involved in their communities. T. J. was one of 405 students who signed up. When I showed up to lead their first retreat, the community leaders gave me this overview of the attending students: "We have a total spectrum represented today, from the student body president to T. J. Ware, the boy with the longest arrest record in the history of town." Somehow, I knew that I wasn't the first to hear about T. J.'s darker side as the first words of introduction.

At the start of the retreat, T. J. was literally standing outside the circle of students, against the back wall, with that "go ahead, impress me" look on his face. He didn't readily join the discussion groups, didn't seem to have much to say. But slowly, the interactive games drew him in. The ice really melted when the groups started building a list of positive and negative things that had occurred at school that year. T. J. had some definite thoughts on those situations. The other students in T. J.'s group welcomed his comments. All of a sudden T. J. felt like a part of the group, and before long he was being treated like a leader. He was saying things that made a lot of sense, and everyone was listening. T. J. was a smart guy and he had some great ideas.

The next day, T. J. was very active in all the sessions. By the end of the retreat, he had joined the Homeless Project team. He knew something about poverty, hunger and hopelessness. The other students on the team were impressed with his passionate concern and ideas. They elected T. J. co-chairman of the team. The student council president would be taking his instruction from T. J. Ware.

When T. J. showed up at school on Monday morning, he arrived to a firestorm. A group of teachers were protesting to the school principal about his being elected co-chairman. The very first communitywide service project was to be a giant food drive, organized by the Homeless Project team. These teachers couldn't believe that the principal would allow this crucial beginning to a prestigious, three-year action plan to stay in the incapable hands of T. J. Ware. They reminded the principal, "He has an arrest record as long as your arm. He'll probably steal half the food." Mr. Coggshall reminded them that the purpose of the ACE program was to uncover any positive passion that a student had and reinforce its practice until true change can take place. The teachers left the meeting shaking their heads in disgust, firmly convinced that failure was imminent.

Two weeks later, T. J. and his friends led a group of 70 students in a drive to collect food. They collected a school record: 2,854 cans of food in just two hours. It was enough to fill the empty shelves in two neighborhood centers, and the food took care of needy families in the area for 75 days. The local newspaper covered the event with a full-page article the next day. That newspaper story was posted on the main bulletin board at school, where everyone could see it. T. J.'s picture was up there for doing something great, for leading a record-setting food drive. Every day he was reminded about what he did. He was being acknowledged as leadership material.

T. J. started showing up at school every day and answered questions from teachers for the first time. He led a second project, collecting 300 blankets and 1,000 pairs of shoes for the homeless shelter. The event he started now yields 9,000 cans of food in one day, taking care of 70 percent of the need for food for one year.

T. J. reminds us that a bird with a broken wing only needs mending. But once it has healed, it can fly higher than the rest. T. J. got a job. He became productive. He is flying quite nicely these days.

~Jim Hullihan

Coach Perry

I can do all things through Christ who strengthens me.
~Phillippians 4:13

My husband Perry was diagnosed with cerebral palsy at age four. At that time, he was falling occasionally when he walked. At the age of twenty years old in 1996, the doctors realized that Perry actually had hereditary spastic paraparesis (also known as familial spastic paraplegia or FSP). It is an inherited neurological disorder characterized by gradual development of stiffness (spastic) and variable degrees of weakness (paraplegia) in the muscle and legs. This disease also causes spasms in the legs, leg cramps, poor balance and fatigue. Perry experiences these symptoms every day. It is not certain right now how his mobility to walk will be affected in the future. At the right time, Perry and I hope our Heavenly Father will bless us with children to love and cherish, even though there is a 50/50 chance they will inherit this disorder.

As a result, Perry walks with a limp, dragging his toes with one foot in front of the other and uses the assistance of a cane. Without his cane, he walks around the house using walls, kitchen countertops and other furniture to help maintain his balance. Even though it takes every effort to walk and he feels tired throughout each day, Perry does not complain. With ongoing research, we hope and pray that his illness will someday be cured.

Despite his handicap, Perry has had a great love for sports

throughout his life. He was determined to play baseball and basketball with his friends when he was in middle school. Even with limitations, I admire him so much because Perry volunteers at the high school he graduated from. The students call him "Coach Perry." His title is Equipment Manager, but he is so much more than that. His dedication to the school is one of the reasons why I love him more each day.

Every football season, he dedicates himself to the team every day. After each practice and each game, he stays to make sure everything is put back where it belongs and then watches the replays with the other coaches. Sometimes I stay with him after the game. Perry has done this for twenty years plus, including four years as a student and he has only missed one game, due to the stomach flu. In December 8, 2006, my new family and I supported him and his school by going to the championship game at the New Orleans Superdome the night before our wedding day! He did not want to miss that for the world. His greatest football experience was in December of 2011, which happened to be the day after our fifth wedding anniversary, when the team went 15-0 and won their first state football championship in school history. All of those years had finally paid off!

Perry also enjoys being involved with other sports. He is the announcer for the boys' baseball team. If there is a function at the school and they need help, you will see him there. Because of everything he does, Coach Perry is well respected by the staff, students, and parents. He was "officially" recognized on May 12, 2007 at the St. Charles Catholic All Sports Banquet with the St. Charles Borromeo Award for loyalty and dedication to St. Charles Athletics. The St. Charles Borromeo Award recognizes members of the school community who have given their time and talents to make the athletic department the best it can be. There have been many students who look up to Perry as a role model. I could not be prouder of him in that moment!

Unfortunately at this time in the year of 2013, Perry feels he needs to step away because of the physical toll on his body due to the responsibilities of his occupation at school. It is uncertain when he will go back to the high school to do small physical tasks in the future.

With my husband's challenges and my own dyslexia and ADD, I was very moved by *Chicken Soup for the Unsinkable Soul*. Every story in this book is special. As I read it, I felt like the stories were encouraging me to not give up during the challenging times in our marriage. It gave me a peace of mind that with our faith and love for each other, Perry and I can overcome obstacles together, being strong for one another, as well as all the other families I have read about.

One story in particular, "Heaven's Very Special Child" by John and Edna Massamilla, grabbed my complete attention. It began in 1954 when a family was taking their handicapped daughter to an institution where doctors felt she should live with other children like her. The girl's mother turned on the car radio and heard a familiar voice. It was a former classmate of hers who had no legs. The next sentence blew me away. It read, "He was now president of an organization employing persons who are disabled."

I can't begin to describe how I felt when I read that sentence. What better way for a person to help those who are disabled, needing employment, when he is disabled himself!

~Michelle Duplessis Prudhomme

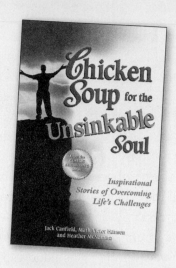

Heaven's Very Special Child

Every child comes with the message that God is not yet discouraged of man.
~Rabindranath Tagore

We were on our way to visit an institution in 1954 with our three daughters: Mary, twelve, Joan, nine, and Ruth, eighteen months old. Because of little Ruth, handicapped since birth, we were making this sad and silent trip. We had been advised to place her in a special home. "It will be less of a burden;" "Ruth will be better off with children like herself;" "Your other children will have a home free of the care of a disabled person."

To break the silence, I flipped on the car radio and heard the voice of a former classmate. I remembered him as a boy without legs. He was now president of an organization employing persons who are disabled.

He told of his childhood and of a conversation with his mother. "When it was time for another handicapped child to be born," his mother explained, "the Lord and his counselors held a meeting to decide where he should be sent... where there would be a family to love him. Well, our family was chosen."

At this, my wife Edna leaned over and turned off the radio, her eyes shining with unshed tears. "Let's go home," she said.

I touched Ruth's tiny face. She looked like a beautiful symbol of innocence. I knew at that moment Ruth was given to us for a purpose. How miraculous it was that the voice of a friend, with whom I'd had no contact for twenty years, should that day speak to me. Mere coincidence? Or was it God's unseen hand helping us hold on to a little girl who would enrich our lives immeasurably in the years that followed?

That night, Edna awoke at three o'clock in the morning with thoughts that demanded to be written. A pad was on the night table, and in the morning we pieced her notes together into the poem "Heaven's Very Special Child":

A meeting was held quite far from Earth;
"It's time again for another birth."
Said the angels to the Lord above,
"This special child will need much love.
Her progress may seem very slow.
Accomplishments she may not show,
And she'll require extra care
From the folks she meets way down there.
She may not run or laugh or play,
Her thoughts may seem quite far away.
In many ways she won't adapt,
And she'll be known as handicapped.
So let's be careful where she's sent,
We want her life to be content.
Please, Lord, find the parents who
Will do a special job for you.
They will not realize right away
The leading role they're asked to play,
But with this child sent from above

Come stronger faith and richer love.
And soon they'll know the privilege given
In caring for this gift from heaven.
Their precious charge, so meek and mild,
Is heaven's very special child."

~John and Edna Massimilla

The Gift of Giving

Wherever a man turns he can find someone who needs him.
~Albert Schweitzer

E ver since the death of my twenty-eight-year-old son Don, Jr., I have given a donation at Christmas or on his birthday in his loving memory. In past years, I had help from the Internet grief support group that I'd found the year of his passing. At Christmas we would pick a family in need and buy them gifts, or make baby blankets and quilts for a hospital, or donate books or art supplies to a school in need. Our projects were varied, and after we voted, we would all chip in to make magic happen in memory of our children.

A few years ago, after our group dwindled down to five and the money wasn't as easy to come by, we decided to discontinue our projects at Christmas time. One of our members lost her husband, so the rest of us voted to send her the remaining money in our Sunshine Fund that we used for our projects. The money helped her pay for his funeral, since his passing was sudden and unexpected. We told each other that we still could do small projects and the money would come out of our own pockets at the time of the donation. If one of the moms wanted to do a project on her child's birthday, we would vote on it and see if we were in agreement and able to help the mom with the expense of her donation.

In the past, I had made several donations on my son's October birthday and had the help of my online friends. I knew, however, that a big donation would put a burden on most of our group since many of us were struggling to keep gas in our cars and food on our tables, and were existing on our Social Security checks alone. With Don's birthday drawing near, I knew it would be difficult to find the money to make a substantial donation in his memory.

Then I remembered a story I'd read and a line from that story kept flashing in my mind: "You're never so poor you have nothing to give." Where was that story? I got out my *Chicken Soup for the Soul* books and began to investigate.

Oh, yes... it had to be in the *Chicken Soup for the Soul: Count Your Blessings* book! Sure enough, I came across the story, (perhaps with a little divine help), titled "Never Too Poor To Give." I knew there had to be a project that I could afford to do. I just had to put on my thinking cap!

Since my husband is dealing with cancer and chemotherapy treatments, we spend a lot of time in waiting rooms. It dawned on me that there were a lot of other people there at the same time as us. Most were waiting to get into their chemotherapy chairs for their treatments. Others were family members, passing the time waiting for their loved ones to finish so they could transport them home.

Books! That's what Drema, who wrote the story, found that she could pass on to others! I had books I had finished, so I gathered them up to take to the chemotherapy rooms and leave for the patients there.

On one of my trips with my husband, I noticed several children in the waiting rooms. That's when I got the idea to create "coloring packs" for them to use as they waited. I could go on the Internet to find free coloring pages and print them out for the children. I also purchased some very reasonable coloring books, which came in "party favor" packs of four for a dollar. I packed Ziploc bags with a coloring book, a few coloring pages, and a handful of crayons. I made them for girls and boys and I used popular movie and cartoon characters. I had such fun doing this, and as I thought of the children receiving them and the smiles on their previously bored faces as they waited, it made me so happy!

As I write this story, October is very near, and my supply of gifts is growing. When my online mom's group heard what I was doing, some sent me crayons and small coloring books, and one mom sent a check to help me buy more printer ink for my pages!

I am excited to take the books to the oncologist's chemotherapy room and the "coloring activity packs" to the hospital waiting area for children to use. I am sure the volunteers there will be happy to give them out as needed! And what a warm feeling in my heart as I carry on our projects to honor our wonderful children, at a very low cost.

It is true. "You're never so poor you have nothing to give." And if my resources run out, I can always give my time. There are people who need rides to chemotherapy.

~Beverly F. Walker

Never Too Poor to Give

No one has ever become poor by giving.
~Anne Frank

"Don't you have any toys you want to share?" I asked my son during our church's Christmas toy drive. "What about all those things in your closet you haven't used in years?"

"I don't have anything," he said. "We're so poor."

We're only "poor" because we refuse to buy him the texting phone he wants for Christmas, which would also require a monthly texting charge.

"You're never so poor you have nothing to give," I found myself saying to him, a phrase my mother often used on me.

How could I help him understand, when I myself still whined about things I wanted, like the *Fowler's Modern English Usage* book that cost nearly $40? I knew Santa Hubby wasn't going to pony up for that one. What about that Vera Wang coat I wanted from Kohl's, the one with the $150 price tag? No, that wasn't happening, either.

At work the next day, one of my students said, "I didn't spell your name right," as she handed me a Christmas gift — a beribboned box of chocolates. No wonder she hadn't spelled it right—I had only worked at the center for a couple of months, and my name is not easy to pronounce, even in English, which is this woman's second language.

The woman had been out of work for months!

"Thank you, Joanna," I said, trying to hold back the tears as I hugged her.

I hadn't expected a gift—I work at an adult education center, where we deal with people every day who struggle economically. The economic downturn is not new to those who come in our doors—those who are laid off, without work, and need an education to get ahead or for a sense of pride. When I was hired, my boss told me she tries to keep snacks around the center and cooks "stone soup" once a week, where whoever can bring something in does, because "You will hear growling bellies here. They give their food to the children before they themselves eat."

"Some of them get food stamps," my boss continued, "but by the end of the month, things are tight. We try not to plan field trips where they would have to pack a lunch because sometimes they just won't show up because they don't even have a sandwich to bring along."

And yet these people, so grateful for a second chance at getting an education, unable to sometimes even afford the gas money to come in, manage to do something for us nearly every week. Some bring in food; others do chores around the center. They help and encourage one another, and us. They give what they are able to give.

When I looked at my Christmas gift from my new friend, I wondered if it had been an offering out of a meager food budget, and I wanted to refuse it. Instead, I said "thank you."

When I brought the candies home to share with my family, I told them just how precious each chocolate was if you thought of how much the unemployed woman's family makes a year. Why, it was the equivalent of a *Fowler's Modern English Usage* book! I said it again, understanding so much better in my heart, "You're never so poor you have nothing to give."

Perhaps the way I could help my son understand best was for me to understand first.

Immediately, I went to my bookshelf and chose several of my favorite novels to share with the center. When I had them boxed, I turned to find my son nonchalantly lugging a white laundry basket of toys he had played with when younger. "I don't want these old things," he said.

I saw among them his beloved Buzz Lightyear and his favorite stuffed dog, Squishy. I set them aside for the toy drive and kissed him on his forehead. He had learned the way I had—by example. Now the students had not only impacted me, but my family as well. Here I had thought I was the teacher, but Joanna and the rest of the students at the center are the ones teaching me. Because you're never so poor you have nothing to give.

~Drema Sizemore Drudge

Hugging Day

You can't wrap love in a box, but you can wrap a person in a hug.
~Author Unknown

One day at church, a good friend gave me a "just thinking of you" gift wrapped in pink tissue paper. It was the original *Chicken Soup for the Soul* and it had just been published. The book was filled with interesting and uplifting stories. I remember I began reading it that very night. I would read an entry or two before going to bed each night. One evening I read a story about hugging called "It Can't Happen Here?" The opening quotation by Virginia Satir said we need four hugs a day for survival, eight for maintenance and twelve hugs a day to grow.

A graduate of one of Jack Canfield's workshops had written a letter to him to describe how she had instituted a "hugs day" at her workplace. She wanted to share with her mentor the positive outcome.

I read this story on a Tuesday. I know it was Tuesday because on Wednesday I walked into my second grade classroom and declared that henceforth every Wednesday would be known as "Hugging Day." I told my second graders everyone needs hugs to live and grow.

I was already a hugger and had always greeted my students with a warm hug each morning. But after reading the story in this new book, I decided that on "Hugging Day" everyone needed to make sure they got at least twelve hugs. I wanted my students to grow. All hugs didn't have to come from me, but I was ready, willing, and able to dole out as many as needed.

My students lined up at my desk with questions and left with a hug. They hugged me before recess and after lunch. They hugged me when they came to school in the morning and when they left for home in the afternoon. The practice spilled over into other parts of the school. Soon the art teacher was helping the children collect their hugs. The gym teacher and music teacher offered their arms to the cause as well. The principal, a long time believer in hugging, dropped by every Wednesday to help make sure the children met their quota. And perhaps best of all, the children in my classroom hugged each other.

Every Wednesday my students counted and charted their hugs to make sure they were getting their fair share. I continued the practice for several years, even after I moved from the second grade classroom and started teaching kindergarten.

Through the years I hugged rich kids and poor kids, smelly kids and clean kids. I wrapped my arms around a boy with a brain tumor and a girl who was deaf. I hugged children with an array of disabilities and diagnosed disorders. I hugged children who were gifted academically and others whose gifts lay elsewhere. I hugged children who were fluent in English and a child who only spoke Chinese. I hugged children coming from all sorts of family situations and living conditions. Hugging Day was a success.

I was cleaning up my classroom one Wednesday afternoon after my newest kindergarten class had gone home. I needed to get everything ready for the next day. I put new activities out on the tables, checked the hamster cage to make sure Houdini was still locked in safe and sound, and set up the calendar center to welcome my students to a new day of school.

"Is Wednesday still Hugging Day?" a soft voice called into the empty classroom.

I looked up to see a tall beautiful blond teenage girl standing in the doorway of my classroom. I will never forget that moment.

"Nicole?" I said, as my former second grader entered. She fell into my arms and began to sob. I hugged her and comforted her as best I could. We sat down in the tiny chairs designed for kindergarten children.

Nicole told me how her father had been killed in a truck accident only a few weeks earlier. We talked, we cried, and eventually we both left that room to go our separate ways.

But I learned something new that day. It doesn't always take four hugs to survive. Sometimes it just takes one.

~Rebecca Waters

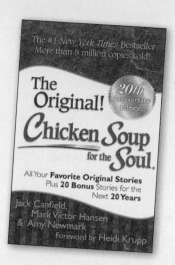

It Can't Happen Here?

We need 4 hugs a day for survival. We need 8 hugs a day for maintenance.
We need 12 hugs a day for growth.
~Virginia Satir

We always teach people to hug each other in our workshops and seminars. Most people respond by saying, "You could never hug people where I work." Are you sure?

Here is a letter from a graduate of one of our seminars.

> *Dear Jack,*
>
> *I started out this day in rather a bleak mood. My friend Rosalind stopped over and asked me if I was giving hugs today. I just grumbled something but then I began to think about hugs and everything during the week. I would look at the sheet you gave us on How to Keep the Seminar Alive and I would cringe when I got to the part about giving and getting hugs because I couldn't imagine giving hugs to the people at work.*
>
> *Well, I decided to make it "hugs day" and I started giving hugs to the customers who came to my counter. It was great to*

see how people just brightened up. An MBA student jumped up on top of the counter and did a dance. Some people actually came back and asked for more. These two Xerox repair guys, who were kind of just walking along not really talking to each other, were so surprised, they just woke up and suddenly were talking and laughing down the hall.

It feels like I hugged everybody in the Wharton Business School, plus whatever was wrong with me this morning, which included some physical pain, is all gone. I'm sorry that this letter is so long but I'm just really excited. The neatest thing was, at one point there were about 10 people all hugging each other out in front of my counter. I couldn't believe this was happening.

Love,
Pamela Rogers

P.S.: On the way home I hugged a policeman on 37th Street. He said, "Wow! Policemen never get hugs. Are you sure you don't want to throw something at me?"

Another seminar graduate, Charles Faraone, sent us the following piece on hugging:

Hugging Is

Hugging is healthy. It helps the immune system, cures depression, reduces stress and induces sleep. It's invigorating, rejuvenating and has no unpleasant side effects. Hugging is nothing less than a miracle drug.

Hugging is all natural. It is organic, naturally sweet, no artificial ingredients, nonpolluting, environmentally friendly and 100 percent wholesome.

Hugging is the ideal gift. Great for any occasion, fun to give and receive, shows you care, comes with its own wrapping and, of course, fully returnable.

Hugging is practically perfect. No batteries to wear out, inflation-proof, nonfattening, no monthly payments, theft-proof and nontaxable.

Hugging is an underutilized resource with magical powers. When we open our hearts and arms, we encourage others to do the same.

Think of the people in your life. Are there any words you'd like to say? Are there any hugs you want to share? Are you waiting and hoping someone else will ask first? Please don't wait! Initiate!

~Jack Canfield

Chapter 6

READER'S CHOICE

Amazing Connections

*Again, you can't connect the dots looking forward;
you can only connect them looking backwards. So you have to trust
that the dots will somehow connect in your future. You have to trust in
something—your gut, destiny, life, karma, whatever. This approach
has never let me down, and it has made all the difference in my life.*

~Steve Jobs

I Was Prepared

Oh, my friend, it's not what they take away from you that counts.
It's what you do with what you have left.
~Hubert Humphrey

We had recently married and we were expecting a baby girl in the summer, but first, I had to say goodbye to my Army husband. He was sent to Afghanistan on March 15, 2011 for a twelve-month deployment.

He didn't have to go, because his military service was ending over the summer. But he wanted to serve in Afghanistan so badly that he extended his duty so he could go.

I used to read *Chicken Soup for the Teenage Soul* and bought every one I could find in the series. When I learned there was a book called *Chicken Soup for the Military Wife's Soul*, I immediately went to buy it and read it every single night.

About a week after I bought the book, I read "Newfound Heroes," a story about a military wife like me who got a call from her husband while he was deployed because he had been shot and seriously injured. While reading the story I kept stopping to think about how I would react if I received a similar phone call. When I read that, despite his injuries, her husband could still walk, I wondered what we would do if my husband called to say he had lost his legs. Our lives flashed before my eyes and I thought about how we would manage, how difficult it would be, and how our lives would change. I imagined the two of us with our little girl, only she was about five and playing at the beach. My husband and I were holding hands and smiling. Everything was okay and it didn't seem so different after all.

I told myself that no matter what, things would be okay. That I would have the strength to stick by my husband through it all. I finished reading this story, closed my book, took a big breath, and fell asleep.

The next day (exactly four weeks after he had left), I received a phone call from my husband. I had been sleeping when he called but I sat straight up to talk to him. He sounded normal and I felt so relieved to hear from him because I hadn't heard from him for about a week.

He asked if I would like to talk to him for a couple of minutes. I said yes, of course. Then he fell silent, and I could tell he had something to say. He told me he was coming home. I was so shocked and confused that I thought maybe a miracle happened and they were starting to send the troops home. I had to ask him why a few times, though, before he told me what happened.

He had been hit by an IED.

In tears, I asked if he was okay. He assured me he was, but it didn't make sense. He had been hit and injured by an IED during his earlier tour of duty in Iraq, but still stayed and finished his tour. I knew they wouldn't send him home if he were okay. Then he told me that he had lost a leg.

Of course I cried. But I also realized this must be so much harder on him and I tried to hold it together as much as I could for him. It wasn't until after we got off the phone that I let myself cry until I couldn't any longer.

After a day of waiting for information, I learned the extent of my husband's injuries. He had lost his right leg from the knee down, his ring finger on his right hand, and the tip of his pinkie. He also sustained multiple shrapnel wounds on his left thigh and both hands.

At some point in the day, shortly after talking to my husband, I realized everything happens for a reason. As unfortunate as this is, my husband still has his life. He came home to me and our unborn child. He got to witness his child being born and he won't have to worry about missing a thing.

My husband was meant to serve in Afghanistan because that's what he always had wanted. He needed to go for his sake. He would have always had regrets if he had decided to not go.

Reading that story in *Chicken Soup for the Military Wife's Soul* was the one that gave me the foresight I needed. It was the one that gave me the strength to see the big picture. It prepared me for what was to come. You never know your strength until being strong is the only option. And you could never guess how you will act in a certain situation; you can only prepare for it. I don't know how I would have reacted if I had not read "Newfound Heroes," and thought about being in a similar situation, the night before my husband's call. It may have been more difficult for me to see the big picture.

We will get through this. And someday, when our daughter is five, we will be at the beach holding hands, smiling, as if nothing ever happened. I just know it.

~Tracy Fitzgerald

Newfound Heroes

No matter what accomplishments you make, somebody helped you.
~Althea Gibson

In September 2003 my husband Bill left for Iraq. This deployment was to be different: he was heading to a war zone where our soldiers were being killed and injured. I tried to calm us all by telling the children and myself that he would be okay. He was an excellent soldier. He was part of a well-trained unit with a good command group. He would be fine. The children were scared, they missed him terribly, but we were managing.

On April 14, 2004, that all changed. The telephone rang, and I heard Bill's voice. He was asking me what I was doing, as if it was a normal call home. I could hear in his voice that something was wrong, and asked him if he was okay. He told me that he had been shot, but that everything would be all right. I felt my stomach drop and my blood run cold, one of my worst fears becoming a reality. He had been hit in the left side, the bullet exiting the right side. When he called, he had just arrived at a Baghdad hospital and been stabilized. Some wonderful individual had given him a satellite phone to call me. He was able to talk for a few precious moments and then had to go. He was being flown out to Landstuhl Hospital in Germany.

As I hung up the phone, a deep sense of panic set in. I had so many questions that I had not thought to ask while he was on the phone; I didn't know when I would hear from him again and didn't know what to do. I have never felt so helpless in my life. I wanted to be by his side; however, that was not possible. The waiting began.

The next day, there was still no word from him. After an hour of inquiries, transfers and wrong rooms, I was finally connected to his room in Germany. He was doing well, in a lot of pain, but alive. The bullet had missed all his major organs. There were shattered bones along the spinal cord, broken ribs and fragments throughout his lower back. It was a bad injury, but he was still able to walk. At that moment, I realized how blessed we were, how miraculous it was that he was able to talk to me at all on the phone.

He arrived home on April 21. The doctors told us that this was going to be a very long recovery but that they believed he would make a full recovery. They also told us how incredibly lucky we were that he was in this condition. The fact that the bullet missed any vital organs was an absolute miracle, and we counted ourselves extremely lucky.

My husband has always been a hero to me, but even more so now — he came home to me. I also found a new set of heroes that day: the soldiers who fought beside him. There was a soldier who lost his own life in that battle. There were others who were wounded beside him. There was the wonderful man who pulled my husband to safety amidst a barrage of bullets. There was the medic who worked on him, keeping him alive until help could arrive. And there were the medical personnel who evacuated him and kept him alive until he could be treated. All these people were heroes to me before, in spirit; however, after this day, they became so in reality. I will never meet them all, will never know most of the men who helped to save his life, but they are my heroes all the same.

~Carol Howard

Postcard from My Past

History never looks like history when you are living through it.
~John W. Gardner

My medical evacuation helicopter crew of four wasn't aware that we were about to be thrust into the middle of a major battle. It was late August 1969 in South Vietnam. The battle would involve four regiments of the U.S. Army's 196th Light Infantry Brigade, two battalions of the U.S. 7th Marines and batteries of the U.S. 82nd Artillery that provided fire support from four firebases located approximately thirty to thirty-five miles southwest of Da Nang. These Americans would be facing 1,500 Communist soldiers.

As operations officer for the 236th Medical Detachment (Helicopter Ambulance), headquartered at Red Beach in Da Nang, I'd assigned myself—from August 20-22—as copilot for our field-site crew at Landing Zone Baldy, twenty miles south of Da Nang. As a rookie pilot, I'd barely been in the unit a month.

In those two and a half days of devastating action, our crew evacuated 150 wounded Americans from the Que Son Valley near Hiep Duc on forty-two missions, fifteen of which were "insecure." This meant that our ground troops couldn't guarantee the safety of the landing zones because the enemy was in close contact or our friendlies were low on ammunition and couldn't provide sufficient covering fire.

On a majority of these insecure missions, helicopter gunships weren't available to cover our unarmed aircraft because there was too much action requiring their services in other parts of this battleground. So our only alternative was to go in alone, because most of the wounded wouldn't have survived if we'd waited for gunships to arrive.

During the morning of August 21st, our UH-1H (Huey) was shot up by enemy AK-47 rifle fire while exiting another insecure landing zone. One of our three patients was wounded for the second time. A burst of enemy fire ripped into a can of oil our crew chief kept under my armored seat, spraying oil over my Nomex flight pants. Another round locked me in my shoulder harness when it clipped a wire on the unlocking device attached to the left side of my seat. We deposited our patients at the Baldy battalion aid station while another helicopter was being flown out for our use.

Less than twenty-four hours later (August 22nd), we were shot up for the second time on another insecure mission while evacuating an African-American infantry staff sergeant who'd been shot in the back. Our medic was wounded in the throat on our way in. An AK-47 round tore out his larynx. Two of our three radios were also shot out and there were a number of bullet holes above my head in the cockpit and other areas of the aircraft.

In the aid station I held our medic's legs while a doctor performed a tracheotomy without anesthesia, because the wound had swollen so quickly he couldn't breathe. Fortunately, he somehow survived but had to endure over a dozen follow-up surgeries... one of which ultimately gave him back a voice.

Thirty-two years later, an intriguing chain of events began that would impact my life. It began with a story titled "The Postcard" by Rocky Bleier with David Eberhart in *Chicken Soup for the Veteran's Soul*. This book caught my attention as I was browsing through displays in a Lincoln, Nebraska bookstore. As I glanced at the first paragraph of his story, the words "Hiep Duc, in the Que Son Valley of South Vietnam," and "August 20, 1969," stopped me in my tracks.

These words instantly brought back decades-old memories of danger, darkness and death.

Since that first paragraph of Bleier's story had caught my attention, I purchased the book, read the entire story and then decided to do some additional research. I'd heard that Bleier had written an autobiography titled *Fighting Back* (with Terry O'Neil). This book covered his early life, the fact that he'd been drafted into the army in 1968 and details concerning his subsequent service in Vietnam in 1969 where he'd been severely wounded in both legs. He also provided the inspiring story of how he'd overcome his wounds, and a right foot that doctors thought—at one point—would have to be amputated, to win four NFL Super Bowls as a running back for the Pittsburgh Steelers in 1974, 1975, 1978 and 1979.

I was able to acquire a copy of the 1995 edition of Bleier's book through an out-of-print book dealer and I sat down to read it as soon as it arrived in 2002.

Before reading the first chapter, I glanced at the "Contents" page. Chapter 7 quickly caught my attention. It was titled "August 20, 1969." That was when things became nearly unbelievable.

On August 20th, Bleier was an M-79 grenadier with the 196th Light Infantry Brigade. He was wounded twice near Million Dollar Hill east of Hiep Duc. His book mentioned that a medevac helicopter had already completed two previous missions to their location that night evacuating other wounded Company C comrades. Bleier was the next to last patient on this third and final flight to be evacuated to Baldy's aid station at 2:00 a.m. on the 21st. That's when it hit me.

I went to my military file and pulled out my combat flight records. Then I retrieved a citation for the Distinguished Flying Cross that our entire crew had been awarded for those two and a half days of action. Everything fit. Our unit's lone field-site was at Baldy and I only assigned one crew there at a time. Hiep Duc and Million Dollar Hill were in our area of operation and I suddenly recalled landing on the same hill three times in one night during that time. There wasn't any doubt we were the medevac crew that had evacuated Bleier and his company comrades that hectic night.

Bleier's *Chicken Soup for the Soul* story made a big difference in my life. I had no idea who we were carrying that night. They were all wounded Americans and it was our responsibility to evacuate them from that dangerous mountaintop.

None of us ever know whose life we will step into or who will step into ours. That's one of the exciting and interesting wonders of life. Ernest Hemingway said, "The world (and also combat) breaks everyone and afterward many are strong at the broken places." Perhaps this is what happened to Bleier, our flight crew and so many others who've survived war. Adversity has a way of introducing us to ourselves.

If I hadn't come across Bleier's story, "The Postcard," in *Chicken Soup for the Veteran's Soul*, I never would have discovered how our crew's efforts—and other doctors and medical personnel—had an impact on football history. I will always be thankful we were given the privilege of assisting those courageous American warriors that night in Vietnam.

~Robert B. Robeson

Stories to Stir the
Pride and Honor the
Courage of Our Veterans

Jack Canfield, Mark Victor Hansen
and Sidney R. Slagter

The Postcard

Faith is the quiet cousin of courage.
~Judith Hanson Lasater

The ambush came out of nowhere and everywhere. My platoon members and I were strung out and moving through the bush near Hiep Duc in the Que Son Valley of South Vietnam. It was August 20, 1969, and, as always, it was hot and wet.

All at once, the distinctive angry staccato of the enemies' AK-47 assault rifles filled the air. It was mixed with a different sound, that of a heavier machine gun. The incoming rounds slapped and tore through the foliage. Adding to the din were the shouts of the platoon sergeant to return fire. Company C of the 196th Light Infantry Brigade was in trouble.

Suddenly, it felt as if someone had smacked me—hard—with a baseball bat on the left thigh. I had been hit by one of the incoming rounds! I tried to scramble out of harm's way, but there was no escape from the withering fire. Then I heard the ear-splitting "ruuump!" of a grenade explosion, and the baseball bat smashed down hard again, this time pounding onto my right leg and foot.

My memory after that is of crawling—for what seemed like

forever. I later calculated that over the course of six hours, I had dragged myself across two miles of ground. I did a lot of thinking and remembering in that time.

At one point during my slow and painful journey, it occurred to me that I'd had the peculiar fortune to have been "drafted" twice. In January 1968, I was a late-round draft pick for the Pittsburgh Steelers, and in November of that year, the U.S. Army drafted me. In my weakened condition, I found this double-draft thing infinitely amusing.

But the joke soon faded, and my mind once again tried to grasp the reason that I was in Vietnam at all. The political reasons for the U.S. being there were easy to understand. The difficult part for a soldier like me to comprehend was my role in this conflict. I had been over all this in my mind many times before, and I always came back to an incident that had happened early on in my tour.

We had come across a village—not even a village, really, but just a couple of hooches inland. There was a family there—kids, an old man and an old lady. I saw that they didn't have anything—except for an old tin can. They had filled the tin can with water and put it on an open fire to boil. When I looked inside the can, I saw a buffalo hoof. That pathetic soup was their sustenance. I decided right then that if I could help these people take a step forward, then my time in the country would be worthwhile.

As it happened, my opportunity to follow through was cut short. My wounds got me evacuated to Tokyo, where the docs told me I had nearly lost my right foot and that I would never play football again. They informed me I was getting discharged with 40 percent disability.

This was not good news. Football was my whole life and dream—a dream that had started in Appleton, Wisconsin, at Xavier High School and matured at Notre Dame, where I had been voted the captain of the Fighting Irish in 1967. There wasn't anything else in my life I wanted to do. Football was something I identified with and that defined me.

It was a black time for me. Wounded and depressed, I tried to contemplate a future without football. Then I received a postcard from Art Rooney, the owner of the Steelers. He had written only, "We'll see you when you get back."

Such simple words, but their impact was immediate. It was then that I determined that I would be back—I would fight this thing with everything I had. The first thing on the program was learning to walk again on what remained of my right foot.

With more patience and resolve than I knew I had, I succeeded. In 1970, I returned to the Steelers and was placed on injured reserve. By the following year, I was on the taxi squad. In 1973, I made special teams. That year, I began running. In 1974, I was still running—but now I wore the Steelers' number 20 jersey.

We won the Super Bowl that year. We won again in 1975, 1978 and 1979. Franco Harris and I ran and ran, setting some modest records along the way.

In 1980, I retired from football, having—against all probability—lived my dream. I have tried to thank providence for my exceptional second chance by serving as a board member of the Vietnam Veterans Memorial Fund and being involved with charities for disabled children. I've also done a lot of professional motivational speaking, hoping to inspire others to overcome any obstacles that may bar their way.

In my talks, I always tell people about Art Rooney, whose faith in me was contagious. As long as I live, I don't believe that I will ever experience more inspirational words than the simple sentence written on that long-ago postcard: "We'll see you when you get back."

~Rocky Bleier with David Eberhart

The Infinite Worth of a Nickel

Don't be discouraged. It's often the last key in the bunch that opens the lock.
~Author Unknown

I looked at the clock as the phone rang. Who was calling so early on a Saturday morning? The caller ID provided no help. "Private." It was probably a sales call.

"Hello?"

The woman on the other end said, "I'm looking for…"

Listening, impatiently, as the caller mispronounced my name, I readied myself to give a polite, but firm, "We're not interested." I was barely paying attention to what was being said when I heard "Chicken Soup" mentioned.

"Did you have a story published in *Chicken Soup for the Soul*?" she had asked.

My curiosity was piqued. "Yes."

"Well, there was an article about you in the paper…"

"Yes," I said again, not sure where my anonymous caller was going with this, and still a bit annoyed by the early morning call.

And then she said: "I think I'm your daughter."

Twenty-three years had gone by since I held my baby close, sang lullabies to her, prayed over her and kissed her sweet face, trying to pour as much love into her as possible in a few short days. Not a week passed I didn't think of Meagan and long to hold her again. As a twenty-three-year-old myself at the time, I carefully weighed my options when I discovered I was pregnant. I decided adoption would be the best option, not only for me, but for my child as well. It was an excruciating choice.

For nearly twenty-two hours, I had struggled to bring this child into the world and as the pain intensified, so did my doubts about my choice. Finally, I had delivered the most beautiful baby girl. Although I had loved her throughout my pregnancy, it was only when I looked into her brown eyes for the first time that I felt *in love* with her. My heart sang with praise for the miracle of her. Tears ran down my cheeks as she was placed into my arms. Meagan Rae, my sweet baby girl.

Three days later, I handed her to a nurse and walked out of the hospital, leaving a large part of my heart with her as I drove away. Everything in me wanted to turn and go back, but I knew it wasn't a time for selfishness. This wasn't about me; it was all about her.

Having two more daughters never took away my grief over losing my firstborn. My children grew up knowing about their half-sister and prayed she would find us someday. On that early October morning, she did.

"Did you ever think about me on my birthday?" Meagan asked. That was an easy one to answer. Every September, I mourned. I bought birthday cards, wrote in them, sealed the envelopes and put them away, hoping that someday I would be able to share them with her. Candles were lit on a yearly birthday cake as my husband, children and I would sing to her empty chair. It was a ritual.

"Did I ever think of you on your birthday?" I repeated her question. "Any number of my friends can answer that one for you." Recounting our yearly tradition to her made all of it worthwhile, no matter how painful it had been.

After being on the phone for nearly an hour, we agreed to meet that afternoon. Raised only ten miles away and in search of me for years, Meagan didn't want to wait another day. Neither did I.

The night before that early morning phone call, I had spent hours searching a birthparent/adoptee reunion website. I kept my updated contact information on the site, making it readily available in case my daughter was searching for me. With tears streaming down my cheeks, I cried, "Meagan, where are you? Why can't you find me?" I prayed for God to bring her to me. More than anything else in my life, I wanted to see my little girl. Crying myself to sleep, I wondered why God wouldn't answer my prayer.

At the same time, Meagan's adoptive mother was up late working on the computer. Suddenly, my name flashed through her mind. She had seen it, upside down, on the adoption papers twenty-three years earlier, but could never remember how to spell it. However, clarity hit at that moment and she typed it into a search engine. A link for a newspaper article appeared on the screen.

Earlier that year, "The Nickel Story" had been published in *Chicken Soup for the Grieving Soul*. It was a touching story about love, loss, and a very special nickel. I wrote about my friends, Frank and Susan, who lived close by and worshipped at the same church as my family. After being published, someone on the staff at Chicken Soup for the Soul suggested I send out a press release about being included in the anthology. After mailing it to several area newspapers, I was actually surprised when one contacted me for an interview, complete with a photograph.

"You have to come home," Meagan's mom had nearly shouted into the phone the night before. "I found her! I found your birthmother!"

Meagan had stayed up all night with her mom, waiting for morning to come so she could finally call me. They read the article, talked about the two sisters she never knew, and discussed her fears. She had no way of knowing I'd been praying for this reunion, nor that her sisters were praying for it as well.

The moment arrived. My heart pounded as I watched Meagan's parents emerge from the van, followed by her brother and his wife, and finally, my daughter—my baby girl. I wasn't prepared for her to be a couple of inches taller than me, filling my arms quite differently than the last time I'd held her. The two families were immersed in hugs and tears—sisters, brother, adoptive parents, birthmother, my husband, Meagan's sister-in-law—all rejoicing in this reunion. We shared pictures and stories. And more hugs. And more joyful tears.

Earlier that morning, Meagan dialed my number.

"Hello."

She heard a stranger's voice, yet somewhere deep inside, there was a familiarity. Who says a nickel can't buy you anything?

~Hana Haatainen Caye

The Nickel Story

Love is a symbol of eternity. It wipes out all sense of time, destroying all memory of a beginning and all fear of an end.
~Author Unknown

"Hey, Red, you owe me a nickel!"

Susan had bumped Frank while he was playing pinball in the bar where she waitressed. A red light flashed TILT and the game was over. Reaching into her apron pocket, Susan pulled out a nickel and flicked it to him, then went back to her work.

"I'm going to marry her someday," Frank told the bartender confidently.

"Sure you are!" he laughed. "She's been here a long time, and I've never known her to even go out on a date. Good luck!" Frank rubbed the nickel between his fingers, knowing it was his lucky charm.

Susan had made a life for herself as a young widow and a single mother. The last thing she was thinking of was complicating her life with a new man.

But Frank's lucky charm worked—Susan knocked his socks off

and stole Frank's heart on their first date. Soon he had not only won her heart, but her daughter's heart as well.

There were many hard times after their wedding. Frank was a military man who was shipped overseas, leaving Susan in the single-mother role once again. Another daughter kept her busy, and both daughters adored their daddy. The years passed by quickly.

Frank loved to tell the nickel story to anyone who would listen. His eyes sparkled as he spoke of his love for Susan. This was a man who truly loved his wife.

Their fiftieth wedding anniversary was a special day. Frank contacted me to do a floral arrangement for the church and a corsage for his bride. They renewed their vows on that Sunday morning following the worship service. Our band surprised them as they walked down the aisle by singing "their" song, "The Sunny Side of the Street." Their walk became a dance as Frank twirled Susan down the aisle. What a celebration! It was a joy to be in their presence.

Soon after this wonderful day, Frank got sick. He offered everyone a smile and continued to glow with his love of Susan. Frank was never one to complain. Having a strong faith, Frank knew he would be with the Lord soon. After a few long months of suffering, he died.

All the seats at the funeral home were taken as we gathered to honor the memory of this dear friend. We were all inspired by him in our own ways. The minister spoke of Frank with such love and respect. We laughed, and our hearts were warmed as he shared memories of this special man. And then he told the nickel story. He said that Frank had called him a week or so before he died and asked to see him. While they visited, Frank took out his lucky charm. He had held onto that nickel for all of these years.

"Frank told me to keep this for him," the minister said as he reached into his pocket and walked over to Susan. "He wanted me to give it to you today and to tell you to hold onto it. He'll be waiting for you at the pinball machine."

~Hana Haatainen Caye

A Cherished Book

Motivation is when your dreams put on work clothes.
~Author Unknown

A few days before Christmas in 2000, a friend and fellow teacher stood before me waving a gift bag. "I've listened to you talk about developing stories and finding the right words and I admire your ceaseless persistence even in the face of rejection. I hope this gift helps in some way." She patted my back and handed me the bag.

"Thank you," I said, wondering how a small, red and white striped bag could contain enough magic to empower my writing career. White tissue paper rustled as I plunged a hand inside and wrapped my fingers around a book. "You can never go wrong with a book," I said, smiling at her while pulling it from the bag. "*Chicken Soup for the Writer's Soul,*" I read aloud. It even sounded inspirational. In awe, I ran my hand over the names of the authors listed on the cover as if I could feel their hearts beating. "I know almost every author listed," I said, hugging the book to my chest. "I can't wait to get home and read this."

The school day flew by and, when the last student walked out the door, I tucked the new book inside my briefcase along with the papers I needed to grade.

At home, I put chicken and potatoes in the oven to bake. Then I walked and fed the dogs, graded papers, and ate dinner with my husband. At last, I turned on the dishwasher and settled down with my new *Chicken Soup for the Soul* book. The encouraging stories by famous authors made me laugh and cry. I felt surrounded by kindred spirits who gave me hope. Halfway through the book I forced myself to shut off the bedside lamp. Snippets of stories flooded my mind before I drifted off to sleep.

The next night I finished the book and dreamed of being a successful writer.

I kept the book near my computer and often reread stories when I needed a lift. The day finally arrived when I could write full-time. But like all new circumstances, it brought with it a different problem — time management. Phone calls, TV shows, and radio programs interrupted my writing time. I cleaned, I baked, I gardened, I canned, I sewed, but I wrote less than when I worked full-time.

One evening, after an exhausting day of mowing the lawn, I picked up *Chicken Soup for the Writer's Soul*, and found "The Flop Artist Writer" by Patricia Lorenz. I didn't know Patricia Lorenz, but after reading her story I knew she understood the pitfalls of poor time management and definitely had something to teach me. I made notes from her story and modified her schedule to fit my own needs.

I started writing and submitting stories to various publications and I began selling stories. My story, "Chocolate Bunnies," was published in *Chicken Soup for the Chocolate Lover's Soul*, in 2007. When the book arrived, I noticed that Patricia Lorenz was the editor. But, by now, enough time had passed that I didn't make the connection that she was the author of "The Flop Artist Writer."

In 2011, I went to a Missouri writing conference and attended a workshop presented by Patricia Lorenz. I mentioned to her that she had edited my "Chocolate Bunnies" story. We spent a good bit of the two-day conference getting acquainted. I knew she was a talented writer and found her to be an excellent instructor and humorous speaker. Before we left the conference, we agreed to keep in touch. She even offered to critique some of my work — an invaluable gift to any writer.

Two weeks after the writing conference, I sat before my computer, composing a short story. The last paragraph was giving me trouble, so I stopped and fixed a cup of tea. I reached for my copy of *Chicken Soup for the Writer's Soul*, and read the subtitle on the cover: Stories to Open the Heart and Rekindle the Spirit of Writers. I needed some "rekindling" right then. I turned to the contents and ran my finger down the list of story titles. I nearly choked on my tea when I discovered Patricia Lorenz was the author of "The Flop Artist Writer."

Because of *Chicken Soup for the Writer's Soul*, Patricia Lorenz mentored me from afar years before I had the pleasure of meeting her in person. No other book has given me that kind of personal connection. It holds a place of honor by my computer and its dog-eared pages are a testament to how much I value and cherish *Chicken Soup for the Writer's Soul*.

~Linda Kaullen Perkins

The Flop Artist Writer

It is not enough to be busy; so are the ants.
The question is: What are we busy about?
~Henry David Thoreau

'd written over forty thousand radio commercials during my career as a copywriter. But when station management moved my workspace to the noisiest room in the building, I decided forty thousand were enough for one lifetime.

Armed with nothing more than a twenty-five-year-old Bachelor of Arts degree in English, I had to face the fact that at age forty-seven the only skill, talent or training I had was that of a writer. In addition to radio and television commercials, I'd written promotional material, newsletters, speeches, brochures, videos, policy manuals and catalogs for numerous advertisers over the years. But I was tired of all that advertising writing. Convincing people to buy things they probably didn't need, and perhaps couldn't afford, did not seem to be the most noble thing I could do with the writing skills God gave me.

So in September, 1992, I left the job that had been paying me a respectable salary to live on my savings while I got serious about the kind of writing I really wanted to do—inspirational articles, books and columns. I decided to become a full-time freelance writer, working in my home.

It was wonderful! I enjoyed leisurely cups of tea in the morning while I watched the *Today* show. I soon realized that I didn't even have to get dressed. I could slop around in my sweatshirt and baggy red pajama bottoms all day if I wanted to.

"What's this?" I said aloud to myself as I flipped TV channels. "A talk show? I love talk shows!" The topics were shocking. Women in their thirties and forties who married teenage boys; men having sex change operations; women murderers; children being indoctrinated into the Ku Klux Klan; women who married prisoners on death row; people who physically abused their elderly parents; fourteen- and fifteen-year-olds who demanded to be allowed to smoke, drink, do drugs and have sex in their own homes. The shows depressed me, but I kept watching, intrigued by real people who would tell all on national TV.

After the talk shows I'd have another cup of tea. Then I'd begin some serious putzing. Water the plants. Paint another sweatshirt for my Christmas gift collection. Talk to my unemployed nurse friend on the phone for an hour. Put a load of clothes in the washer. Feed the birds. Make spaghetti sauce. Run errands.

"Whoa, lunch time already?" Time for another TV talk show. More phone calls. Well, you get the picture. Very often I didn't get to my writing room until 3:00 p.m., and more often than not I didn't get there at all. But I was having a ball. After Christmas I took up cross-country skiing. Mother Nature cooperated with more snow than we'd had in years.

That winter I also welcomed hosts of out-of-town friends and relatives and spent days doing "white glove inspection" cleaning before my houseguests arrived.

After weeks of not setting foot inside my writing room or even turning on my computer, I started to feel like a slug. But I kept busy running errands, cleaning house, watching more TV talk shows and, yes, I even started taking mid-afternoon naps.

One day at the drugstore I picked up three candy bars, favorites of my thirteen-year-old son Andrew, my only child still at home. My other three were all full-time college students, living away from home, so mothering Andrew had become my sole occupation from 4:00 p.m. until 8:00 a.m. the next morning. When I got home I sat down at the kitchen counter, flipped on the TV and decided it would be fun to send Andrew on a treasure hunt for his candy. I cut a sheet of paper into eight pieces. On the first I wrote, "There's a tasty prize for you at the end of the Mama Lorenz treasure hunt. The first clue is at the place that rhymes with bears."

Taped to one of the upper stairs was the next clue. "Clue number three is not on this floor. But it is near the door. Look up!" Andrew ran upstairs and down looking for and finding his clues, laughing all the way. He was having as much fun on his treasure hunt as I had writing and hiding the clues.

Clue number eight said, "You're tired, right? Go to bed. Hug your pillow. Dream sweet dreams and enjoy your prize. I love you. Mom." He found the candy inside his pillow.

After a big hug and giant "Thanks, Mom!" Andrew stood next to the kitchen counter where I was sitting watching Oprah on the kitchen TV. My son put his arm around my shoulders, held out the eight slips of paper with the treasure hunt clues, and paused for a moment before he said, "So, Mom, is this what you do now instead of earning money?"

His simple question hit me hard. The eight clues I'd written for Andrew's little treasure hunt were the first words I'd actually written in months. I'd found every excuse imaginable to avoid real writing, the kind of writing that could help me earn an income.

I walked to the bathroom and looked at myself in the mirror. I was a single woman, flop artist. I'd gained fifteen pounds since I'd quit my job. I felt brain dead. I knew that writing silly little treasure hunt clues for my seventh-grader was not what the good Lord had in mind when He gave me the ability to write.

I knew I had to get back in shape physically, mentally, spiritually and professionally. On the white message board next to the front door, I wrote five lines in bold, black marker:

FIVE MILES, FIVE DAYS
FIVE GLASSES OF WATER
FIVE MINUTES OF SCRIPTURE
FIVE ARTICLES TO READ A DAY
FIVE ARTICLES MAILED EACH WEEK

It was my prescription for my new career and my new life. I would ride my exercise bike five miles a day, Monday through Friday. I would drink at least five glasses of water a day to flush out all the sugary foods I'd been eating and to help get my body back in shape. I would start each morning with five minutes of scripture or prayer. I'd been meaning to read the Psalms, one by one, for years. Now I would do it. If I kept the Bible on the kitchen counter, I knew I'd pick it up and start reading each morning.

I needed to catch up on reading and turn off the TV. Books, magazines and newspapers were stacked on my coffee table, abandoned in favor of those ridiculous TV talk shows. My new promises to myself included reading at least five articles or chapters each day, especially the ones in my professional writer's magazines.

And finally, five manuscripts in the mail each week meant that I had to get busy in my writing room every single day. I had to write. I had to rewrite and rework articles, stories and essays that I'd written in previous years and get them in shape to send to editors. My goal was to rewrite old pieces or write new ones to the tune of at least five a week and then put them in the mail to editors.

By the end of the next week I'd put a dozen manuscripts in the mail, some newly written, some I was trying to sell as reprints. I started writing more and searching for new markets on a daily basis.

I even started dressing for work. My new routine consisted of breakfast, reading and finishing my second cup of tea by 9:00 a.m., riding my exercise bike at least five miles (and often seven or eight) a day, showering, getting dressed (no pajamas allowed at work!) and being on the job in my writing room by 10:00 a.m. each weekday morning.

I still had time for a treasure hunt with Andrew every once in a while, but my five-step plan taught me that I had a lot more to share with him when he came in the door at 4:00 p.m. than silly treasure hunt clues. My own treasure hunt for more structured, more successful, work-at-home writing so far has reaped six books, dozens of newly published articles and stories, a syndicated column and a speaking career to boot. But the best part of all is the knowledge that who I am is truly based on what I do with the talent God has given me. And what I do is write. Every day.

~Patricia Lorenz

A Match Made in Heaven

No friendship is an accident.
~O. Henry

When my copy of *Chicken Soup for the Soul: A Tribute to Moms* arrived in the mail I tore open the wrapper and hugged it tight as if it were my mother in the flesh. I knew it was as close as I was going to get. Mom was gone four years by 2008 when this particular *Chicken Soup for the Soul* book was published. Having one of my favorite stories about her, "The Autumn Leaves of Summer," nestled between the front and back covers rated pretty high on my threshold for thrills.

That afternoon I settled down in a comfy chair with a pot of tea and a few ginger snaps at my side. Then I set about the delicious task of devouring every story. I'd hardly gotten started when I came across a tale entitled "Tea for Two," by Terri Elders. At age six, a case of chicken pox prevented Terri from cavorting about the neighborhood with her siblings and other assorted ghosts and goblins on Halloween. The prospect of Terri having any Halloween fun at all seemed grim indeed. Terri's lovely and kindhearted mother, who understood all too well the disappointment of a sick little girl on the second most popular kid holiday of the year, came to the rescue. With a few props and a little imagination, Terri's mother turned a spoiled Halloween into an enchanting tea party for two, creating a treasured memory for Terri.

I related to Terri's story in a big way. For me the culprit was a case of measles that left me banished to bed on my seventh birthday, and far away from my first grade classroom where cupcakes and schoolyard games had been planned to celebrate my big day. I passed the hours alternating between naps and intense bouts of disappointment. All the while my resourceful and sympathetic mother, using a few props and a little imagination, created the most astonishing hobbyhorse carousel birthday cake you could ever imagine. It was quite a delightful surprise for a feverish forlorn kid and to this day remains a cherished memory.

By the time I'd finished Terri's story I felt compelled to contact her. The portrait of her mother that Terri had painted with words was exquisite and so vividly reminded me of my own sweet mother that I wanted to meet Terri, even if only via e-mail. So I flipped to the back of the book and found Terri's biography notes, which included her e-mail address. And so it began.

I sent my first e-mail to Terri Elders in January 2008 explaining who I was and how much I appreciated her story. Terri responded the same day. We chatted about the similarities our mothers shared and how much we revered and missed them. I told Terri that even though her mother and mine had never met I suspected that somewhere in heaven they'd become good friends.

That was five years ago. We've been corresponding almost daily since. Though our shared passion for writing is a big part of our relationship, and brought us together from the start, it is not the core of our friendship. Somewhere along the way we found other common ground—the love of a tasty yet undeniably simple recipe, a properly made dry martini, a well written novel, a common dislike for household chores, all things penned by Lennon and McCartney, chocolate-covered… anything, and any project whatsoever that Johnny Depp has seen fit to make his own. The ties that bind Terri and I stretch across three thousand miles and almost twenty years difference between her age and mine.

It's not all fun and games though. When Terri's late husband was diagnosed with pancreatic cancer that progressed quickly, we communicated several times a day. I shared her anguish and sorrow at seeing Ken suffer and rapidly slip away. And likewise when my sister was diagnosed with breast cancer two years ago, Terri was there every day to listen to my fears, support me and share our joy when my sister emerged victorious over cancer.

Still we are not without our differences. Terri is outgoing and always on the move. I am a self-proclaimed recluse. Sometimes just reading her schedule exhausts me. Terri is a world traveler. I am always happiest in my own back yard. I am into crafts in a big way. Terri—well I've explained a hot glue gun to her three times now and she still doesn't get it. Terri will be taking classes until she draws her last breath. I can't even think of the word "school" without breaking out in a sweat. Yes, we differ to a great degree but that is part of what keeps things interesting between us.

Terri, a lifelong fan of Charles Dickens came east last year to Philadelphia where she celebrated the 200th anniversary of his birth with the Philadelphia chapter of the Charles Dickens Fellowship. After all the e-mails, greeting cards, and Christmas surprises that have crossed between us, Terri and I finally met in February of 2012. It was a grand event celebrated with good food, good wine and plenty of laughter.

The story "Tea for Two" has made a remarkable impact on my life because it led to a wonderful and lasting friendship. I'd like to think Terri's mother and mine had a hand in drawing us together and who's to say they didn't? However it came about, I'm awfully glad I opened the book and found "Tea for Two," the story that brought me my dear friend and writing companion Terri Elders. It is truly a match made in heaven.

~Annmarie B. Tait

Tea for Two

Every problem has a gift for you in its hands.
~Richard Bach

My sequined purple princess costume remained in its tissue paper wrappings on the top shelf of my bedroom closet, as I perched in my pink flannel pajamas on the window seat, peering out the bay window at the neighborhood witches, ghosts, and cowboys scurrying by.

On October 31, 1944, we didn't expect any knocks at our front door, festooned not with the jack-o'-lantern cutout I had made in my first-grade classroom the week before, but with a stark black-and-white quarantine sign that shouted, "Contagious Disease, Chicken Pox!"

Daddy had taken my unaffected older sister and little brother to Grandma's house for a party earlier that evening, leaving Mama and me home alone. I had finished reading all the stories in the newest edition of *Children's Activities*, tired of cutting out paper dolls from the old Sears catalog, and longed to be outside. Mama had promised me a special treat, but I couldn't imagine what could replace the thrill of joining the troops of children wandering door-to-door in the autumn twilight with their rapidly filling pillowcases. No Hershey bars, candied apples, or popcorn balls for me this year. *I don't care*, I told myself, because though the itching had ceased, I had yet to regain my appetite anyway.

I heard Mama turn on the radio in the kitchen, and then heard her call to me, "Time to get dressed!"

Glancing down at my pajamas, I wondered what she could mean, but scooted off my seat and trudged to the kitchen. On the back of one of the chrome dinette chairs hung Mama's fur chubby, a kind of short jacket that represented the essence of elegance to me those days. I used to love to watch Mama get dressed for special evenings, in her chiffon dresses always topped by the chubby.

"Put it on," she said, pointing to the jacket. "We are going to play tea party, and I am going to be the hostess, while you will be my guest." She draped a string of pearls around my neck, as I shrugged into the jacket. I noticed that the table had been set with her best Blue Willow cups and saucers, and that an empty platter had been placed next to the toaster.

Though I could not venture all the way out, Mama opened the door a crack so I could at least knock on the outside, right below the Quarantine sign. "Oh, Miss Terri, it's so good of you to call this evening. It's tea time," she announced. "And even though you are my guest, I'm going to ask you to make the meal, since you have such a special touch with cinnamon toast."

I'd seen the bakery truck make its delivery earlier, and had wondered what had been left on our doorstep. Now Mama opened the breadbox and pulled out a loaf of sliced raisin bread. She placed the sugar bowl, the butter dish, and the red tin of cinnamon on the counter, and lifted the chubby from my shoulders. Then she opened her *Searchlight Recipe Book* to page forty-four, handed me the yellow plastic measuring spoon set, and said, "Let's see how you do reading that recipe."

I was the best reader in my class, so I stumbled only on "substitute" and "proportion" as I read aloud the instructions.

"Cinnamon Toast: Spread freshly toasted bread with butter or butter substitute. Spread generously with sugar and cinnamon which have been blended in the proportion of one teaspoon cinnamon to a half of cup sugar."

While I watched the raisin bread brown in our two-sided toaster, Mama put her tea kettle on to boil, and told me a story about the birds on the Blue Willow china. She said that an angry Chinese father had been trying to catch his daughter who was running away with a boyfriend. Before he could catch them, they had been transformed into birds and flew away together. I rubbed my finger across the birds on the saucer. "When you grow up, your father won't chase away your boyfriends," she said with a little laugh. "And now that you're learning to cook, it won't be too much longer before you are grown up for every day, not just for Halloween." I smiled. It was true. I was learning to cook.

Though I hadn't been hungry all day long, the smell of the cinnamon sugar seemed to reawaken my appetite, and I ate my entire slice and half of Mama's, and even managed a swallow or two of my milk tea. When my sister returned later that evening with the candied apples that Grandma had sent, I accepted one, but insisted I wasn't really hungry, since I had cooked and eaten a meal earlier.

Mama's prediction came true, too, as I became engaged just a dozen years later. And at my wedding shower in 1955, she presented me with a black leatherette bound *Searchlight Recipe Book*. I turn the yellowed pages today to page forty-four, and again recall the delicious aroma of cinnamon toast as I remember the year that trick or treat became tea for two.

~Terri Elders

READER'S CHOICE

Meet Our Contributors
Meet Our Authors
Thank You
About Chicken Soup for the Soul
Reading List

Meet Our Contributors

Debbie Acklin is a frequent contributor to the *Chicken Soup for the Soul* series. She loves to network with other authors and travel with her family. Wish her luck as she expands her writing career with an attempt at a first novel.

Kathleene S. Baker and husband Jerry reside in Plano, TX with three pooches: Hank, Samantha and Abby. She has contributed to many publications, anthologies and writes regularly for *Southern Tour Magazine* and *Frank Talk* magazine. And she is a co-creator of the *Not Your Mother's Book* anthology series. Learn more at www.txyellowrose. com.

Teri Batts is a Christian published author and has been married for thirty-seven years with two sons, three beautiful granddaughters and another grandbaby on the way. Teri writes true-life short stories, poems, political opinion and blogs. Her writing style includes a sense of humor that will keep you coming back.

Carole A. Bell is a licensed professional counselor. Her ministry is helping families become what God wants them to be. She writes, speaks, and consults about parenting issues. Since 1999, she has written a weekly Christian parenting column for the *Plainview Daily Herald*. Read her blog at www.ParentingfromtheSource.com.

Valerie D. Benko is a Communications Specialist from western Pennsylvania. She is a frequent contributor to the *Chicken Soup for the Soul* series and other anthologies and journals, such as *Not Your Mother's Book* and *Recovering the Self: A Journal of Hope and Healing.*

Rocky Bleier of Appleton, WI graduated from Notre Dame, was drafted by the Pittsburgh Steelers, was drafted again by Uncle Sam and sent to Vietnam. He was severely wounded in his legs and feet; overcame his injuries, rejoined the Steelers and played twelve seasons, winning four Super Bowls and rushing for a thousand yards in one season.

Ginny Dent Brant is an educator, counselor, writer, soloist, Christian speaker and Bible teacher who resides with her husband Alton in Clemson, SC. She is the author of *Finding True Freedom: From the White House to the World*, which was endorsed by Chuck Colson. For more info go to www.ginnybrant.com.

Sally Willard Burbank has practiced medicine for over twenty years in Nashville. She is the married mother of two college students. She is seeking publication for three completed novels and she has written a book and a blog about her humorous and touching experiences as a doctor: patientswewillneverforget.wordpress.com.

Jim C., Jr. LCSW's sobriety date is 11-1-84. He has a master's degree in social work from University of Maryland and has been in the addiction treatment field for twenty-seven years. Jim's private practice includes working with impaired physicians, PA's, pharmacists and professional athletes. He has two beautiful daughters, Katie and Emily!

Maisha C. is a high school student who immigrated to the USA at the age of eight. She hopes to someday become a successful writer. Some of her other favorite activities are ice-skating, painting, and reading.

Maisha wants to inspire other girls (or women) to stand up for their rights.

Hana Haatainen Caye, speaker and writing instructor, is agency principal for Speechless, a copywriting and voice-over business in Pittsburgh. With over twenty-five children's books published, she is an award-winning poet and author of short stories. Hana's non-fiction book, *Vinegar Fridays*, evolved from her blog, Green Grandma. Learn more at www.wordsinyourmouth.com.

Emily Parke Chase is the author of six books, including *Help! My Family's Messed Up* (Kregel, 2008). When not writing, Emily speaks at writers' conferences and women's retreats. She has blogged extensively about her cousin's woodworking skills at her website. Visit her at emilychase.com.

Jane McBride Choate has dreamed of being a writer since she was in grade school. After marrying, she started banging out stories on an ancient typewriter. She's since upgraded to a laptop. Being published in the *Chicken Soup for the Soul* series is a dream come true.

Carol Commons-Brosowske is a native Texan. She has been married to the love of her life, Jim, for thirty-nine years. They have three children and four dogs. Carol would love to have more. Dogs, not children. Besides writing, she loves quilting. She writes a weekly column for a national magazine.

Michele Ivy Davis lives in Southern California where she is a freelance writer. Her stories and articles have appeared in a variety of magazines, newspapers, and law enforcement publications. Her debut young-adult novel, *Evangeline Brown and the Cadillac Motel*, won national and international awards. Visit her at www.MicheleIvyDavis.com.

Drema Sizemore Drudge is an MFA student at Spalding University and has been published in *The Louisville Review*, *Chicken Soup for the Soul*, *ATG*, *Mother Earth News*, *Penumbra*, and other publications. She is currently working on a novel inspired by a recent trip to Paris. Contact her at http://dremadrudge.wordpress.com.

Terri Elders, LCSW, lives near Colville, WA, with two inspirational dogs and three narcissistic cats. Seventy-five of her stories have appeared in anthology series, including several *Chicken Soup for the Soul* books. She can be friended on Facebook and contacted via e-mail at telders@hotmail.com.

Sandy Ezrine died in 2002. Her bio as it appeared in 1996 listed her as an author, trainer and management consultant. For twenty years she had worked with foundations, universities, federal agencies and private corporations. Sandy specialized in organizational development, employee motivation and problem solving.

Jayne Jaudon Ferrer is an author and speaker based in Greenville, SC. Her work is fun and family-friendly. Her newest book is *The Art of Stone Skipping and Other Fun Old-Time Games*, with a Christmas novel in the works for 2014. Other works include four collections of "reality" poetry. Visit www.JayneJaudonFerrer.com for more information.

Tracy Fitzgerald married her best friend in December of 2010 and their first daughter was born the summer of 2011. Tracy is a stay-at-home mom and enjoys painting pottery, traveling and spending time with her family.

In 2005, when she contributed her story, **Hattie Frost** was a student at Miami University in Oxford, OH, where she was studying to become a special education teacher. She was actively involved in Alpha Pi Omega, a coed service fraternity, as well as many other organizations. In her spare time, she enjoyed writing.

J. Fullerton has been writing for her own self-expression for years.

She aspires to help others with the fragile and vulnerable places in the mind, helping them to find defining moments of transformation and then investing this information into creative communication. E-mail her at beyewhole@yahoo.com.

Patricia Gallegos lives in the beautiful Pacific Northwest. She inspires young authors through teaching writing classes, and works at Washington State University. She is a freelance writer finishing her first book, *In My Shadow: Inspiring Goals, Life's Dreams, Your Legacy*. She can be reached via e-mail at pattygallegos@comcast.net or at www.patriciagalwrites.com.

Nancy B. Gibbs is a writer and motivational speaker living in Cordele, GA. She is the author of nine books, has contributed numerous stories to the *Chicken Soup for the Soul* series, writes devotions, newspaper articles and stories, anthologies, magazines and Sunday school papers. She would love to speak at your event. Learn more at www.nancybgibbs.com.

Liz Graf is a retired high school biology teacher with three grown children. She loves translating the world through the writer's word. Liz is married to her high school sweetheart and writes in Palm Coast, FL. She hopes you have a Sunshine Day. E-mail her at linesbyliz@gmail.com.

Judythe Guarnera, a retired non-profit program director in the fields of health and aging, is grateful that she is too old to die young. She connects with people through her volunteer work as a mediator and through her writing. She is active in SLO NightWriters, a local writing organization.

Joseph P. Guerrero is an aspiring cartoonist. He is a non-violent offender striving to make the necessary changes needed so that once released he may become a positive, successful member of society. He welcomes correspondence and may be contacted at #1195944,

Haynesville Correctional Center, P.O. Box 129, Haynesville, VA 22472.

Carol Goodman Heizer resides in Louisville, KY. She received her Master's of Education from the University of Louisville. She is a five-time published author whose books have sold both in the United States and overseas. E-mail her at cgheizer@insightbb.com.

Rebecca Hill and Tom Caufield live in Los Angeles. She and her friend Dominique work at Channel Road Inn and the Inn at Playa del Rey. Rebecca's stories have appeared in previous *Chicken Soup for the Soul* anthologies and in *Redbook* magazine. Her novel is entitled *Confessions of an Innkeeper*.

Megan Hjelmstad graduated from West Point in 2007 and spent five years as an Army Officer before embracing life as a stay-at-home mom. She resides in Colorado with her husband and three kids, where she's mastering the art of domesticity and writing about life's little adventures. E-mail her at megan@positivelyimperfect.com.

When **Carol Howard** contributed her story in 2005, she was working on her associate's degree, in addition to being an avid reader and a writer. She had three wonderful children and was happily married to her own personal hero. Carol was writing a historical romance novel. E-mail her at williamandcarolhoward@yahoo.com.

Jim Hullihan is an internationally recognized film producer and leadership retreat designer whose Motivational Media Assemblies programs annually appear before millions of people. As the creator of America's first digital magazine for teens, *Sweet! Digizine*, and the LeaderONE program, Jim is a leading motivations expert for U.S. secondary education.

Jeanette Hurt still visualizes her goals, and as an award-winning author, wife and mom, she's achieved many of them. Her latest book is *The Complete Idiot's Guide to Dehydrated Foods*. Tweet her at JHurtAuthor, or visit her online at www.jeanettehurt.com.

Jennie Ivey lives in Tennessee. She is the author of numerous works of fiction and nonfiction, including stories in several *Chicken Soup for the Soul* collections. Visit her online at www.jennieivey.com.

Mimi Greenwood Knight is a freelance writer living in South Louisiana with her husband, David, and their four spectacular kids. She enjoys gardening, baking, karate, knitting, Bible study, and the lost art of letter writing. Mimi is blessed to have essays in two dozen *Chicken Soup for the Soul* books.

Janey Konigsberg lives in Rye Brook, NY with her husband Don. They are very active grandparents to their twelve grandchildren. Janey received a bachelor's degree in English from Adelphi University. She was a caregiver for her elderly mom, Rosie, who passed away just before her 100th birthday.

Continuing to write throughout his teen years, **Christopher Laddish** went on to study journalism at San Francisco State University. He is currently a freelance writer and photographer based in the Bay Area. You can find links to his current work on his blog at laddish. wordpress.com.

Tom Lagana is coauthor of *Chicken Soup for the Prisoner's Soul*, *Chicken Soup for the Volunteer's Soul*, *Serving Productive Time*, *The Quick and Easy Guide to Project Management*, and *Serving Time, Serving Others*. Contact him at P.O. Box 7816, Wilmington, DE 19803 or e-mail TomLagana@yahoo.com. Learn more at www.TomLagana.com.

Jeannie Lancaster is grateful for the tender mercies and blessings found in each day. She dedicates her story to her husband, who danced with her through forty-three years of rain and sunshine, joy and sorrow.

Ginger LeBlanc works in public relations and lives with her husband, her son and her feisty wiener dog in Baton Rouge, LA. E-mail her at lovemydox@gmail.com.

Aletheia D. Lee has earned three degrees in education from Atlanta Christian College and Walden University. She teaches English as a Second Language to elementary students. She lives with her husband and three children in Douglasville, GA. This is her fifth story to be published. E-mail her at aleavitt09@gmail.com.

Lynne Leite is a writer, speaker and storyteller. Her stories have appeared in several *Chicken Soup for the Soul* books. Lynne gets her inspiration from her faith and family, and she is blessed by both! She is currently working on her first book. Contact her at www. CurlyGirl4God.com.

Gregg Levoy, author of *Callings: Finding and Following an Authentic Life* and *This Business of Writing*, is a former adjunct professor at the University of New Mexico, and former reporter for *The Cincinnati Enquirer* and *USA Today*. His writing has appeared in *The New York Times Magazine*, *The Washington Post*, and others. E-mail him at callings@gregglevoy.com.

Bobbie Jensen Lippman is a prolific human-interest writer. She currently writes "Bobbie's Beat" for the *Newport News-Times*, Newport, OR. She has been a hospice volunteer for over thirty years. She lives with her husband, Burt, their dog Charley, and a shelter cat named L.S. (Lap Sitter). She may be reached at Bobbisbeat@aol.com.

Linda Lohman is a frequent contributor to the *Chicken Soup for the Soul* series. She thanks God daily for a bounty of supporting friends and family. Living in Sacramento, CA, she loves life in retirement. Her hobbies include beading, reading, and walking her Yorkie, Lucy. E-mail her at lindaalohman@yahoo.com.

Patricia Lorenz is the author of thirteen books including *The 5 Things We Need to Be Happy*. She also has contributed to nearly sixty *Chicken Soup for the Soul* books. She's a professional speaker who travels the country, often speaking about one of her favorite topics: "Humor for the Health of It." Contact her at www.PatriciaLorenz.com.

Mandie Maass is a certified life coach who has dedicated herself to motivating and encouraging others to become their very best person. She loves reading, writing, and most of all spending quality time with her husband and three boys. She is currently writing a book on experiencing fullness of life.

James C. Magruder has bachelor's (BBA) and master's degrees (MBA) in marketing. He manages the Marketing Communications department in a Fortune 200 firm. He enjoys hiking, biking and the martial arts, having earned a third-degree black belt in karate. He blogs at www.thewritersrefuge.wordpress.com.

Tim Martin is the author of *There's Nothing Funny About Running*, *Summer With Dad*, and *Wimps Like Me*. Tim has completed nine screenplays and is a contributing author to numerous *Chicken Soup for the Soul* books. E-mail him at tmartin@northcoast.com.

John and Edna Massimilla wrote the poem "Heaven's Special Child" soon after the birth of their third daughter, Ruth, in 1952. Edna, who liked to write poetry since childhood, seemed to make her personal project to continue this talent from then on, with concern for all mentally retarded children. Her husband, Rev. John, devoted his ministry to this cause, becoming chaplain of Delaware's institution for the disabled. When columnist Ann Landers printed "Heaven's Special Child" in her column, the Massimillas received thousands of letters from parents and other caregivers; they answered them all.

Hanoch McCarty, Ed.D., is a professional speaker, trainer and consultant specializing in motivation, productivity and the improvement of instruction on every level. He combines fresh insights, useful data, and best current practice presented with high energy and much appropriate humor. He can be reached at 12970 Self-Esteem Ln., Galt, CA 95632.

Kathleen Swartz McQuaig shares stories shaped by her deep faith. As a writer, speaker, teacher, wife, and mother, she lives to encourage others. After earning her master's degree in education and living in military communities stateside and abroad, Kathleen and her family settled in Carlisle, PA. Learn more at www.KathleenSwartzMcQuaig. com.

Jacquie McTaggart lives in Independence, IA with her husband, Carroll. She teaches literacy workshops, does staff development training, operates an interactive website at www.TheTeachersDesk. com, and is a frequent keynote speaker at reading and early childhood conferences. Jacquie has two sons and six grandchildren.

Brad Meltzer is the #1 New York Times bestselling author of *The Fifth Assassin*, as well as the bestsellers *The Inner Circle*, *The Tenth Justice*, *Dead Even*, *The First Counsel*, *The Millionaires*, *The Zero Game*, *The Book of Fate* and *The Book of Lies*. He is also the host of *Brad Meltzer's Decoded* on the History Channel. But to see what's far more important, please go to: www.BradMeltzer.com. P.S. He still loves Marshall's.

Janet Miracle is a retired teacher and librarian. She lives in Kentucky with her husband Carson. She received a bachelor's degree from the University of Maryland and master's degrees from Eastern Kentucky University. The mother of three grown children and two grandchildren, Janet enjoys gardening, traveling, and listening to music.

Kevin Nastu is happily married and a fun-loving father of two wonderful kids. Kevin is an avid player of the drums, loves concerts and stand-up comedy. Kevin's motto is why frown and cry when you can smile and laugh! E-mail him at kevinmnastu@gmail.com.

Catina Noble received her Bachelor of Arts in psychology from Carleton University in 2009. She lives in Ottawa, Ontario with her four children. Catina enjoys reading, writing and taking photos. Catina plans on writing a novel at some point. E-mail her at catina. noble@yahoo.ca.

Linda O'Connell, a seasoned preschool teacher from St. Louis, MO, enjoys a good laugh, dark chocolate and long walks with her husband. Her inspirational stories have been published in fifteen *Chicken Soup for the Soul* books and many other publications. Linda blogs at lindaoconnell.blogspot.com.

Ava Pennington is an author, speaker, and Bible teacher. She has published numerous magazine articles and contributed to twenty-three anthologies, including sixteen *Chicken Soup for the Soul* books. Her newest book, *Daily Reflections on the Names of God: A Devotional*, will be released October 2013. Learn more at www.AvaWrites.com.

Saralee Perel is an award-winning columnist/novelist and multiple contributor to Chicken Soup for the Soul. Her book, *The Dog Who Walked Me*, is about her dog who became her caregiver after Saralee's spinal cord injury, the initial devastation of her marriage, and her cat who kept her sane. Contact her at sperel@saraleeperel.com or www. saraleeperel.com.

Linda Kaullen Perkins taught second grade at Washington Elementary in Sedalia, MO. Her writing has appeared in *Chicken Soup for the Chocolate Lover's Soul*, *Chicken Soup for the Soul: Kids in the Kitchen*, *Country Woman* magazine, *Woman's World* magazine, and various other publications. E-mail her at lindaperks2@gmail.com or www.lindakperkins.com.

Brittany Perry was born and raised in West Virginia. Her mother Deanna Dick was her role model and taught her to write. She also had help from Pamela Frailey and Leann Likens, who were her best teachers. She attended the 2007 West Virginia Governor's School for the Arts and Concord University. E-mail her at ilovebeingmommy91711@hotmail.com.

Lori Phillips received her BA in communications/journalism and her master's degree in education. She is the online editor for Bellaonline.com's Dreams and Marriage sites. Her e-book titles are available through Amazon. Contact her through her Bellaonline.com sites or lori@reallifehelpbooks.com. Follow her on Twitter @tweetdreams4u, @flutterby03 and @BellaMarriage.

Rebecca Pippert is a prominent speaker, bestselling author and evangelist, the founder of Salt Shaker Ministries: a global evangelism training ministry. Becky is the author of nine books, including the modern classic, *Out of the Salt Shaker*. Becky and her husband are ministering in the UK and Europe. Contact her at Becky@saltshaker.org.

Michelle Duplessis Prudhomme is dedicated to her husband, Perry, helping him with his daily needs. They are strong in their faith and blessed with everything they have. She misses her two beloved cats and Golden Retriever. Michelle also helps others work at home; to join her team and work from home, contact her at www.luvourfam.com.

Robert Robeson is a professional member of the National Writers Association, the Distinguished Flying Cross Society and the Military Writers Society of America. He retired from the U.S. Army as a lieutenant colonel, has a BA in English from the University of Maryland and has completed extensive graduate journalism work.

Marcia Rudoff, author of *We Have Stories—A Handbook for Writing*

Your Memoirs, is a writing instructor and newspaper columnist in Bainbridge Island, Washington. She enjoys freelance writing for anthologies, newspapers and magazines when not playing with grandkids, watching baseball, or enjoying friends.

Glenna Salsbury provides keynotes and seminars nationally and internationally. She graduated from Northwestern University and holds a master's degree from UCLA and Fuller Seminary. A member of the National Speakers Association, Glenna has received the highest awards given among professional speakers. Glenna can be reached at glennasalsbury.com.

Theresa Sanders is honored to be a frequent contributor to the *Chicken Soup for the Soul* series. An award-winning technical writer, she managed a documentation and training department before turning to creative endeavors. She lives with her husband near St. Louis. Connect with Theresa on Facebook: www.facebook.com/pages/Theresa-Sanders/208490939276032, LinkedIn: www.linkedin.com/pub/theresa-sanders/50/245/b26, or e-mail her at TheresaLSanders@charter.net.

Virginia Satir (1916-1988) was an American author and psychotherapist, known especially for her approach to family therapy and her work with Systemic Constellations. She is widely regarded as the "Mother of Family Therapy." Her best known books are *Conjoint Family Therapy*, 1964, *Peoplemaking*, 1972, and *The New Peoplemaking*, 1988.

Donna Finlay Savage is a pastor's wife who loves encouraging women. When she isn't writing or teaching, she's trying to simplify her life, see more joy, and conquer her addiction to chocolate. Her phone contains over 100 photos of her grandson. Connect with Donna at donnasavagelv@cox.net or www.donnasavage.blogspot.com.

Angela Sayers was a twenty-year-old cancer patient who sought to raise awareness for pediatric cancers, especially osteosarcoma. She loved books, writing, playing online *Scrabble*, and her cat, Charles Fitzpatrick The Third.

John Wayne Schlatter is a freelance contributor to the *Chicken Soup for the Soul* series. His book, *Gifts by the Side of the Road*, was released in 2012. Sponsored by Showpath Promotions, he speaks at schools throughout the country on "Creating a Culture of Civility." Visit him at www.giftsbythesideoftheroad.com.

When **Sophfronia Scott** published her novel, *All I Need to Get By*, with St. Martin's Press, one reviewer referred to her as "one of the best writers of her generation." Her work has appeared in *Time*, *People*, *More*, NewYorkTimes.com, *Sleet Magazine*, *Numéro Cinq*, *Saranac Review* and *O, The Oprah Magazine*.

Georgia Shaffer is a certified life coach, a licensed psychologist in Pennsylvania, and the author of *12 Relationship Mistakes Women Make... And How to Avoid Them*. As a professional speaker, she loves to encourage cancer survivors and healthcare givers. For more information, visit www.GeorgiaShaffer.com or e-mail her at Georgia@GeorgiaShaffer.com.

Ritu Shannon is a working mom of two who has recently rediscovered her passion for writing. She is thankful to her children who are her literary inspirations. She dreams of one day moving to Maui with her husband and kids and working as a writer or blogger from the beach. E-mail her at ritushannon@yahoo.ca.

Annabel Sheila calls Moncton, New Brunswick home and it's there she writes about the splendour of nature, the serenity of the ocean, and the wonder of love with a passion that comes from the heart of an author who is one with her muse! E-mail her at annabelsheila@live.ca.

Susan Elizabeth Smith received her BA in Recreation Administration in 2007. She belongs to numerous honor societies and graduated salutatorian from high school in 2002. She currently works as a CSR, loves animals of all kinds and currently lives with her rescue guinea pig and rescue cat.

Mike Staver is an internationally respected coach and speaker. His book *Leadership Isn't for Cowards* was published in June 2012. He is a Certified Speaking Professional (CSP) and was most recently chosen as one of the forty hottest business speakers in America by *Meetings & Conventions* magazine.

Annmarie B. Tait resides in Conshohocken, PA with her husband Joe Beck. Annmarie is published in several *Chicken Soup for the Soul* volumes, *Reminisce* magazine, *Patchwork Path*, and many other anthologies. She also enjoys cooking, crocheting, and singing Irish and American folk songs. E-mail Annmarie at irishbloom@aol.com.

Robert Tell's poetry and other work have appeared in many periodicals. A full-length poetry book, *Bard Memorial Hospital*, as well as Tell's novels, memoir, stories and poetry are widely available in both print and e-book editions. Information about Tell and his work can be found on his website bobtell.com.

Penelope Vazquez moved to Los Angeles in 2002 to become a professional dancer. She has toured with artists around the world. She lives a fulfilled life as a mother and wife. She enjoys teaching dance to kids and continues to fulfill her passion as a professional dancer by doing local gigs every now and then.

Beverly Walker lives in Tennessee and cares for her husband, who is battling cancer. She enjoys scrapbooking pictures of grandchildren and family memories, and has been published in many *Chicken Soup for the Soul* books.

Rebecca Waters taught in the field of early childhood education for nineteen years before becoming a professor of teacher education at Cincinnati Christian University. She is now a freelance writer, novelist, and speaker. E-mail her at rwaters.author@gmail.com or visit her blog at rebeccaawaters.blogspot.com.

Sarah Winkler received her Bachelor of Arts degree in English from the University of California, Davis. She loves to read, write, and travel. She is a self-professed coffee addict with a huge collection of books and never lacks imagination. E-mail at sarahlwinkler@yahoo.com.

Susan Yanguas lives in Maryland and is a writer/editor for the federal government. She enjoys painting, reading, and working with animals. The first book in her mystery novel series will be published this year.

Dominique Young spends each day expressing herself artistically through dancing, baking, writing, photography, gardening or innkeeping. Her hopes for Morning Bird Homemade Baked Goods are for them to reach and nourish all who find and need them. E-mail her at morningbird333@yahoo.com.

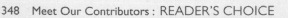

Meet Our Authors

Jack Canfield is the co-creator of the *Chicken Soup for the Soul* series, which *Time* magazine has called "the publishing phenomenon of the decade." Jack is also the co-author of many other bestselling books.

Jack is the CEO of the Canfield Training Group in Santa Barbara, California, and founder of the Foundation for Self-Esteem in Culver City, California. He has conducted intensive personal and professional development seminars on the principles of success for more than a million people in twenty-three countries, has spoken to hundreds of thousands of people at more than 1,000 corporations, universities, professional conferences and conventions, and has been seen by millions more on national television shows.

Jack has received many awards and honors, including three honorary doctorates and a Guinness World Records Certificate for having seven books from the *Chicken Soup for the Soul* series appearing on the New York Times bestseller list on May 24, 1998.

You can reach Jack at www.jackcanfield.com.

Mark Victor Hansen is the co-founder of Chicken Soup for the Soul, along with Jack Canfield. He is a sought-after keynote speaker, bestselling author, and marketing maven. Mark's powerful messages of possibility, opportunity, and action have created powerful change in thousands of organizations and millions of individuals worldwide.

Mark is a prolific writer with many bestselling books in addition to the *Chicken Soup for the Soul* series. Mark has had a profound influence in the field of human potential through his library of audios, videos, and articles in the areas of big thinking, sales achievement, wealth building, publishing success, and personal and professional development. He is also the founder of the MEGA Seminar Series.

Mark has received numerous awards that honor his entrepreneurial spirit, philanthropic heart, and business acumen. He is a lifetime member of the Horatio Alger Association of Distinguished Americans.

You can reach Mark at www.markvictorhansen.com.

Amy Newmark is Chicken Soup for the Soul's publisher and editor-in-chief, after a thirty-year career as a writer, speaker, financial analyst, and business executive in the worlds of finance and telecommunications. Amy is a *magna cum laude* graduate of Harvard College, where she majored in Portuguese, minored in French, and traveled extensively. She and her husband have four grown children.

After a long career writing books on telecommunications, voluminous financial reports, business plans, and corporate press releases, Chicken Soup for the Soul is a breath of fresh air for Amy. She has fallen in love with Chicken Soup for the Soul and its life-changing books, and really enjoys putting these books together for Chicken Soup for the Soul's wonderful readers. She has co-authored more than five dozen *Chicken Soup for the Soul* books and has edited another three dozen.

You can reach Amy with any questions or comments through webmaster@chickensoupforthesoul.com and you can follow her on Twitter @amynewmark or @chickensoupsoul.

Thank You

What a fun project this was! We felt like we were throwing our own 20th anniversary party as we read the positive stories from our readers and put this unprecedented collection together.

This is a thank you that spans twenty years, as we are grateful to the various contributors whose stories, many of which are from the original *Chicken Soup for the Soul*, proved timeless enough to be cited as favorites by our readers. We are grateful to those thought leaders, whose stories have held up so well, and we also appreciate all the readers who sent in their new stories about how our old stories have changed their lives.

We owe a special thanks to our editor Barbara LoMonaco, who was the perfect person to read the submissions for this book as she has been with Chicken Soup for the Soul since almost the beginning. Our assistant publisher D'ette Corona is also an "old timer," despite her youth, and she worked closely with Barbara to evaluate the stories and prepare the manuscript after we had made our final choices. Our editors Madeline Clapps and Kristiana Pastir worked hard to proofread and prepare the manuscript for our Creative Director and book producer, Brian Taylor at Pneuma Books, who did a masterful job putting together this manuscript that blends the old with the new.

~Amy Newmark

Improving Your Life
Every Day

Real people sharing real stories—for twenty years. Now, Chicken Soup for the Soul has gone beyond the bookstore to become a world leader in life improvement. Through books, movies, DVDs, online resources and other partnerships, we bring hope, courage, inspiration and love to hundreds of millions of people around the world. Chicken Soup for the Soul's writers and readers belong to a one-of-a-kind global community, sharing advice, support, guidance, comfort, and knowledge.

Chicken Soup for the Soul stories have been translated into more than 40 languages and can be found in more than one hundred countries. Every day, millions of people experience a Chicken Soup for the Soul story in a book, magazine, newspaper or online. As we share our life experiences through these stories, we offer hope, comfort and inspiration to one another. The stories travel from person to person, and from country to country, helping to improve lives everywhere.

Share with Us

We all have had Chicken Soup for the Soul moments in our lives. If you would like to share your story or poem with millions of people around the world, go to chickensoup.com and click on "Submit Your Story." You may be able to help another reader, and become a published author at the same time. Some of our past contributors have launched writing and speaking careers from the publication of their stories in our books!

Our submission volume has been increasing steadily—the quality and quantity of your submissions has been fabulous. We only accept story submissions via our website. They are no longer accepted via mail or fax.

To contact us regarding other matters, please send us an e-mail through webmaster@chickensoupforthesoul.com, or fax or write us at:

Chicken Soup for the Soul
P.O. Box 700
Cos Cob, CT 06807-0700
Fax: 203-861-7194

One more note from your friends at Chicken Soup for the Soul: Occasionally, we receive an unsolicited book manuscript from one of our readers, and we would like to respectfully inform you that we do not accept unsolicited manuscripts and we must discard the ones that appear.

How to Find the Books Mentioned in This Volume

We hope you enjoyed these stories. To read more, here is a list of all the books mentioned in this volume, along with their print and e-book ISBNs. Happy reading!

A 2nd Helping of Chicken Soup for the Soul
Print ISBN: 9781623610357
e-book ISBN: 9781453285596

Chicken Soup for the Cancer Survivor's Soul
Print ISBN: 9781623610395
e-book ISBN: 9781453285916

Chicken Soup for the Caregiver's Soul
Print ISBN: 9781623610203
e-book ISBN: 9781453282120

Chicken Soup for the Christian Family Soul
Print ISBN: 9781623610876
e-book ISBN: 9781453285411

Chicken Soup for the Girl's Soul
Print ISBN: 9781623610319
e-book ISBN: 9781453282236

Chicken Soup for the Grieving Soul
Print ISBN: 9781623611019
e-book ISBN: 9781453282267

Chicken Soup for the Military Wife's Soul
Print ISBN: 9781623610289
e-book ISBN: 9781453282335

Chicken Soup for the Mother's Soul
Print ISBN: 9781623610456
e-book ISBN: 9781453285978

Chicken Soup for the Mother & Daughter Soul
Print ISBN: 9781623611095
e-book ISBN: 9781453282076

Chicken Soup for the New Mom's Soul
Print ISBN: 9781623610586
e-book ISBN: 9781453281901

Chicken Soup for the Prisoner's Soul
Print ISBN: 9781623610968
e-book ISBN: 9781453282366

Chicken Soup for the Recovering Soul
Print ISBN: 9781623610210
e-book ISBN: 9781453285220

Chicken Soup for the Soul
Print ISBN: 9781611599138
e-book ISBN: 9781453282380

Chicken Soup for the Soul: A Tribute to Moms
e-book ISBN: 9781453285022

Chicken Soup for the Soul: Count Your Blessings
Print ISBN: 9781935096429
e-book ISBN: 9781611591385

Chicken Soup for the Soul: Family Caregivers
Print ISBN: 9781935096832
e-book ISBN: 9781611592023

Chicken Soup for the Soul: Find Your Happiness
Print ISBN: 9781935096771
e-book ISBN: 9781611591965

Chicken Soup for the Soul: Food and Love
Print ISBN: 9781935096788
e-book ISBN: 9781611591989

Chicken Soup for the Soul: Hope & Healing for Your Breast Cancer Journey
Print ISBN: 9781935096948
e-book ISBN: 9781611592115

Chicken Soup for the Soul: Inspiration for the Young at Heart
Print ISBN: 9781935096719
e-book ISBN: 9781611591934

Chicken Soup for the Soul: My Resolution
Print ISBN: 9781935096283
e-book ISBN: 9781611591460

Chicken Soup for the Soul: Say Hello to a Better Body!
Print ISBN: 9781935096894
e-book ISBN: 9781611592122

Chicken Soup for the Soul: Shaping the New You
Print ISBN: 9781935096573
e-book ISBN: 9781611591620

Chicken Soup for the Soul: Thanks Dad
Print ISBN: 9781935096467
e-book ISBN: 9781611591415

Chicken Soup for the Soul: Thanks Mom
Print ISBN: 9781935096450
e-book ISBN: 9781611591408

Chicken Soup for the Soul: The Power of Positive
Print ISBN: 9781611599039
e-book ISBN: 9781611592184

Chicken Soup for the Soul: Think Positive
Print ISBN: 9781935096566
e-book ISBN: 9781611591316

Chicken Soup for the Soul: What I Learned from the Dog
Print ISBN: 9781935096382
e-book ISBN: 9781611591477

Chicken Soup for the Teacher's Soul
Print ISBN: 9781623611071
e-book ISBN: 9781453281949

Chicken Soup for the Teenage Soul
Print ISBN: 9781623610463
e-book ISBN: 9781453281918

Chicken Soup for the Unsinkable Soul
Print ISBN: 9781623610838
e-book ISBN: 9781453282359

Chicken Soup for the Veteran's Soul
Print ISBN: 9781623611033
e-book ISBN: 9781453286005

Chicken Soup for the Woman's Soul
Print ISBN: 9781623610432
e-book ISBN: 9781453282113

Chicken Soup for the Writer's Soul
e-book ISBN: 9781453285831

Chicken Soup for the Soul

www.chickensoup.com

for the Soul